# 'RIGHTEOUSNESS' IN THE SEPTUAGINT OF ISAIAH: A CONTEXTUAL STUDY

SOCIETY OF BIBLICAL LITERATURE
SEPTUAGINT AND COGNATE STUDIES SERIES

Edited by
Harry M. Orlinsky

Number 060408

'RIGHTEOUSNESS' IN THE SEPTUAGINT OF ISAIAH:
A CONTEXTUAL STUDY

by
John W. Olley

SCHOLARS PRESS
Missoula, Montana

# 'RIGHTEOUSNESS' IN THE SEPTUAGINT OF ISAIAH:
## A CONTEXTUAL STUDY

by
John W. Olley

Published by
SCHOLARS PRESS
for
THE SOCIETY OF BIBLICAL LITERATURE

Distributed by
SCHOLARS PRESS
Missoula, Montana 59806

# 'RIGHTEOUSNESS' IN THE SEPTUAGINT OF ISAIAH:
# A CONTEXTUAL STUDY

by

John W. Olley
Chung Chi College
The Chinese University of Hong Kong

Library of Congress Cataloging in Publication Data

Olley, John W
    (Society of Biblical Literature Septuagint and cognate studies series ; no. 8 ISSN 0145-2754
    A revision of the author's thesis (M.Th.), Melbourne College of Divinity, 1975.
    Bibliography: p.
    Includes indexes.
    1. Bible. O. T. Isaiah. Greek—Versions—Septuagint. 2. Justice—Biblical teaching. 3. Tsdk
(Hebrew root) I. Title. II. Series: Septuagint and cognate studies ; no. 8.
BS1514.G7S47  1977            224'.1'048                          78-3425
ISBN 0-89130-226-3

Printed in the United States of America
1 2 3 4 5 6
Edwards Brothers, Inc.
Ann Arbor, Michigan 48104

TABLE OF CONTENTS

PAGE

PREFACE                                                              ix

INTRODUCTION                                                          1

I.   GENERAL ASPECTS OF METHODOLOGY AND BACKGROUND                    3
     1. Semantic Issues, 3; 2. The Septuagint:
     A. General, 5; B. The Book of Isaiah, 8;
     3. Jewish Greek? 9; 4. Previous studies on
     δικαιοσύνη and δικαιοῦν in the LXX, 12;
     5. צדק in the Old Testament, 14; 6. Nature,
     Method of Investigation and Contribution of the
     Present Study, 17.

II.  CLASSICAL AND HELLENISTIC (NON-JEWISH) GREEK USAGE              21
     1. Introduction, 21; 2. Plato, 22;
     3. Aristotle, 27; 4. Other Greek Sources,
     32: 4:1. Aeschylus, 33; 4:2. Sophocles,
     34; 4:3. Herodotus, 34; 4:4. Thucydides,
     36; 4:5. Aristophanes, 37; 4:6. Xenophon,
     37; 4:7. Polybius, 38; 4:8. Dionysius
     Halicarnassensis, 38; 4:9. Plutarch, 39;
     4:10. Inscriptions, 39; 4:11. Papyri, 39;
     5. Some conclusions, 40.

III. THE BOOK OF ISAIAH: VERB FORMS                                  45
     1. The Hiphil of צדק, 45: A. 5:23, 45;
     B. 50:8 (50:4-9)*, 46; C. 53:11, 48.

     2. The Qal of צדק, 51: A. 43:9 (43:8-15),
     51; B. 43:26, 53; C. 45:25 (45:18-25),
     54.

     3. Other occurrences of δικαιοῦν, 59:
     A. 1:17, 59; B. 42:21, 60.

     4. Summary and Conclusions, 61.

IV.  THE BOOK OF ISAIAH: NOUN FORMS                                  65
     1. Introduction, 65.

     2. (ה)צדק/ἐλεημοσύνη, ἔλεος: A. 1:27
     (1:21-28), 66; B. 28:17a (chap. 28), 68;
     C. 56:1, 71; D. 59:16b (chap. 59), 72.

---

* A passage in parenthesis signifies that all occurrences of
  the root צדק and of δικαιο-words in the passage are
  discussed here.

3. δικαιοσύνη translating other than
(π)PTS: A. 33:6 (33:5-15), *79*;
B. 61:8 (chap. 61), *80*; C. 63:7
(chaps. 63, 64), *86*; D. 38:19;
39:8 (chaps. 36-39), *91*.

4. PTS/κρίσις: A. 11:4 (11:1-5), *95*;
B. 51:7 (51:1-8), *96*.

5. (π)PTS/δίκαιος: 5:1: τὸ δίκαιον,
*101*; 5:2: Other instances of
δίκαιος: A. 32:1 (chap. 32), *103*;
B. 41:10 (41:1-13), *105*; C. 54:17
(54:11-17), *107*; D. 58:2, *109*.

6. Summary and Conclusions, *111*: 6:1:
A note on the translation, *111*;
6:2: (π)PTS, *112*; 6:3: δικαιοσύνη,
*112*.

V. SOME OTHER RELATED GREEK WORDS IN ISAIAH 119

1. δίκαιος, *119*; 2. Positive σεβ-words,
*119*; 3. ἀδικ-, ἀνομ- and ἀσεβ-words, *120*.

VI. CONCLUSIONS 125

1. Methodology, *125*; 2. Jewish Greek?
*125*; 3. Significance for the rest of the
LXX and the NT, *127*.

APPENDICES

I. Frequency and distribution of Hebrew words
and their Greek translation equivalents. 129

II. A comparison of modern translations of all
occurrences of the root PTS in Isaiah. 133

III. τὸ ἔλεος, ἡ ἐλεημοσύνη in non-Jewish Greek
and LXX. 141

IV. The translation of TON in Isaiah. 143

V. Israel and the Nations. 147

NOTES 153

ABBREVIATIONS 163

BIBLIOGRAPHY 167

INDEX OF BIBLICAL REFERENCES 183

INDEX OF NON-BIBLICAL GREEK SOURCES 191

*To*

*Colleagues and Students*

*Theology Division*
*Chung Chi College*
*The Chinese University of Hong Kong*

*1968 - 1977*

PREFACE

In a work such as this one is always conscious of
building on the endeavours of so many and of receiving in
countless ways inspiration, criticism, guidance and encouragement.

An earlier version was a research thesis presented in
April, 1975 to the Melbourne College of Divinity for the Theol.
M. degree. Appreciation is rightly first expressed to my
advisors, initially the Rev. E. L. Randall of St. Barnabas'
Theological College, South Australia, and for the major part
Dr. J. J. Scullion, S.J., of the Jesuit Theological College of
Australia. In certain areas advice and help has been willingly
given by Dr. K. J. McKay, Classical Studies Department, and
Dr. J. A. Thompson, Middle Eastern Studies Department, The
University of Melbourne. My debt to Dr. Thompson is even more
extensive as it was he who introduced, enthused and guided me
in my basic Old Testament studies and who first suggested the
topic that led to the present work.

Subsequent examiners and readers of the manuscript,
unfortunately (?) all anonymous, have made many careful
comments and suggestions for improvements. The Editor of this
series, Professor Harry Orlinsky, has been most encouraging and
has spent much time in making many penetrating and helpful
comments. For the time and effort all have spent, especially
when distance requires writing and not discussion, they cannot
adequately be shown appreciation. Needless to say, I have not
always agreed with their views, although anyone who wishes to
compare this work with the earlier thesis will see just how
much change has been made!

From fellow faculty and students of Chung Chi College,
The Chinese University of Hong Kong, have come stimulus and
insights as one continually grapples with the problems of
translating biblical words in another culture. Septuagintal
problems come to life! The work also could not have been done
without the help of staff and use of facilities of libraries of

universities and theological colleges in Hong Kong, Sydney and
Melbourne.

My involvement at Chung Chi has been as a member of the
Australian Baptist Missionary Society, seconded to the American
Baptist Churches Board of International Ministries.  Both
bodies have made possible various special arrangements and
financial support for this research.

The most tedious aspect of any work must be the typing,
especially when much Greek and Hebrew is included.  Mrs. S. Ho
not only typed the original thesis but has now willingly and
accurately typed the revised, and still difficult, script.

All have been involved and have guarded me from some
errors.  But much still needs correction and development by
others.  So the thanks must go again to the Editor of this
Series who has been willing to have the work published and to
Scholars Press for making such a publication possible.

Finally, a special word of appreciation must be made to
my wife, Elaine, for her patient encouragement and to David,
Linda and Catherine who kept wondering, "When will daddy
finish?"

J. W. O.

Hong Kong
November, 1977

INTRODUCTION

"With an alien tongue the Lord will speak to this
people."
Isaiah 28:11 *RSV*

While not the original intention of the prophet, these
words aptly describe the situation of Jews in Alexandria under
the Ptolemies with regard to their scriptures. For many Hebrew
had become a strange tongue, and God's word was to come to them
in Greek, the language of their foreign rulers and neighbours.
In such a setting the LXX had its origin.

Many problems come to the fore as one considers the LXX,
not least of which being those concerning the translators'
knowledge of both Hebrew and Greek and their theological views.
Certainly one cannot assume that the translators always both
understood and conveyed the sense of the Hebrew, nor can one
make assumptions concerning the "Jewishness" of their Greek.

The purpose of the present study is to investigate the
translation of the Book of Isaiah, in particular seeking to
determine how passages in which the root צדק occurs were understood and what was the intended meaning of δικαιοσύνη and
related words.

Chapter I provides a brief survey of various issues and
topics which are basic to our purpose, concluding with a
statement of methodology which emphasises the need for
*contextual* study, i.e., for taking into account the *LXX*
context. Chapter II is an investigation of Hellenistic usage
that has not been influenced by Jewish background so as to
provide a standard for measuring the "Jewishness" of Isaiah LXX
usage.

Chapters III and IV form the central part. As our
concern is to apply and illustrate a method of study the order
of presentation is governed by that method. Thus each verse or
passage is discussed on its own, while noting comparisons with
other passages. Conclusions and summaries of observable
patterns are left to the end of the chapter. In other words,

each chapter presents a series of exegetical investigations in an order suggested by the method rather than by the conclusions. Nevertheless the reader may like to read the conclusions of each chapter first to alert him to those issues which contextual study showed to be important.

Chapter V demonstrates the value of investigating other words in the semantic field, including opposites.

The concluding chapter does not repeat the conclusions of the preceding chapters but contains further general observations and suggestions for further study.

# CHAPTER I

## GENERAL ASPECTS OF METHODOLOGY AND BACKGROUND /1/

1.   SEMANTIC ISSUES.

Any discussion of the use of words in the Bible must
take account of the issues raised by Barr, 1961.  His
criticisms of etymologising, of the confusion between
synchronic and diachronic study, of the confusion between word
and concept, and of the language-culture link seen by many /2/
are well-known.  A lengthy discussion and criticism of Barr is
in Hill: 1-22, 294-300.  As a linguist, Tångberg gives a
helpful discussion of Barr's linguistic philosophy.  He refers
to Barr as an "eclectic structuralist" in that he uses both
American structuralists (beginning with L. Bloomfield) and
European linguistics (e.g., de Saussure).  He notes that Barr
has received much sympathy from Bible translators such as Nida
and the Summer Institute of Linguistics/Wycliffe Bible
Translators.  Certainly the stress upon the importance of the
sentence as the conveyor of meaning and upon the need to
determine the ways in which a word is used in relationship is
most necessary.  Barr has continued to write on these matters
and has endeavoured to give positive guidelines (1968a, b,
1969, 1972).

While there are areas of disagreement and differences
of emphases between Barr and Hill, in practice there are
certain agreements which are pertinent to our study:
(a)    there is linked with each word some area of thought to
which the word is a pointer or semantic marker (e.g., Barr,
1961: 217; Hill: 12f);
(b)    it is the context, both literary and cultural, which
determines the meaning of the word in that context.  As Barr
points out, one obtains the meaning of a word by investigating
how it is used in context, its syntactic and semantic
relationships.  Although Hill criticises Barr for being
"formalistic," neglecting psychological and sociological

3

factors (10f, 296), Barr, 1968b, returns the criticism, stating that Hill is too "formalistic," relying mainly on statistics.

On the complex question of the relationship between word and concept, Hill is quite scathing in his criticism of Barr. Nevertheless, amongst linguists there is increasing recognition of the need to examine the semantic field of a word /3/, and it is precisely this aspect which Hill neglects (see the criticisms by Hughes). At the same time he does recognize the importance of the context for narrowing the meaning when he refers to the responsibility of the user of *TWNT* to "choose the correct (or most nearly correct) meaning in the context with which he is dealing" (13). Surely this means that one has to examine the word-combination, the word-in-context which Barr is concerned to stress.

The question of the relationship between language and culture is quite complex — Barr recognizes a link but describes it as "logically haphazard" (1972: 11-19) — but many would concur with the conclusion of Henle:

> "All we have contended is that certain linguistic
> features make certain modes of perception more
> prevalent or more probable, not that they
> completely rule out others ... Language is *one*
> of the factors influencing perception ... This
> influence need not be primary or unique or
> compelling, but neither is it negligible." (17f)

One is led naturally to the question of the difficulties of translation. Barr (1961: 266) agrees that there is likely to be some loss of meaning in translation, although Hill overstates the case when he refers to the possibility of "fundamental loss" (13). To be preferred is the conclusion of Tångberg:

> "Translation is possible because every language is
> capable of producing an infinite number of sentences
> even though vocabulary items and grammatically
> permissible constructions are limited in number ...
> 'Languages differ not so much as to what *can* be
> said in them, but rather as to what is *relatively
> easy* to say.'" (309 /4/)

While such discussion has greatly assisted modern translation, in the LXX we are faced with ancient translations made without the benefits of modern linguistic science. We have to look at the translations and seek to determine how the translators saw their task, and why they used certain words and

grammatical structures and not others. We shall, however, make
one assumption: that the translators believed that the words
and structures they used were at least reasonably capable of
conveying the meaning they saw in the original, allowing for
individual theological views and linguistic abilities. This
does not mean that they necessarily agreed with the meaning
they saw (see, e.g., Orlinsky, 1975: 103-108).

2.    THE SEPTUAGINT.

A.    GENERAL:

In recent years there has been a resurgence of interest
in Septuagintal studies. A major work is Jellicoe, 1968, which
includes a 31-page bibliography of works since 1900, demand has
warranted a reprint of Swete, and Brock, Fritsch and Jellicoe
have produced a valuable bibliography (Brock, 1973). Reviews
of current study have been given by Orlinsky, 1941, 1947; Katz,
1954, 1961; Wevers, 1954, 1968; Eissfeldt: 701-15; Jellicoe,
1969, 1974: xiii-liv; Tov, 1976a; and Kraft, 1976. Significant
is the formation of the International Organization for
Septuagint and Cognate Studies (see *BIOSCS*; Fritsch, 1972a; and
Kraft, 1970, 1971).

The greatest effort necessarily has been spent on text-
critical studies, with the production of various critical texts
and much discussion on the various textual traditions and the
relationship with MT and Qumran scrolls (Orlinsky, 1959, 1961).
Some have recognized the link with NT textual criticism, e.g.,
Jellicoe, 1968: 353-358; Metzger: 2-3. The complete
unreliability of the references to LXX in *BHK* must be stressed
(Orlinsky, 1961: 114-121, and references there to the work of
C. C. Torrey, M. L. Margolis, J. Ziegler and Orlinsky himself).
There is a general acceptance of the Lagardian hypothesis of a
single LXX *Vorlage* over against the multiple "versions" view of
Kahle (Orlinsky, 1941; Jellicoe, 1968: 59-73, 1974: xxi-xxiv,
54-157).

It is recognized that much needs to be done in lexical
studies. See especially Kraft, 1972, and Tov, 1976b. Caird,
1968, 1969, begins by looking at LXX references in *LSJ*, while
J. A. L. Lee looks at LSJ *Sup*. A major work is that of Daniel,
of which an extended review and discussion of principles is

given by Jacques.  See also the articles of Gehman.

Even greater is the need in theological studies.  Brock, 1973, lists few articles on theological issues, while the works of Jellicoe and Wevers say almost nothing about lexical and theological aspects.  Ziegler in the introduction to his major work on Isaiah (1934) specifically leaves until a later date questions of the distinctive theological concepts of the LXX. In 1948 Seeligmann only briefly discusses theological issues in Isaiah (95-121), while Orlinsky, 1956, discusses anthropomorphisms and anthropopathisms in Isaiah LXX.  Little else, however, has been done, so warranting the plea of Fritsch for more theological studies of the various books of the Septuagint:

> "Scholars must pay more attention to the theology of the LXX ...  (It) represents the first attempt to translate the language of revelation into another linguistic medium ...  Behind the problems of translation technique lies the deeper question, What determined the translators' choice of a particular term by which they rendered the Hebrew word? ...  The LXX reflects much of the theological ferment which was going on within Judaism at this time."  (1972a: 5; cf. 1971, 1972b)

It is this plea that needs to be stressed and in which the present writer wishes to join.

In this connection Kraft warns concerning simplistic terminology such as "*the* language of *the* LXX," as one needs to take account of variations in Greek rendering in various books (1970: 387, n.1).  It is failure to do this which is a major weakness of studies such as *TWNT*, Dodd, Hill, and Ziesler.  It is common-place in biblical scholarship today to assert the close link between Greek words in the N.T. and Hebrew words in the O.T., recognizing too the key place of the LXX (cf. Tov, 1976a: 16-17).  And yet rarely is the LXX treated with the same exegetical seriousness as MT or NT.  One could cite many cases where it is assumed that, because a given Hebrew word is rendered by a certain Greek word (or words), therefore the Greek word has the same connotation as the Hebrew.

Certainly the first translation of the OT into Greek was a major undertaking.  Several writers have recently considered possible reasons for the translations and models which the translators may have had to give some guidance in their work

(Bickerman: 167-200; Brock, 1969, 1972; Rabin; Jellicoe, 1968: 29-73, 314-37). Brock follows Bickerman and Rabin in seeing the likely models as the court dragoman (ἑρμηνεύς), "who served as an oral interpreter in legal and commercial transactions," and the written translations of legal documents.

Although the Letter of Aristeas sees the impetus for the translation as coming from Ptolemy II, this is much debated (Gooding; Jellicoe, 1968: 29-58, 1974: 158-225). Bickermann, amongst others, sees the translation of the Torah as part of a general policy adopted by the Greeks (including Ptolemy II) of translating oriental law-codes. Brock observes, however, that the LXX is the only long oriental religious text to be translated into Greek, despite, for instance, Greek interest in Zoroaster (1972: 14). Bickerman refers to this "unique" feature of the LXX (198), but does not relate this to his earlier argument: "Ptolemy II was interested in books ... A multitude of volumes purporting to *report* the doctrines of Zoroaster was assembled in the Alexandrian library" (174, emphasis mine).

It seems more likely that the origins relate to the inner needs of the Jewish community. Thackeray (1921) sees the origin in liturgical needs. Bickermann, followed by Brock, rejects this, stating that the continuous reading of the Torah in the synagogue was hardly current as early as the 3rd century B.C., although there was use of certain passages. Associated also with the synagogue and (with Brock, 1972: 16) providing the main incentive for a translation would be the need in teaching. It seems almost certain that a translation into Greek was needed because for so many Alexandrian Jews Hebrew had become a foreign tongue and thus the LXX was welcomed by them (Hanhart, 1962; Sevenster: 83ff). Whether the immediate need be liturgical or, more likely, educational, it is Jewish needs rather than Egyptian initiative which is significant. This is unquestionably the case for books outside the Torah.

Certainly the Torah was translated first with other books following at the hands of different translators whose translation techniques and knowledge of Hebrew and Greek varied considerably (Thackeray, 1902 a, b, c, 1906; Orlinsky, 1975). In the classification of the various books given by Thackeray

(1909: 13-14, 1929: 2729-31) only the Pentateuch, Joshua (part), Isaiah and I Maccabees are listed as "good *koine* Greek."

The question as to whether to adopt a literal (i.e., word for word) or free translation must have been of great concern to the first translators, as it has been to subsequent Bible translators. Orlinsky stresses that "one did not deal lightly with the text of Holy Writ" (1975: 103). Brock refers to the compromise in the Pentateuch which is neither consistently free nor consistently literal, although specifically legal passages tend to be more literal, as also in secular translations into Greek in Egypt (1972: 20).

The difficulties involved in translation and the differences between "what was originally expressed in Hebrew" and the "sense when translated into another language" are expressed at an early date in the Prologue to the Wisdom of Ben Sirach. It is with aspects of these difficulties and differences as they occur for one translator, the translator of the Book of Isaiah, that this present investigation is concerned.

B.    THE BOOK OF ISAIAH:

Any discussion of the LXX of the Book of Isaiah is greatly indebted to the studies of Ottley, Ziegler, and Seeligmann. In addition there are the brief works of Thackeray (1902c) and Orlinsky (1956).

Among these writers there is general agreement that the whole book is by one translator, except perhaps chapters 36-39 (Orlinsky, 1956: 200, 1974: 89-90, 107; Hurwitz), and that the LXX *Vorlage* is compatible with MT except in a few debatable instances. A detailed discussion of the relationship between LXX, MT, and $Q^a$ is given by Ziegler (1959). While Gray (1910) and Baumgärtel /5/ argue for two translators, the studies of Ziegler (1934: 1-45) and Seeligman (39-42) give much evidence to support the single translator view. The present study also gives no evidence requiring two translators (except perhaps for chaps. 36-39). We shall thus regularly refer to "the (Isaiah) translator".

There is also general agreement that the Isaiah translation is early, possibly first after the Hexateuch (so

Thackeray), and that, as a translation, it is to be sharply
distinguished from the rest of the prophetic books. Although
Seeligmann (70-94) argues that Isaiah follows Psalms, Ezekiel
and the Minor Prophets our study suggests independence of these
books, thus supporting Thackeray's arguments for early date.
Most refer to the translator's "incompetence" — Katz regards
him as being "completely unequal to the task" (1954: 200-01) —
and to his habit, when faced with difficulty, of using
favourite "stop-gap" words (listed in detail in Ottley, 1: 50,
and Ziegler, 1934: 13-14). At the same time little attention
has been given to Thackeray's conclusion that "he employs a
Greek which much more nearly approaches the classical style
than the Greek of the more painstaking translators of the other
prophetical books" (1902c: 583). Seeligmann (42f) notes his
large Greek vocabulary. Although certain Hebrew constructions
do occur this would seem to reflect the fact that this is a
translation.

The evident freedom which the translator has seen fit to
exercise means that it is easier to see his own theological
predilections. In the course of our study several instances
shall be observed where it is evident that it is his general
understanding of a passage which has affected his translation
rather than any inability to understand the underlying Hebrew:
i.e., it can be seen that he must have known the meaning of the
words in a particular verse, but has altered the syntax or
otherwise translated less literally in order to carry on the
general tenor of the passage as he interprets it (cf. Ziegler,
1934: 7-8). Nevertheless, the task of being the first to
translate a prophetic book must have been exacting (cf.
Thackeray, 1929: 2730).

Both the early date and the style make it of value to
examine the theological thought of the translator of the Book
of Isaiah.

3.    JEWISH GREEK?

As a result of investigations of non-literary papyri,
inscriptions and ostraca (see Deissmann; Moulton and Milligan),
it became common-place to assert that the language of the LXX
and NT had close affinities with vernacular *koine* Greek. For
the LXX Thackeray could say that "'Biblical Greek,' once

considered a distinct species, is now a rather discredited
term" (1929: 2722). This consensus has been gravely disputed,
especially by Turner (Hill's lexical studies follow him) and,
to a lesser extent, by Gehman. (For general discussions, see
Vergote; Bauer, 1957; Colwell.)

It is necessary to distinguish among various questions:

(1)     To what extent is the *syntax* of the LXX either a
        translation syntax or a reflection of spoken language?

(2)     Why did the various translators choose the *words* they
        did, and to what extent was the Greek word used with a
        Hebrew meaning?

(3)     To what extent did the varieties of LXX *syntax* give rise
        to changes in subsequent language use, spoken and/or
        written (such as NT)?

(4)     To what extent did the use of certain Greek *words* in
        certain LXX contexts give rise to later semantic
        changes?

(1) and (2) relate to the translation process, (3) and
(4) to subsequent impact. (It is of interest to compare
answers to these same questions applied to the early English
versions.) It would appear that in much discussion to date
there has been a confusion of these four areas, with data and
conclusions pertinent to one area being used uncritically to
justify statements in another. Our investigation is limited to
the translation process. Here one must be alert to variations
both among translators and also within the work of a single
translator. Thus, for instance, Brock argues that in the
Pentateuch the "very inconsistency (wavering between use of
natural Greek expression and a syntactic calque on the
original) argues against the existence of Jewish Greek" (1972:
32).

Of relevance to all these areas are the characteristics
highlighted by Rabin: "automatic response translation,"
rendering source-language words mechanically by the receptor-
language word on which the translator hit when he first met the
source-language word, and "semantic tolerance" shown by a
hearer who is able to absorb, due to context, unusual words or
senses of words (8-13) /6/. Hill suggests that such semantic
tolerance "might introduce new elements into that language -
producing something of a 'new sub-language.'" /7/ This appears
to be a moderating of his earlier enthusiastic endorsing of a
Jewish Greek in the LXX itself. An awareness of the

translation process seems also to be behind Gehman's
moderating of earlier statements. Thus in 1951 he refers to
the "pronounced Hebrew cast" of the Greek of the LXX and argues
that, if the translation made sense to Hellenistic Jews, then
this was because this was already a familiar way of speech -
surely a *non sequitur* (compare again the analogy of early
English versions) (1951: 90). To be preferred is his 1972
conclusion, that the translators had "a high respect for the
original ... *Consequently* in many instances they wrote a
Hebraic Greek" (1972: 45; emphasis mine). (See also his
conclusions in 1953: 148. His view now approaches that of
Orlinsky, 1974, 1975: 103-108.) Gehman is willing to see a
closer link between Hellenistic word usage and LXX choice of
words than are either Turner or Hill.

The present study is mainly concerned with area (2)
described above, viz., the reasons why a translator used
certain words and what meaning he saw in those words in their
context. In this regard we note the categorization given by
Caird of classes in which any word or expression found in the
LXX may fall:

"1.     Well-attested Greek usage which adequately renders the
        Hebrew;

2.      Well-attested Greek usage which inadequately renders the
        Hebrew, because the translator for reasons of his own
        decided to alter or improve the original;

3.      Well-attested Greek usage which points to a misreading
        of the Hebrew text or a variant reading;

4.      The only or earliest surviving instance of a piece of
        current Hellenistic speech;

5.      An instance of semantic change induced by the new
        associations which the Greek term has acquired by being
        placed in a Hebrew context;

6.      A neologism ... because the translator knew of no Greek
        equivalent;

7.      A strained or unnatural usage, produced by mechanical
        methods of translation;

8.      A transliteration from the Hebrew;

9.      ... Textual corruption in the Greek ..."   (1968: 455)

It should be observed that one Greek word or expression may
come under different categories in various occurrences.

Further, there should be added another category:

2a.     Well-attested Greek usage which inadequately renders the
        Hebrew because the translator understood the Hebrew in a

Greek sense.

Stress must be placed on examination of the *LXX context* of individual words as it is this that helps us to see the intention of the translator. Also, in relation to area (5) - subsequent semantic change of Greek words - it must be remembered that these words were read and heard in their *LXX* context.

4.    PREVIOUS STUDIES ON ΔΙΚΑΙΟΣΥΝΗ AND ΔΙΚΑΙΟΥΝ IN THE LXX.

Much attention has been given to the meaning of δικαιοσύνη and δικαιοῦν in the NT, especially in Pauline literature. In most cases account has been taken of classical Greek and LXX usage, and here issues raised in the previous section are pertinent. On the part of many, these studies are related to the Hebrew צדק and there is considerable debate as to the extent to which Paul's usage is a reflection of Hebrew or of classical Greek usage, especially for the phrase, δικαιοσύνη θεοῦ /8/.

While in most cases the LXX is rightly seen to provide a link between MT and NT usage, it is generally treated in a mechanical manner on the basis of word-translation statistics with the unexpressed (and unrecognized?) assumption that the LXX context has the same meaning as MT (so particularly Schrenk, 1935; Hill: 104-09; and Ziesler: 52-69). Further, no account is taken in any of these works (except that of Seeligmann) of possible variations among translators, and often the LXX is treated indiscriminately with inter-testamental literature. When the LXX has been treated in its own right the studies have been brief, but often contain valuable insights.

For LXX use we may note the following conclusions of studies to date.

A.    ΔΙΚΑΙΟΥΝ.

Most writers describe two main uses in classical Greek: that with an impersonal object, with a meaning such as "deem, declare to be right," and that with a personal object, "treat justly, do justice to." The second use is seen to be predominantly with the negative sense, "punish, condemn," and contrasted with LXX positive emphasis, "vindicate" or "acquit, declare righteous," including cases where the object is an

unrighteous person. (So Dodd: 51-53; Schrenk, 1935: 211-14;
Hill: 101-02, 106-09; Ziesler: 47-48, 52-58; and Watson.
Snaith, 1944: 162-66, sees any forensic or judicial sense as
being "very attenuated," but he has been effectively answered
by Watson.) Of note is the use of the passive δικαιοῦσθαι to
translate the Qal of צדק.

Hill sees a complete disjunction between secular Greek
and LXX usage: "The verb δικαιόω is not found with its secular
Greek meanings in the LXX: it has to be interpreted in terms of
the Hebrew roots it renders" (109). Dodd and Ziesler, however,
are willing to see some links. Dodd sees the meaning
"vindicate" as being a possible development from the neutral
sense "treat justly" observable in the passive used by
Aristotle, and both Dodd and Ziesler regard the meaning
"acquit" as possibly coming from a shift in the use of the
meaning with an impersonal object, "deem right," applied to a
personal object. Both recognize the meaning, "acquit" with
"the guilty" as object, as being an unnatural usage: a secular
Greek reader would see a sense, "condemn."

While Hill (109) and Ziesler (58) conclude that δικαιοῦν
has to be interpreted in accordance with the Hebrew, Dodd
comments that "the close connection of δικαιοῦν with the
narrower sense of 'justice' very largely obscures the full
meaning of הצדיק and gives to the Greek-speaking world a
thinner and poorer substitute for this characteristic Hebrew
idea" (53).

One of the purposes of this study is to re-examine both
secular Greek and LXX usage.

B.    ΔΙΚΑΙΟΣΥΝΗ.

There is general consensus as to the meanings of
δικαιοσύνη in classical Greek, referring to "righteousness" as
a virtue, or more narrowly to "justice," expressed in social
duties and related to conformity to some norm (although some
aspects of this require further investigation: see Chapter II).
Dodd sees the LXX use of δικαιοσύνη to translate צדק as being
inadequate:

> "Two aspects of צדק are polarized into δικαιοσύνη
> and ἐλεημοσύνη. In place of the comprehensive
> virtue of צדקה, we have justice on the one hand,
> mercy on the other. Similarly, in reference to

God, instead of thinking of a צדק which included
the element of grace, the Greek reader of the Old
Testament was obliged to think here of justice,
there of mercy." (56-57)

Most writers, however, regard the fact that the overwhelming majority of instances of צדק(ה) are translated by
δικαιοσύνη to be evidence of considerable semantic overlap.
The use of δικαιοσύνη to occasionally render אמת, חסד, and
משפט, seen as covenant words, is also used to support this
contention. Thus, for example, Ziesler "can see no reason to
assume any different range of meaning (for δικαιοσύνη) from
that of *ts-d-q*" (64; so essentially Schrenk, 1935: 195f; Hill:
104-09; Stuhlmacher: 108-112; Ziesler: 59-68; and Cranfield:
94f).

Of particular note is the LXX use of δικαιοσύνη
referring to God. Hill makes much of this, stating as his
first point in summarising the "considerable expansion and
change" which the δίκαιο-words underwent: "The words were
employed to refer to God's character, attitude and actions. In
classical Greek usage, δίκαιος, etc., were not terms used of
the divine, except at a very early date" (108f; cf. Stuhlmacher: 102-05 and references there). This statement, in
itself, is unexceptional, but Hill's emphasis is clearly seen:

> "There is nothing in Greek thought lastingly
> comparable to the idea of the 'righteousness
> of God,' and consequently no development of the
> meaning of δικαιοσύνη towards 'victory' or
> 'salvation.' This significance was added to
> the word in biblical Greek usage through the
> LXX translator's use of it to render צדקות־יהוה."
> (103; cf. 300)

It is especially the last sentence that is much debatable and
concerning which our study will make some contribution, as part
of a larger investigation of semantic overlap between צדק(ה)
and δικαιοσύνη in the LXX of Isaiah.

5.      צדק IN THE OLD TESTAMENT.

This century there have been several studies on the root
צדק in the Old Testament /9/. Mention should be made of the
summary of earlier studies given in Schmid, Reventlow (neither
discuss English-language material), and Scullion (1971: 335-
337).

Schmid and Reventlow highlight the two streams that have

been evident in modern studies. The older stream (continuing
to today /10/) emphasises the idea of "conformity to a norm,"
this frequently being forensic. Over against this is an
emphasis upon "relationship" leading to the description,
"Gemeinschaftsverhältnis" and a translation of צדק(ה) as
"Gemeinschaftstreue" /11/. Arising out of the latter has come
the question as to whether צדק can ever refer to the punitive
activity of Yahweh. This is particularly denied by Cazelles,
von Rad, Horst and Stuhlmacher, but strongly argued for by
Dunner.

It is to the debate on these issues that Schmid makes a
major contribution (with further development by Reventlow,
1971). In an examination of both Hebrew and Canaanite usage he
finds the root used in 6 areas: "Recht, Weisheit, Natur/
Fruchtbarkeit, Krieg/Sieg über Feinde, Kult/Opfer und
schliesslich Königtum" (14; see 13-65). He shows how these are
brought together in kingship as the other five areas are linked
with the rule of the king (see Psalm 72 and other passages
referred to, 83-89). Thus, while others have seen צדק as an
*Ordnungsbegriff* (e.g., Jepsen), his particular contribution is
to link this with the king-ideology, in which the king serves
as the son or representative of Yahweh, the "summus deus"
(166-69). He describes צדק as being *related* to *Weltordnung*,
with the "Grundbedeutung" being probably "recht, richtig, in
Ordnung" (67).

Schmid is thus able to bring together those uses of
צדק(ה) which have suggested the idea of norm and those which
have pointed to relationship, to take account of uses in both
salvation and forensic contexts, and to include all of the
specific uses referring to Yahweh, communities, individuals,
ritual and things. At the same time it is from the context
that one is to determine the particular meaning, the
"Konkretion" of צדק:

> "Das Substantiv צדק bezeichnet ursprünglich die
> kosmische Ordnung, die sich in Weisheit, Recht
> usf. konkretisiert und vom König im Rahmen des
> Irdischen gewährleistet wird, צדיק dementsprechend
> das in diesem Horizont ordnungsgemässe oder sogar
> ordnungschaffende Verhalten oder Handeln." (67) /12/

It is on this basis that one can speak of "recht, in Ordnung
sein." It is a strength of his work that he recognizes

varieties within the OT: "Die Vokabel ist konstant, der
Begriff, das Verstandnis der Vokabel, ist variabel. Was
'recht', 'in Ordnung' ist, ergibt sich ... aus der Theologie
des jeweiligen Autors" (169). In deutero-Isaiah צדק points to
"die Heilsordnung Jahwes" (168). In answering those who deny a
punitive aspect, he concludes, "Zur Wahrung der Ordnung gehört,
dass der רשע, der sich selbst ausserhalb der Grenzen des Kosmos
begeben hat, umkommt. So ist selbst das Verderben des Frevlers
Vollzug der heilvollen Ordnung" (179).

A study such as Schmid's enables us more adequately to
recognize the variety in the uses of צדק and reminds us to look
more carefully at the contexts of each occurrence, beginning
with the concrete use. The Book of Isaiah is particularly
interesting because of the variety: in chaps. 1-39 there are
contexts referring to the reign of the king, covenant-community
behaviour, and forensic situations; in chaps. 40-55, to
salvation and military victory, as well as community behaviour,
linked with Yahweh's purposes in creation; and in chaps. 56-66,
there are salvation contexts as well as those referring to the
moral and ritual behaviour of the people of Israel /13/.

Of particular relevance to our study is the use in
chaps. 40-55 of צדק(ה) almost as a synonym of salvation and
prosperity. This is stressed by many, including commentators
on these chapters (e.g., Descamps: 1446, 1459f; Snaith, 1944:
87-91; Eichrodt, 1961: 246f; von Rad, 1962: 372; Justesen: 56f;
Hill: 91f; Schmid: 132f; Ziesler, 29f; and Scullion). There is
debate as to whether this meaning is also to be seen in chaps.
56-66: Scullion argues for continuity, essentially in agreement
with Schmid (134-37).

The concern of all of these studies has been mainly the
nouns. The verb forms are usually interpreted on the basis of
the understanding of the root, and in light of the context.
Unlike the nouns, most uses of the verbs appear to be in
forensic situations (KB; Ziesler: 18-22). Thus the Qal has
been given meanings such as "be in the right, be just," and the
Hiphil, "declare to be just, vindicate," and perhaps "deliver."
Further discussion will be left to the contextual studies on
the various passages in Isaiah where the verb occurs.

6.    NATURE, METHOD OF INVESTIGATION AND CONTRIBUTION OF THE
      PRESENT STUDY.

The present study builds upon and contributes to the
various current issues in Biblical research which have been
outlined in the preceding sections.

The main aim is to determine how one of the LXX
translators, namely the Isaiah translator, interpreted one
important Hebrew root, צדק: what he understood to be the
meaning of the Hebrew words he read and of the Greek words he
used, in their respective contexts.

The choice of צדק and of the Book of Isaiah is for
inter-related reasons:

   (a)  there is need for closer examination of LXX
        interpretations of the contexts of צדק-words, to
        further understand the meaning intended by the
        translators in their use of δικαιο-words;

   (b)  it is especially in Isaiah that צדק is used in a
        variety of contexts;

   (c)  because of characteristics of the Isaiah
        translation the translator's theology is more
        evident.

In Isaiah, as elsewhere in the LXX, the translation of
the nouns (ה)צדק is predominantly δικαιοσύνη, and of the verb,
δικαιοῦν (hiphil translated by the active, qal by the passive),
although there are instances of other translations (refer to
Appendix I for statistics).

*The method of investigation* is as follows:

(1)  To determine secular Greek usage of δικαιο-words, apart
     from Jewish influence.  This is necessary so that one
     can compare the translator's usage with that in non-
     Jewish secular Greek, so enabling a better understanding
     of possible Jewish influence on the translator's
     language.

(2)  In the Book of Isaiah, to look at each occurrence of the
     verbs, צדק and δικαιοῦν, and at each "unusual"
     translation of nouns (i.e., instances of departure from
     (ה)צדק = δικαιοσύνη).

(3)  In each case, to examine the occurrence in its literary
     context (this may be a single verse, a group of verses

or a whole chapter, as deemed relevant), determining (a) what is the meaning of the MT, as seen by various modern exegetes, and (b) how the translator interpreted the context, in light of which his understanding of particular words may be seen.

(4)     Within such a context there are often cases of (ה)צדק = δικαιοσύνη or of some other translation of note. Thus the occasion where the context is discussed, by reason of (2), will also be the occasion for the discussion of these other translations.

In this way, investigation in detail is made of 41 out of 61 instances of (ה)צדק, and 30 out of 50 instances of δικαιοσύνη. This includes 25 of the 45 instances where (ה)צדק = δικαιοσύνη (chaps. 1-39: 8 out of 15; chaps. 40-55: 8 out of 16; 56-66: 9 out of 14). A check has shown no reason to suspect that there is any difference in the uses in the passages not examined in detail.

(5)     (a) As (ה)צדק is occasionally translated by words other than those related etymologically to δικαιοσύνη, account must be taken of how these Greek words are used elsewhere in Isaiah.

(b) As δικαιοσύνη occasionally translates words other than (ה)צדק, account must be taken of how these words are translated in other contexts in Isaiah.

*The major contribution* of this investigation is in its emphasis upon and practice of the need, when investigating LXX word usage, to examine *both* the LXX and MT literary context, recognizing also differences among translators. More attention is paid to reasons why the translator used "unusual" translations, in terms of (5) above.

It is apparent that this is not a complete investigation of the semantic fields of צדק and δικαιο-words. Thus it is strictly not a complete investigation of the translator's concept of "righteousness" or "justice" (the limitations of these English words are recognized). To do so would require taking account of other ethical, judicial and soteriological words in both Hebrew and Greek. Nevertheless, the investigation of the translator's handling of certain important words, with attention given to exegesis of passages, does enable several major observations on the translator's theology and his understanding of certain words.

Our results contribute also to the discussion of the use of Greek words in a Judeo-Christian setting, especially when one observes the frequent use made of LXX Isaiah by NT writers. Of course, a discussion of *later* usage must take into account other LXX books and inter-testamental writings, including the works of Philo and Josephus. Nevertheless, such investigations would not affect our study, which is of the Isaiah translator's usage compared with Hellenistic usage outside of Jewish influence. Their value lies in providing information on other Jewish-Greek usage.

The contextual investigation of secular Greek literature provides insights into usage there, this in turn being significant for our discussion of LXX usage.

# CHAPTER II

## CLASSICAL AND HELLENISTIC (NON-JEWISH) GREEK USAGE

1.     INTRODUCTION.

Of Greek words related etymologically to the simple noun δίκη (Chantraine 1:283f), those used in the Septuagint of Isaiah include the adjectives, δίκαιος and ἄδικος, the verbs, δικαιοῦν and ἀδικεῖν, and the nouns, δικαιοσύνη, ἀδικία and ἀδίκημα.

To determine the meaning of these words in various contexts, ideally one should undertake a complete synchronic description of the associative fields of these words in Hellenistic Alexandrian writers contemporary with the Isaiah translator.  As our concern is to determine usage apart from Jewish influence, we are limited, however, to mainly earlier Greek writings whose usage may be assumed to give a reasonable indication of non-Jewish Alexandrian usage.  For this reason we shall examine mainly Plato and Aristotle, taking special note of places where they seem to present or reflect popular usage. A further limitation lies in the scope of this present work: we limit ourselves to the uses of the words listed above, although some observations will be made on other words.

It will be seen that we include the ἀ-privative forms: their usage provides valuable information concerning the meaning of the positive forms (so Chantraine).  It is of note that Aristotle begins his discussion on "Justice" by referring to ἄδικος (*EN* V.i. 1129a).  Sawyer, refers to the value of opposition between lexical items (83), but Schrenk (1935), Dodd, and Ziesler make no mention of the negative forms, while Hill makes only one reference (101).

Taking Plato and Aristotle separately, we shall look at their discussions relating to "justice" /l/ and observe their use of words in context.  Note is taken of the strictures raised by Barr (1961).  Our concern is mainly word usage, but it must be said that both Plato and Aristotle regarded

21

themselves as considering concepts which were associated with
the words and as explicating the use of the words in harmony
with the concepts.

Other writers shall then be considered where it is
believed their usage is relevant. This will be especially
necessary for the verb forms. (Texts and translations, unless
otherwise stated, are from the appropriate volumes in Loeb.)

2.    PLATO.

The main discussion of δικαιοσύνη is in the *Republic*,
where, in his conclusion in Book IV, Plato endorses a common
view that "to do one's own business and not be a busibody is
δικαιοσύνη" (433a). Plato gives this a new basis by showing
that, when each of the three classes of society performs its
proper function, this is δικαιοσύνη and makes the city δίκαια
(434c). Conversely, ἀδικία is "the interference with one
another's business of three existent classes and the
substitution of the one for the other" (434b-c).

He argues from the state to the individual and uses the
same description of the harmonious working together of parts to
elucidate the meaning of δικαιοσύνη and ἀδικία for the
individual (441c-444e). His use of δικαιοσύνη as "psychic
harmony" seems to have no link with ordinary use or with other
philosophers and so need not concern us here (for his argument
here, see Sachs, Demos and Vlastos). What is significant is
that when he gives examples of the kinds of actions which a
just man will not do, each example involves actions in
relationships with society and the gods, such as embezzlement,
sacrilege, theft, "adultery, and neglect of parents and of due
service of the gods" (442e-443a). There is also a close
relationship between one's action and one's self. Not only
does a man whose self is characterised by "justice" perform
"just" actions, but also "just" actions produce "justice" and
"unjust" "injustice" (444c).

Having proved his major point concerning the intrinsic
benefits of "justice," Plato goes on to consider rewards in
this life and after death. He speaks quite explicitly of the
religious context: "For by the gods assuredly that man will
never be neglected who is willing and eager to be righteous,
and by the practice of virtue be likened unto god so far as

this is possible for man" (X.612c), and conversely for the
unjust man (613b). A similar idea is seen in *Lg*. IV.716d,
where conduct appropriate in the State in which law is supreme
is that which is "dear to God and in his steps."

In judgement after death the specific examples of "doing
wrong" (ἀδικεῖν) to a person are: being the cause of many
deaths, betraying cities and armies and reducing them to
slavery, being a participant in any other iniquity, and
especially impiety (ἀσέβεια) towards the gods and parents and
self-slaughter. Such wrongdoers are opposed to those who have
"done deeds of kindness," have been "just and holy" (δίκαιοι
καὶ ὅσιοι), and have shown piety (εὐσέβεια) to the gods and
parents (X.615a, b; cf. *Phd*. 113d-114b).

Turning briefly to other writings of Plato we may note
the following:
*Euthyphr*. 11e-12e is a lengthy discussion of the relationship
between δίκαιος and ὅσιος. The conclusion is, that τὸ ὅσιον is
the species of τὸ δίκαιον which has to do with the service of
the gods. This agrees with several statements in the *Republic*
which include piety to the gods as an example of just deeds.
*Cri*. 49b links very closely the law of the state and just or
unjust actions: "Granted it was unjust to condemn him to death,
can it ever be right for him to escape by breaking the law? ...
One must not even do wrong when one is wronged" (ET by
Tredennick). Similar are *Ap*. 37b and *Grg*. 469b, c ("μᾶλλον
ἀδικεῖσθαι ἤ ἀδικεῖν").

There are several statements concerning popular under-
standings. In *R*. I.331c-e, Cephalus thinks of "justice" as
essentially involving "just acts," and in particular, "not to
cheat any man even unintentionally or play him false, not
remaining in debt to a god for some sacrifice or to a man for
money," and concurs with the view attributed to Simonides
"that it is just to render to each his due." While Plato feels
that the definition of Cephalus is too imprecise (Plato himself
is opposed to classifying specific acts *per se* as "just" or
"unjust"), he does refer to the task of rulers as seeing that
"no one shall have what belongs to others or be deprived of his
own" (*R*. IV.433e).

The Sophist view is presented by Thrasymachus: "I affirm

that the just (τὸ δίκαιον) is nothing else than the advantage
of the stronger" as rulers enact laws to their own advantage
(*R.* I.338c-e) /2/.

Glaucon presents the view that justice is "a compromise
(μεταξύ) between the best, which is to do wrong with impunity,
and the worst, which is to be wronged and be impotent to get
one's revenge" (*R.* II.359a).

Finally there is the speech of Agathon praising Eros in
*Smp.* 196b: Eros "neither to a god gives nor from a god receives
any injury (οὔτ'ἀδικεῖ οὔτ'ἀδικεῖται) /3/, nor from men
receives it nor to men gives it ... (since) Love wins all men's
willing service; and agreements on both sides willingly made
are held to be just by 'our city's sovereign the law.'"  The
speech of Eryximachus in *Smp.* 188a distinguishes two kinds of
love: one is "orderly" and "guilty of no wrong (οὐδὲν
ἠδίκησεν)," being closely linked with "harmony," whereas the
"wanton-spirited Love ... wreaks great destruction and wrong
(ἠδίκησεν)," including "pestilences and diseases in beasts and
herbs, frost and hail."  While allowing for the poetic
language, the close link between ἀδικεῖν and lack of harmony is
evident.

We may summarise Plato's discussion of "justice" as
follows:

(a) Justice involves action in conformity with the laws
of the state, even if one considers the laws unjust
(in which case one should seek to have the laws
changed).

(b) The function of justice (and of laws) is the
enabling and maintaining of harmonious relations
within the state.

(c) Justice and just acts involve responsibilities to
gods, parents, other citizens, and the state, and
in general is concerned with what is due to a
person or god.

(d) Just acts are approved by the gods because they too
are just.

(e) Where illustrations are given of just actions or of
the deeds of just men or cities, they are of
actions which maintain harmony.  Conversely, unjust
actions disrupt the harmony; and an unjust man
should be punished so that "the brutish part is
tamed and the gentle part liberated" (*R.* IX.591b),
this punishment being the task of rulers (*R.*
IV.433e).

These points would be generally accepted by Plato's contem-

poraries, albeit with varying emphases. Specifically Platonic
is:

(f) δικαιοσύνη for the individual involves an order and
balance within one's self.

While Plato puts much emphasis on maintaining the right
balance between the constituents of the state or elements of
the individual, there is little explicit information on where
the balance is to be struck. His description of actual acts is
quite traditional. [Further discussions are in the
introductions to the translations of the *Republic* by Shorey
(Loeb) and H. D. P. Lee, and in Shorey, 1918, 1971.]

FURTHER COMMENTS ON SEMANTICS.

(1)    δίκαιος and άδικος are used frequently to describe
people, the state and deeds in contexts relating to (a)-(e)
above. Vlastos (86) highlights two uses of "just": one as a
relational predicate (the way a person habitually relates
himself to others), and the other a group-predicate (applied to
a group whose members are "just" in the first sense). With
most of this use Plato's contemporaries would agree. Plato's
particular concern with the subjective aspects means that his
use is broader in its ethical connotation. Often words such as
"just," "fair," "right," "righteous" (and their opposites)
would be appropriate English translations.

(2)    δικαιοσύνη and άδικία are the corresponding abstract
nouns, referring to the quality (either virtue/vice or
condition) of a city or person whose life is characterised by
such actions. In *R*. IV.443d-444a, the use of δίκαια/άδικα to
describe actions which maintain/destroy the "single controlled
and orderly whole" of the *individual* is recognized by Plato as
being somewhat forced /4/. But this only emphasises that such
use for the *State* is normal: actions are δίκαια when they help
to maintain the δικαιοσύνη of a state, δικαιοσύνη in turn
referring to a situation when everyone performs his proper
function, doing his own business, much of this being prescribed
by laws; and a person who so acts can be described as δίκαιος.

(3)    The verb δικαιοῦν is used only three times by Plato,
whereas άδικεῖν occurs many times, in both active and passive
forms.

In most of the occurrences of άδικεῖν the immediate

context shows clearly that it involves doing something which harms another person and is contrary to the law of the city. Thus, e.g., *Ap.* 19b: Socrates "ἀδικεῖ καὶ περιεργάζεται in that he inquires into things below the earth and in the sky, and makes the weaker argument defeat the stronger and teaches others to follow his example" /5/. When the meaning to be conveyed is "harm," with *no* sense of injustice, then βλάπτειν is used, e.g., *R.* I.335e (cf. *Cri.* 49) in a debate on whether "it is just to harm (βλάπτειν) the unjust." *Smp.* 196b links ἀδικεῖν and laws that define what is δίκαιον, while *Smp.* 188a links ἀδικεῖν with lack of harmony (both quoted above). When the opposite of ἀδικεῖν is spoken of, the usual way is μὴ(οὐ) with ἀδικεῖν or ἀδικεῖσθαι (e.g., *Lg.* 829a; *Smp.* 188a, 196b; *Ap.* 37b).

Two of the three occurrences of δικαιοῦν refer to a quote from Pindar, *Fr.* 169.3, given fully in *Grg.* 484b, "νόμος ... ἄγει δικαιῶν τὸ βιαιότατον ὑπερτάτᾳ χειρι," while *Lg.* IV.715a refers to "τὸν Πίνδαρον ἄγειν δικαιοῦντα τὸ βιαιότατον." There are two separate questions here: Pindar's meaning and Plato's use (see Dodds: 270; also supporting text as quoted). In *Gorgias* Callicles is quoting Pindar in speaking about "natural justice." Later (488b) we read, "Repeat what you and Pindar hold natural justice to consist in: is it that the superior should forcibly despoil (ἄγειν) the inferior?" This suggests "declare to be right" for the meaning of δικαιοῦν [Dodds, "making just"; W. Lamb (Loeb), "justifies"].

Pindar's meaning is more contentious. Many have seen a sense as in Plato: J. Sandys (Loeb), "justifies"; LSJ "set right," but changed in *Sup* and now included under "pronounce and treat as righteous, justify, vindicate." This has been disputed, especially by Pavese who argues for the meaning "bring to justice" since, "in the few instances where the verb governs a noun (as distinct from infinitive or clause), it always means 'to bring to justice,' i.e., 'to punish'" (57-59, 69-71). Lloyd-Jones has effectively replied to this on the basis of the total context in Pindar, reaffirming "making just." We would add that Pavese's proposed meaning occurs only with a personal object. Thus Pindar's use, as well as Plato's, is similar to that which we shall observe in other writers /6/.

The other occurrence of δικαιοῦν is in *Lg*. XI.934b (here passive). Compensation must be paid "in all cases where one man causes damage to another by acts of robbery or violence ... (so that) both he himself and those who behold his punishment (τοὺς ἰδόντας αὐτὸν δικαιούμενον) may either entirely loathe his sin or at least renounce such conduct" [so R. G. Bury (Loeb); LSJ: "chastise, punish," but *Sup*: "brought to justice."]. Here we observe a corrective aspect: δικαιοσύνη must be maintained, so there is probably in δικαιοῦν here the dual sense of "brought to justice" and "punish so as to prevent continuation of unjust acts."

If such is the meaning of δικαιοῦν with a personal object in Plato's time, this would explain its rarity in Plato, as he rarely discusses the trial of wrongdoers and is rather concerned with the acts of citizens to each other. Thus, while one can wrong (ἀδικεῖν) another, contrary to law, the opposite is not δικαιοῦν but either μὴ ἀδικεῖν or δίκαιος εἶναι.

3.   ARISTOTLE.

The main discussion is in the *Nicomachean Ethics*, Bk. V, with comments in the *Eudemian Ethics* and *Rhetoric*. [See H. Rackam (Loeb); Joachim; and Hardie, especially ch. X, "Justice."] *Rhetorica ad Alexandrum* shall be treated separately as there is real doubt as to its being written by Aristotle, although it is contemporary with Alexander.

Aristotle commences with the two kinds of people to whom ἄδικος applies: ὁ παράνομος ("the man who breaks the law") and ὁ πλεονέκτης καὶ ἄνισος ("the man who takes more than his due /7/, the unfair man"). Thus ὁ δίκαιος will be ὁ τε νόμιμος καὶ ὁ ἴσος, and τὸ μὲν δίκαιον ἄρα τὸ νόμιμον καὶ τὸ ἴσον, τὸ δ᾽ἄδικον τὸ παράνομον καὶ τὸ ἄνισον (*EN*. V.1129a31ff). Accordingly, one sense of "just/unjust" is "lawful/unlawful." Because laws are determined by a legislature for the common interest of all or of a ruling class, so "just" can be "applied to anything that produces and preserves the happiness (ἡ εὐδαιμονία) ... of the political community" (1129b17-19; cf. VIII.1160a11-14). The law also prescribes certain conduct, "commanding virtues and forbidding vices" (1129b19-25). "Justice (δικαιοσύνη) then in this sense is perfect Virtue,

though with a qualification, namely, that it is displayed
towards others" (1129b26f). Thus Aristotle approves the view
expressed by Thrasymachus in Plato, *R*. I.343c, that, of all the
virtues, Justice alone is another's good (1130a3f). Hardie
comments:

> "Aristotle's meaning here is unclear. Most
> virtues and vices are manifested in actions which
> affect, and often are in their nature intended to
> affect, others; liberality for example. Perhaps
> what Aristotle has in mind is that, when we say
> that an act is injurious or wrong, we are not
> merely saying that it manifests an ethical fault;
> we are saying that it is an offence or trans-
> gression against a fellow citizen of a kind which
> can lead to prosecution in the courts." (185f)

We would add to this, that Aristotle thinks of "justice" in
terms also of one's responsibilities as a member of a community
(1130a1-5).

Aristotle's main concern is not with this universal
(ἡ ὅλη) sense of justice/injustice (linked with law), but with
the particular (κατὰ μέρος) sense as a part of virtue/vice
(linked with δίκαιος/ἄδικος as ἴσος/ἄνισος). Both kinds
however are "exhibited in a man's relation to others" (1130b1).
Particular justice is involved with (a) "the distribution of
honour, wealth, and the other divisible assets of the
community," and (b) "supplying a corrective principle in
private transactions," both "voluntary" (buying, selling, etc.)
and "involuntary" (theft, adultery, etc.) (1130b30-1131b9). He
seeks to establish "due proportion," not equality, and
concludes: in such distribution, "Justice (δικαιοσύνη) is that
quality in virtue of which a man (ὁ δίκαιος) is said to be
disposed to do by deliberate choice that which is just (το
δίκαιον)" (1134a1-6).

A close link between "justice" and "law" is frequently
seen elsewhere in Aristotle's writings. Of note are the
definitions in *Rhetoric*: "Justice (δικαιοσύνη) is a virtue
which assigns to each man his due in conformity with the law,
... injustice (ἀδικία) claims what belongs to another, in
opposition to the law" (I.1366b9f); "let injustice (τὸ ἀδικεῖν)
be defined as voluntarily causing injury (τὸ βλαπτεῖν) contrary
to the law" (I.1368b6; cf. *EN*. V.1135a31). At the same time,
while written laws should be as detailed as possible to "leave

as little as possible to judges" (*Rh.* I.1354a31-b12), there are
limits where the law is defective and erroneous due to its
absoluteness and generality and here "equity" is needed (*EN.*
V.1137a30ff). The function of a judge is to "restore equality"
acting as a "mediator" (*EN.* V.1132a6-25).

It is the role of a ruler to see that "justice" fulfils
its function of producing and preserving the well-being and
harmony of the community. "A just ruler ... labours for
others, which accounts for the saying that 'Justice is the good
of others'" (*EN.* V.1134a35-b7; cf. 1136b32ff on the unjust
ruler). Associated is the close link made between "justice"
and "friendship," e.g., *EN.* VIII.1159b25-1162a33 (chaps.
ix-xii) and *EE.* VII.1234b18-31.

While it is not our purpose to discuss in detail
Aristotle's analysis, we observe that, compared with Plato, he
is not concerned with the subjective aspects of δικαιοσύνη, but
with its practical expression in the community, especially in
its particular sense as one of the virtues. Like Plato he
distinguishes clearly voluntary and involuntary acts (see
later).

Parallelling our earlier summary of Plato, we may
summarize Aristotle's discussion as follows:

    (a)   Justice involves actions in conformity with the
laws of the community; the function of a ruler is
to administer these laws to which he himself is
subject.

    (b)   The function of justice (and of laws) is the
enabling and maintaining of the common advantage of
the community, which means that everyone receives
his due. (He does not include responsibilities to
the gods.)

    (c)   Justice and just acts involve responsibilities to
other members of the community, and are concerned
with what is due to each member, in terms of "the
Mean" and "the Good" (see Hardie, chaps. II, XI, on
these terms).

    (d)   Due to the idea of "the Mean," the doing of
beneficial deeds and the refraining from wronging a
person are both emphasized. "Corrective justice"
involves a penalty that must be paid to restore the
correct balance in community relationships, and
this is determined by judges.

While the logical structure, centering on the idea of "the
Mean," is specifically Aristotelian, the nature of his
discussion suggests that other aspects of word usage would be

familiar to his contemporaries.

FURTHER COMMENTS ON SEMANTICS.

(1)    The link between noun and adjective forms is clearly seen in *EN*. V.1129a6-10:

> "We observe that everybody means by Justice (δικαιοσύνη) that moral disposition which renders man apt to do just things (πρακτικοί τῶν δικαίων), and which causes them to act justly (δικαιοπραγοῦσι) and wish what is just (τὰ δίκαια); and similarly by Injustice (ἀδικία) that disposition which makes men act unjustly (ἀδικοῦσι) and wish what is unjust (ἄδικα)."

Earlier quotes from 1129a31ff, dealing with the common understanding of the adjectives, are also relevant. δίκαιος/ἄδικος are uniformly used of people and actions and refer to law-conformity/law-breaking and "fairness"/"unfairness." Aristotle's theoretical structure does not alter the common use of the words in contexts in which one wishes to speak of "fairness," but rather explicates the contexts in which it is appropriate to speak thus.

(2)    As does Plato, Aristotle frequently uses the verb ἀδικεῖν, both with and without a personal object, and in both active and passive forms. It is used both for "voluntarily causing injury (τὸ βλάπτειν ἑκόντα) contrary to the law" (*Rh*. I.1368b6) and for "having too much (τὸ πλέον ἔχειν)," with ἀδικεῖσθαι being τὸ ἐλάττον τοῦ ἀγαθοῦ, in terms of distributive justice (*EN*. V.1133b30f; cf. 1131b19).

The usual opposite of ἀδικεῖν (active) is either μὴ ἀδικεῖν (e.g., *EN*. IV.1123b32; V.1136b32; *EE*. VII.1234b28), or, more positively, δικαιοπραγεῖν (e.g., *EN*. V.1129a8, quoted above; 1136a2-5. 19). Like ἀδικεῖν, δικαιοπραγεῖν is always "voluntary" (*EN*. V.1136a4, 19).

The verb δικαιοῦν occurs only five times in all of Aristotle's writings, each being in the passive voice (4 times δικαιοῦσθαι and once δικαιοῦνται) in the brief discussion in *EN*. V.1136a18-31. The passive is used as a deliberate antithesis to ἀδικεῖσθαι, and as the passive equivalent of the active δικαιοπραγεῖν: "ἀδύνατον γὰρ ἀδικεῖσθαι μὴ ἀδικοῦντος, ἢ δικαιοῦσθαι μὴ δικαιοπραγοῦντος" (line 30; cf. line 19). The passive thus means "be treated justly."

We must ask why Aristotle refrains from using the active

δικαιοῦν. He seems to regard it as not an appropriate word to describe the actions of ὁ δίκαιος. A clue is provided in his distinction between the nouns, δικαίωμα and δικαιοπράγημα. The passage (*EN*. V.1135a9-13) is here quoted in full as it also shows the use of ἀδίκημα:

διαφέρει δὲ τὸ ἀδίκημα καὶ τὸ ἄδικον καὶ τὸ δικαίωμα καὶ τὸ δίκαιον· ἄδικον μὲν γάρ ἐστι τῇ φύσει ἢ τάξει; τὸ αὐτὸ δὲ τοῦτο, ὅταν πραχθῇ, ἀδίκημά ἐστι, πρὶν δὲ πραχθῆναι, οὔπω, ἀλλ'ἄδικον. ὁμοίως δὲ καὶ δικαίωμα (καλεῖται δὲ μᾶλλον δικαιοπράγημα τὸ κοινόν, δικαίωμα δὲ τὸ ἐπανόρθωμα τοῦ ἀδικήματος).

From this passage it is evident that Aristotle would reserve the active δικαιοῦν for correcting or rectifying acts of injustice /8/. For the active doing of just deeds in general δικαιοπραγεῖν is preferred. It is seen also that the -μα ending denotes the performance and completion of a concrete act. Subsequently emphasis is placed upon the voluntary (ἑκούσιος) character of this act (1135a20; 1135b11-1136a5): ἀδίκημα is done knowingly, either unpremeditated, in which case the person is not ἄδικος, or deliberately, in which case the person is ἄδικος καὶ μοχθηρός.

3.1    *RHETORICA AD ALEXANDRUM.*

Of main interest is chapter IV, on forensic oratory. In 1426b30ff there is the juxtaposition (referring to actions) of "unjust" (ἄδικοι), "illegal" (παράνομοι) and "detrimental to the mass of citizens" (τῷ πλήθει τῶν πολιτῶν ἀσύμφοροι). Similarly, in 1427a26f, there is "ἔννομον καὶ δίκαιον καὶ καλὸν καὶ συμφέρον τῇ πόλει."

In 1427a30 it is suggested that, in defending a person, one should "define injustice (ἀδικία) as the deliberate commission of evil (τὸ ἐκ προνοίας κακόν τι ποιεῖν)." This puts a closer connection between act and character than does Aristotle (*EN*. V.1135b11-1136a5), but is however a rhetorical device, as in 1427a36f: "Also say that unjust conduct (ἀδικεῖν) is peculiar to wicked people (πονηρός)" (Schrenk, 1933:157, overlooks the context). The use is thus not in conflict with the Aristotelian definition. Similarly, when one's task is accusation, one should not allow a person to say he has made a mistake (ἐξαμαρτάνειν; cf. Aristotle, ἁμάρτημα, an injury done without evil intent), and thus by implication, μὴ ἀδικεῖν, otherwise everybody would "do wrong on purpose" and then put up the defence that he "made a mistake" (1427a12ff). The usage here is consistent with Aristotle.

In 1421b36ff δίκαιον is defined as "the unwritten custom (ἔθος) of the whole or greatest part of mankind, distinguishing honourable actions from base ones." "Honourable actions" are also called τὰ δίκαια and listed as "to honour one's parents, to do good to one's friends and to repay favours to one's benefactors" (1422a1). This description is similar to the popular view presented in Plato's *Republic* (I.331c-e, 334b), except that there is no mention of obligations to the gods.

Finally we note that in 1443a22 it is assumed that "the law is laid down for the public benefit."

Thus in several ways *Rhetorica ad Alexandrum* reflects the popular usage of words obtained from our investigations into the writings of Plato and Aristotle.

4.    OTHER GREEK SOURCES.

Our investigation of Plato and Aristotle, along with *Rhetorica ad Alexandrum*, has provided much information concerning popular usage of the words being studied. One could continue and investigate several other writers, but here we briefly consider, the popular orator, Isocrates.

Although Isocrates frequently discourses on δικαιοσύνη and το δίκαιον, nowhere does he give definitions. δικαιοσύνη is amongst "the most sovereign virtues" which lead to great benefit for the life of man (*Nicocles* 29f; *On the Peace* 32; cf. *To Demonicus* 15). To keep harmony in the state and in the household is a work of δικαιοσύνη (*Nicocles* 41). Similarly το δίκαιον is that which is secured by laws, is practised by men of character, constitutes the chief concern of all well-regulated states, decides wars and preserves the life of man (*Archidamus* 35). Thus a ruler shows δικαιοσύνη by being concerned for the greatness of the state and the advance of its prosperity, and not seeking to gain prosperity for himself through base means, but treating people justly (*Nicocles* 31-34, 45). While δικαιοσύνη cannot be taught (*Against the Sophists* 21, *Antidosis* 274-5), there is value in wanting to speak well since

"when anyone elects to speak or write discourses

which are worthy of praise and honour, it is not
conceivable that he will support causes which are
unjust (ἄδικος) or petty or devoted to private
quarrels, and not rather those which are great and
honourable, devoted to the welfare of man and our
common good." (*Antidosis* 276)

In his thinking there is a close link between the
practice of δικαιοσύνη and rewards, especially from the gods.
This is seen clearly in *On the Peace* 35:

"They are of all men most afflicted with unreason
who concede that justice (δικαιοσύνη) is a way of
life more noble and more pleasing to the gods than
injustice (ἀδικία), but at the same time believe
that those who follow it will live in worse case
than those who have chosen the way of evil." (Cf.
*To Demonicus* 39, *Antidosis* 282)

Isocrates' use is thus similar to that which we have
already observed in Plato and Aristotle. Accordingly we shall
not go into further detail for the use of the nouns and
adjectives in other writers.

The occurrences of δικαιοῦν in Plato and Aristotle,
however, are so few, it is necessary to look at writers over a
larger time period to elucidate the usage of the verb. Our
concern will be c. 500 B.C. to A.D. 100, spanning either side
of the probable date of translation of the various books of the
Septuagint. This excludes some writers and papyri which
receive considerable discussion in *TDNT* (e.g., Dio Cassius).
Also excluded are Jewish writings as our aim is to determine
Greek usage apart from Jewish influence. We shall not look
further at the understanding of "justice" except in so far as
this may be of help in elucidating the use of δικαιοῦν.

Our remarks shall be brief, concentrating on representative passages and those where there is some disagreement
as to the meaning in that context /9/.

4.1    AESCHYLUS.

The verb δικαιοῦν occurs only once (*Ag.* 393), in the
phrase, μελαμπαγὴς πέλει δικαιωθείς. Traditionally the verb
has been translated "proved, tested" as in LSJ and Dodd (48, n.
1). LSJ *Sup* has altered to "brought to justice." Fraenkel (1:
115; 2:202-3) shows that the imagery is not that of the
"testing" a metal, but rather that of the shining surface of a
bronze vessel which looks fine initially, but soon becomes

dark: "Only after the guilty man has received due punishment
will those who were deceived in their opinion of him in the
time of his prosperity see clearly the blackness and worthless-
ness of his character" (2:206; similarly Rose: 2:33). Thus the
context suggests the meaning "brought to justice, punished and
so shown to be what he really is (cf. Italie, "iudicare")."

All three occurrences of ἀδικεῖν are in the phrase, τὸ
μὴ ἀδικεῖν (Eu. 85, 691, 749). The general sense of the phrase
is "doing what is just and fair," particularly referring to
those in positions of responsibility. In Eu. 691 such actions
follow from "reverence" and "fear" of the gods.

4.2    SOPHOCLES.

δικαιοῦν occurs 8 times, each use being with an
infinitive or other impersonal object. In all contexts
reference is to some action being right or appropriate, i.e.,
δικαιοῦν means "deem right, think appropriate." When the
subject is God (Ph. 781) this may suggest "approve," while,
when the subject is human, there is generally present in the
context the idea of some "right" behaviour for those circum-
stances which leads to a willingness or unwillingness to act
(e.g., Aj. 1072, Tr. 1244) or to a claim as a right the doing
of some action (OT 575, 640). The "right" behaviour may be
linked with law (Aj. 1072) or custom (θέμις; OC 1642), or may
be that expected by the gods (Tr. 1244).

ἀδικεῖν occurs 3 times. Ant. 1059 refers to giving
false prophecy to gain money. In OC 174, Storr (Loeb)
translates, "let me not suffer (μὴ δῆτ᾽ ἀδικηθῶ) for my
confidence in you." This is possible, but in view of line 142,
"regard me not as a lawless one," the sense is rather, "let me
not be treated wrongly." Ph. 1035f states, "Perish you shall
for the wrong you have wrought (ἐδικηκότες) against me, if the
gods regard justice (δίκη)."

4.3    HERODOTUS.

δικαιοῦν occurs 31 times, 28 of these having as object
some action, usually in the form of an infinitive explicitly
stated. In most cases the meaning is clearly "deem or think
right, appropriate" in a particular setting or relationship.

For 3 of these 28 occurrences (2.172; 3.118; 6.86)

Schrenk (1935: 211) and LSJ say that the meaning has become
"consent, allow, agree." It is debatable whether this is
warranted. 2.172 refers to the Egyptians' reaction after the
hitherto despised new king Amasis used an acted metaphor
(changing a gold laver to a statue of a god): now δικαιοῦν
δουλεύειν, they "thought it fitting to serve him." 3.118
speaks of rightness of a particular action in terms of a law on
the basis of which Intraphenes desired (ἤθελε) to enter the
king's palace alone. The setting of 6.86 is that, because the
Athenians were not willing (βουλόμεναι) to return some men to
one king, they said that "as two kings had put the men in their
keeping, they thought not fit (δικαιοῦν) to restore them to one
without the other" (for Herodotus, Powell, 1949, is used).
Certainly in the two latter instances what is being stated is
not a matter of willingness (this is conveyed in the context by
other words) but of reasons for the "rightness" of an action.
Similarly in the first instance it is a matter of "fitness."

The remaining 3 (of 31) instances (2 active, 1 passive)
refer to some form of punishment inflicted by a ruler on
wicked-doers. In 1.100 we read of Deioces, a δικαστής: "and
the people wrote down their suits (τὰς δίκας) and ... he judged
(διακρίνων) them ... If he heard of any man that did wrong
(ὑβρίζοντα) he sent for him and chastened (ἐδικαίου) him
according to the desert of his offence (ἀδικήματος)." δικαιοῦν
is here clearly "punish as a result of judgement." 3.29 refers
to priests who were "punished" (ἐδικαιεῦντο) because Cambyses
regarded them as being guilty of mocking him with false
statements. The use in 5.92b, part of an oracle, is clear in
that the child who becomes ruler of Corinth avenges ill-
treatment given to his parents: δικαιώσει refers to
"chastising."

ἀδικεῖν is used 35 times: 13 in an absolute sense,
"commit wrong," and 22 with a person as object (4 of these
implied; 8 by use of the passive), "wrong" someone. The act of
wrongdoing varies, from disobedience of a ruler, to treating a
stranger unfairly in an athletic contest, to murder (e.g.,
1.112, 121, 155; 2.160; 7.10e). The idea of being the
initiator of wrong is frequently used when speaking of a city,
country or king which commences war without a just cause (e.g.,

3.21; 4.119; 6.87; 7.9). In each case the context shows that
the "wrongness" is in relation to some "correct, just, fair, or
normal" behaviour expected in a given situation or relationship.

## 4.4 THUCYDIDES.

δικαιοῦν occurs 12 times, 11 of these being with an
impersonal object (implied in 3). As in other writers the
impersonal use has a sense such as "deem to be right." Only
occasionally is this with a legal sense, e.g., II.71, where the
Plataeans ask to live in independence "as Pausanias granted
that to us as a right (ἐδικαίωσεν)" (cf. II.67) /10/.
Conversely, in V.105 the Athenians regard something as a right
apart from considerations of τὸ δίκαιον. They later argue that
the gods equally act on the rule that the relationship between
stronger and weaker forces overrules any question of τὸ
δίκαιον. Thus there is a sense in which the Athenians can
"deem right" their request (Gomme et al.: 4:162-65) /11/.

The only other instance of δικαιοῦν is in III.40 where
the context points to a meaning of the middle, "pass sentence
on oneself, bring judgement on oneself" (LSJ; Gomme et al.:
2:310):

> "If you take my advice (Cleon exhorting the
> Athenians to attack the Mytilenaeans) you will not
> only do what is just (τὰ δίκαια) to the Mytilenaeans
> but also what is expedient for us; but if you decide
> otherwise you will ... bring a just condemnation on
> yourselves (δικαιώσεσθε); for if these people had a
> right (ὀρθῶς) to secede, it follows that you are
> wrong (οὐ χρεῶν) in exercising dominion."

As in Herodotus, so in Thucydides, ἀδικεῖν is used (more
than 100 times) in a variety of situations in a general sense
of "do wrong" or "wrong (someone)." Often a sense of
"injustice" is quite evident (e.g., I.37, 42, 43, 53; II.71).
Explicit is I.77: "Men it seems are more resentful of injustice
(ἀδικούμενοι) than of violence (βιαζόμενοι); for the former,
they feel, is overreaching by an equal (πλεονεκτεῖσθαι) whereas
the latter is coercion by a superior." This thought was
observed earlier in V.89ff and has similarities with Aristotle.

Reference to gods in these contexts is rare. Apart from
the discussion between the Athenian envoys and the Melians
mentioned earlier, the only other allusion is in II.5 where the

Plataeans said that the Thebans "had done an impious act (ὅσια) in trying to seize their city in time of peace and they bade them do no injury (ἀδικεῖν) outside the walls (to Plataeans living outside). The Thebans withdrew without doing injury (ἀδικήσαντες)."

## 4.5    ARISTOPHANES.

There are no instances of δικαιοῦν, but ἀδικεῖν occurs 37 times. The uses are similar to those observed in other writers. Of note is *Pl.* 429-460 (4 occurrences) where Poverty is certainly being harmed, but Chremylas argues that it cannot be "doing an injustice (ἀδικεῖν)" if thereby good is brought to mankind. In *Nu.* 1080 the argument is advanced that an act which is similar to that of Zeus cannot be "unjust."

## 4.6    XENOPHON.

Nowhere is δικαιοῦν used, but ἀδικεῖν occurs frequently in a variety of contexts, again often specifically referring to an "injustice."

*"The just," "the pious" and the gods*.

Xenophon commonly distinguishes between το ἀσεβές and τὸ ἄδικον. For example, in *Cyr.* VIII.8.7 he writes περὶ μὲν θεοὺς ἀσέβειαν, περὶ δὲ ἀνθρώπους ἀδικίαν (cf. *HG* II.3.53; *Ap.* 22), and in *Mem.* IV.6.4, 6 are the two definitions, ὁ τὰ περὶ τοὺς θεοὺς νόμιμα εἰδὼς ... εὐσεβής, ... δικαίους ... εἶναι τοὺς εἰδότας τὰ περὶ ἀνθρώπους νόμιμα. That δίκαιος/ἄδικος is used with reference to community relationships is supported by examples of τὸ δίκαιον/τὰ ἄδικα: Socrates proclaimed τὸ δίκαιον in that he scrupulously obeyed all that the laws required (*Mem.* IV.4.1); things that are called δίκαια are ἃ οἱ νόμοι κελεύουσιν (6.6); and ἡ ἀδικία or τὰ ἄδικα include lying, deceit, evil-doing, selling into slavery (2.14f), "perjury or calumny or stirring up strife between friends and fellow-citizens" (4.11).

Schrenck has misinterpreted Xenophon when he concludes: "The differentiations in these passages show that ἄδικος can imply the violation of what is socially right as distinct from what is religious ... The relationship to God is not sovereignly determinative in the field of ethics" (1933: 150).

in support he also quotes *Mem*. I.4.19: ἀπέχεσθαι τῶν ἀνοσίων τε
καὶ ἄδικον καὶ αἰσχρῶν. However, the basis on which Socrates
kept his companions from these acts was by stressing the
relationships with the gods who see and hear all things and pay
heed to man's needs! Further, in the discussion in *Mem*. IV.4.
19ff on unwritten laws that are uniformly observed in all
countries, it is stated that the laws are ordained by the gods
"for among all men the first law is to fear the gods." In the
incident recorded in *HG* IV.3.20 (similar to *Ages*. 2.13)
concerning the enemy (Thebans) who had taken cover in the
temple, "he did not forget the deity but ... would permit them
(his soldiers) to do no wrong (ἀδικεῖν)." Finally there is
*Mem*. I.1.1: ἀδικεῖ Σωκράτης οὓς μὲν ἡ πόλις νομίζει θεοὺς οὐ
νομίζων.

Thus for Xenophon a man is called ἄδικος or he ἀδικεῖ
when he acts in such a way as to harm his fellow-man or disrupt
the harmony of the community, but this is in a context of laws
ordained by the gods. A failure to observe aspects of one's
responsibilities to the gods would be ἀδικεῖν if it harmed
others or the community as a whole, although there will be
other private acts that are merely ἀσέβεια.

4.7    POLYBIUS.

In III.31 is the cry: "How can anyone when wronged
himself (ἀδικούμενος) or when his country is wronged find
helpmates and allies" (31.5). There is a need to find "τὸν
ἐλεήσοντα ... τὸν συνοργιούμενον ... τὸν δικαιώσοντα" (31.9).
Here δικαιοῦν appears to have the sense of "righting an
injustice." Thus Paton (Loeb) has "join us in being avenged on
our enemies" and Schrenk (1935: 212) "to represent the cause of
someone, to secure him justice" (linked with the passive use in
Aristotle *EN* V.1136a18ff).

4.8    DIONYSIUS HALICARNASSENSIS.

In *Antiquitates Romanae* 10.1, when people came to the
kings for δίκη, "whatever they decreed (δικαιωθέν) was law."
This is a passive of the common use of δικαιοῦν, "deem right,"
the stronger connotation, "decree" (Carey, Loeb), "ordain"
(LSJ), "prescribe" (Schrenk, 1935: 211), coming from the
context.

4.9   PLUTARCH.

Of the 10 occurrences of δικαιοῦν listed by Wyttenbach, 9 are with an impersonal object with the range of meanings noted in other writers.  II.294c and I.349a (*Cato Ma.* 21.4) refer explicitly to judicial decisions: in the former, an arbitrator in a dispute decides, and, in the latter, the decision is to put someone to death.  Schrenk is misleading in describing the use as being "of the execution of the death sentence" (1935: 211): δικαιοῦν itself is act of deciding, with the death sentence as the impersonal object.

The only occurrence with a personal object is the passive use (II.565b) referring to one being "chastised" by Dike.  The context (564f) refers explicitly to this being corrective, for those who can be "healed" of evil deeds and passions.

δικαιοπραγεῖν occurs 8 times: opposite to ἀδικεῖν (II.135f, 818a, 964b) and παρανομεῖν (I.81b = *Solon* 5.3); and as a virtue linked with φρονεῖν and σωφρονεῖν (II.776d), τὸ φρονεῖν and τὸ εὖ ζῆν (II.439a), and φιλεῖν and ἀληθεύειν in the affairs of society (II.791c, twice).

4.10   INSCRIPTIONS.

In the Greek of the Rosetta stone (*OGI* I.90) the act of violating the temple is twice referred to using ἀσεβής (lines 23, 26) and once using ἀδικεῖν (line 27) with no apparent distinction.

Deissmann states, "We find the synonyms ἄδικος, 'unjust', and ἀσεβής, 'impious', in inscriptions from the Delphinium at Miletus both before and after the Christian era" (114).  From the phrases given by Deissmann /12/ it appears that one is ἄδικος in the sight of the gods for breaking an oath, i.e., one has perhaps brought the gods into an agreement involving two parties and so when the agreement is broken the gods are also involved.

4.11   PAPYRI.

Within the time period we are considering, there are only two instances of δικαιοῦν known to me. *PTeb.* 444 (1st Century A.D.) is a fragment of a contract and refers to an amount "deemed fair or just," and therefore "fixed" (Moulton

and Milligan; Schrenk, 1935: 211). *PRyl.* 119.14f (A.D. 54-67)
refers to the judgement of a prefect concerning "the right" in
a case brought before him. This comes under the general sense,
"deem right," the specific meaning coming from the context,
"declare 'the right' to be" (LSJ, "pronounce judgement," as in
Thucydides II.71; Moulton and Milligan, "awarding a verdict in
the courts, ... 'decided'"). The decision is given as the
object of δικαιοῦν.

As in these two cases, so in the overwhelming number of
instances where ἀδικεῖν and τὸ δίκαιον occur the context is a
dispute relating to contracts, money and property. Petitions
abound with an introductory formula such as ἀδικοῦμαι (ὑπο)
/13/ and ending with a phrase such as διὰ σὲ τοῦ δικαίου τύχω
/14/. It is the function of some judicial authority to
determine τὸ δίκαιον /15/. It thus seems a natural extension
to use δίκαιος for "standard" or "correct" measures, i.e.,
those legally determined or defined /16/.

Other uses of the words we are studying are rare:
δικαιοπραγεῖν is in the fragment *PTeb.* 183 (2nd Century B.C.);
only two cases have been noted of ἀδικεῖν in the active with a
personal object, *PMich. Zen.* 58.10 and *PMerton* 4.9 (both 3rd
Century B.C.); and no cases of δίκαιος/ἄδικος applied to
persons have been noted, except δίκαιος in a fragment, *PHib.*
147.

5. . SOME CONCLUSIONS.

*Noun and adjective forms.*

1.    (a)   τὸ δίκαιον refers to that which is just, right or
fair, the particular reference being provided by the context.
It is often related to laws or to decisions of rulers or judges
whose responsibility it is to determine τὸ δίκαιον in cases of
dispute. The reference is to socio-political relationships and
to external actions; it may refer to "what is due" to another,
to one's "right."
(b)   ἄδικος functions as a strict antonym with reference to
specific acts. The specific acts or decisions which may be
described as δίκαια are generally given negatively in terms of
those which are ἄδικα.
(c)   The person whose life (in general) conforms to τὸ

δίκαιον can be described as δίκαιος, while one who wilfully
does not conform is ἄδικος.

2.    δικαιοσύνη/ἀδικία occur as abstract nouns, referring to
the general quality or virtue/vice of a community or person,
which exhibits itself in acts that are δίκαια/ἄδικα.  We might
compare the conclusions of Havelock: "δικαιοσύνη was coined
sometime during the fifth century ... to denote the notion of
morality as an attribute of a person, or as a set of habit-
patterns resident in him" (51).  "It generally becomes
effective in social and political contexts" (67).

(a)    As with δίκαιος/ἄδικος, δικαιοσύνη/ἀδικία can be
characterised by reference to (1) law-conformity, and (2) not
taking more than one's due.

(b)    The popular criterion of what ultimately constitutes
δικαιοσύνη is that which brings about and maintains harmony,
balance and happiness of the whole society, each man having his
due.  To accomplish this laws and law-enforcement are
essential.  Thus rulers and judges both have important roles in
effecting and maintaining δικαιοσύνη in a community.

(c)    While Plato is concerned with δικαιοσύνη in terms of
harmony within a person, the general use with reference to an
individual is simply to a virtue seen in external, social acts.

(d)    When one considers suitable modern English translations
of δικαιοσύνη, it is evident that "justice" is most suitable in
forensic contexts, while "righteousness," "integrity" or
"uprightness" can be used in broader contexts.

(e)    Plato's discussion on the relation between δίκαιος and
ὅσιος, and on the role of the gods in judgement after death,
the comments in Thucydides and Isocrates, and the use of ἄδικος
and ἀσεβής in inscriptions would appear in general to be
consistent with Xenophon's use of τὸ ἄδικον and τὸ ἀσεβές: τὸ
δίκαιον refers to man's public responsibilities for the well-
being of the community, including actions regarding temples and
public ceremonies, with laws being ultimately ordained by the
gods.  Aristotle alone is silent on this.

*Verbs.*

1.    ἀδικεῖν is very common, having as its subject either an
individual or community.  It is used (a) without an object in
the broad sense, "do wrong," (b) with a personal object /17/,

"to wrong (a person or community)," and (c) in the passive, "to be wronged." Such "wrong" is opposed to what is τo δίκαιον in that situation or relationship, i.e., ἀδικεῖν has a variety in usage corresponding to that of δίκαιον. There is always involved in the context some reference to what is unlawful or unfair, and there is frequently "harm" to the object. (βλαπτεῖν is used for "harm" with no sense of wrong or injustice.)

2.      The use of δικαιοῦν is more complex.

(a)     The great majority of occurrences are with an infinitive or other impersonal object (action, attitude, decision, etc.). Some general thought of "deem right or appropriate" is present, although the context provides other nuances, e.g., for a ruler or judge, "declare or decide what is right," and for a claimant in a case or argument, "claim to be right." Its usage is broader than contexts in which δίκαιος is appropriate (e.g., in arguments involving a stronger and weaker city) and it seems to have become a set idiom. In this use it may be compared with ἀξιοῦν. Thus, against Ziesler (48), it would appear irrelevant to use this idiom to explicate the LXX use outside the idiom.

(b)     In only 13 instances in the literature studied (spanning 500 years!) is δικαιοῦν used with a personal object, including 9 instances of the passive. We include the instance of the active verb in Polybius as its meaning there belongs in this category. Schrenk's reference to "widespread usage" (1935: 211) applies only to Jewish material.

Aeschylus, *Ag.* 393 (passive): a guilty man who appeared to
        prosper is brought to justice, punished, and so shown to
        be guilty.

Herodotus, 1.100 (active); 3.29 (active): people are punished
        following judgement; 5.92b (active): a ruler avenges
        unjust treatment.

Thucydides, III.40 (passive): the city brings judgement on
        itself by admitting that it was wrong to exercise
        dominion over another people.

Plato, *Lg.* XI.934b (passive): an evildoer has to pay
        compensation for robbery or violence, and this also
        deters others.

Aristotle, *EN* V.1136a18-31 (passive, 5 times): passive

passive equivalent of δικαιοπραγεῖν.

Polybius, III.31 (active): an unjustly attacked people make a plea for help.

Plutarch, II.565b (passive): an evildoer is punished to be "healed."

Apart from Aristotle, in each case an "unjust act" has been committed, or a "wrong" situation exists. Some action is required to restore τὸ δίκαιον or δικαιοσύνη. Frequently this can be done by punishing the evildoers, and so δικαιοῦν with evildoers as object conveys the thought of "punish," this being corrective (and for Plato, educative).

If it were not for the apparently casual use in Polybius (204-122 B.C.), it may have been possible to conclude that the meaning of δικαιοῦν had become only "punish," and to regard Aristotle's use as unusual (as does Dodd: 50, n. 1). Taking into account Aristotle's full discussion, along with Polybius, it seems most likely that δικαιοῦν has the general dynamic sense of "*doing* (to a person, or in absolute sense) *what is necessary to correct an act or state of injustice*," the particular sense being provided by the context. This provides a much more satisfactory explanation of Aristotle's active use of δικαιοπραγεῖν than to assume that a positive connotation for δικαιοῦν was unusual and accords with his use of δικαίωμα. It also fits in with our observations on usage elsewhere /18/.

(c)    It is thus seen that (1) the syntactic constructions for ἀδικεῖν and δικαιοῦν are different, and (2) they are not strict antonyms (against Hill: 100). However, both ἀδικεῖν and δικαιοῦν (apart from use with impersonal object) always retain legal connotations.

# CHAPTER III

## THE BOOK OF ISAIAH: VERB FORMS

1. HIPHIL OF צדק.

The three occurrences in Isaiah of the hiphil of צדק (5:23; 50:8; 53:11) are all translated in the LXX by an active form of δικαιοῦν.

A. 5:23:

MT: מצדיקי רשע עקב שחד וצדקת צדיקים יסירו ממנו

LXX: οἱ δικαιοῦντες τὸν ἀσεβῆ ἕνεκεν δώρων καὶ τὸ δίκαιον τοῦ δικαίου αἴροντες.

The sense of MT is certainly "who acquit /1/ the guilty for a bribe, and deprive the innocent of his right" (*RSV*). רשע and צדיק are used in a juristic sense, not religious (cf. Duhm). Thus it is of note that LXX uses ἀσεβής and δίκαιος, apparently following the Pentateuchal precedent. The use of τὸ δίκαιον reflects the forensic setting of the whole verse.

The LXX of the first half of the verse is very close to Exod 23:7: οὐ δικαιώσεις τὸν ἀσεβῆ ἕνεκεν δώρων. This is an additional instance of a link between the Exodus and Isaiah translations, other links being noted by Thackeray (1902c), Ziegler (1934: 103), Seeligmann (45-49), and Brockington. It is significant that in both cases ἕνεκεν δώρων occurs. In Exodus the phrase has been added by LXX, perhaps influenced by the reference to "bribe" at the beginning of v.8 (in both LXX and MT). Note also that in v.7 MT uses 1st person, referring to God, while LXX has 2nd person. The addition strongly suggests that δικαιοῦν τὸν ἀσεβῆ without any further qualification would, to the Exodus and Isaiah translators, *not* mean "acquit the godless" (contrary to previous commentators). The meaning, "acquit," is provided by other semantic markers. Thus here the sense is: "You shall not 'treat justly' the wicked with a 'justice' that is influenced by a bribe." This is seen to be consistent with our conclusions regarding classical Greek usage of δικαιοῦν with a personal object. At

the same time, if one wished to say "acquit" in an original
Greek writing, ἀπολύειν would be more natural. Thus the use of
δικαιοῦν in this context in both Isaiah and Exodus would appear
to be due to צדק in MT.

*Note*: The only other occurrence in MT of הצדיק רשע is Prov
17:15 /2/:

MT:     מצדיק רשע ומרשיע צדיק
LXX:    ὃς δίκαιον κρίνει τὸν ἄδικον, ἄδικον δὲ τὸν δίκαιον

Snaith (1944: 166) makes much of the use here of κρίνειν
"to  make clear the forensic sense," so supporting his view
that in LXX (as in Biblical Hebrew) the forensic sense of
δικαιοῦν "is sometimes very attenuated." This has been rightly
criticised by Watson (259f), followed by Hill (107). Their
argument however is flimsy: "The translator wanted a verb which
could be used in both halves of the sentence and δικαιοῦν could
not so be used." On the basis of our discussion, it would not
be possible to use δικαιοῦν in *either* half! To say δικαιοῦν
τὸν ἄδικον without further qualification would mean "punish the
wicked" and δικαιοῦν τὸν δίκαιον "acquit the righteous."

B.    50:8:

MT:     קרוב מצדיקי מי יריב אתי נעמדה יחד מי בעל משפטי יגש אלי:
LXX:    ὅτι ἐγγίζει ὁ δικαιώσας με· τίς ὁ κρινομενός μοι;
        ἀντιστήτω μοι ἅμα· καὶ τίς ὁ κρινομενός μοι; ἐγγισάτω
        μοι.

The setting is the commonly recognised third "Servant Song"
/3/. The forensic language of the verse is quite evident (in
addition to צדק, ריב and שפט, נגש and קרב also frequently occur
in litigation contexts as shown by Falk), and continues an
affirmation of confidence in Yahweh. There is no disagreement
among scholars with the view that מצדיקי is Yahweh as the one
who will defend his cause and vindicate him. His message has
been rejected and he has been treated as a criminal, but he is
sure Yahweh is on his side.

     In the LXX translation of vv.4-11 there are various
items of note:
(1)    παιδεία in v.4 (A: σοφία; MT: למודים) and v.5 (אדני
יהוה/ἡ παιδεία κυρίου) appears to reflect Israel's experience
of the Exile and Diaspora. [The use παιδεία to translate מוסר
in 26:16 and 53:5, in contexts of suffering, suggests that the

translator saw παιδεία, the instruction or training from God, as coming not only from the Law but also through Israel's historical experience (cf. elsewhere in LXX: Jer 2:30; 5:3; Prov 3:11; see also Bertram). Seeligmann discusses aspects of the translation which suggest the Diaspora experience (110-20), but identifies παιδεία with prophesying (109)⅃ Through her experiences she has received παιδεία, and now seeks to pass this on to others but in doing so has received abuse. This historical experience also appears to be reflected in the following three points.

(2)    There is an oscillation in vv.4-9 between present, aorist and future forms, e.g., אדני יהוה יעזר לי is translated in v.7 κύριος βοηθός μου ἐγενήθη and in v.9 κύριος βοηθεῖ μοι.

(3)    In v.9 ירשיעני is translated κακώσει με, thereby missing the legal connotation of MT, as also in 54:17, תרשיעי/ ἡττείσεις, the only other instance of הרשיע in Isaiah. (Nowhere else in LXX are either of these words used to translate רשע.) LXX appears to say that the sufferings of v.6 are going to end because all will see that God is with "me."

(4)    The question arises, for the LXX translator who are "I" and "you"? In Appendix V the relation between Israel and the nations is discussed. It is there argued that LXX has more emphasis on Israel's task in the presence of the surrounding nations. In several passages, including chap. 51, there is a call to others to become proselytes or else face destruction. It thus seems most likely that here also in LXX "I" refers to Israel and "you" to the nations (unlike MT). This is reinforced by the use of "you" in v.9b, and by the whole translation of vv.10f, especially the last sentence, "These things have happened to you because of me." There is the duality of both punishment and a call to "trust in the name of the Lord."

(5)    At the beginning of v.8 LXX has ὅτι, which seems to interpret the following phrase as a reason for οὐ μὴ αἰσχυνθῶ, or more likely gives a reason for saying, τίς ὁ κρινομενός μοι. In either case ὅτι serves to show that δικαιώσας is to be understood in a favourable sense. The aorist participle does not refer to past action (against Ottley, "he that justified me"), but to some completed act of undefined time - past,

present, or future: "he who sees that justice is done to me"
(for this understanding in terms of *Aktionsart*, cf. BDF sect.
318, 339; and McKay). A narrower "declare that I am in the
right" seems both inadequate in the LXX context, (1)-(3) above,
and more limited than the corrective connotation of Classical
Greek.

C.   53:11:

MT:   מעמל נפשו יראה ישבע בדעתו יצדיק צדיק עבדי לרבים ועונתם
      הוא יסבל:

LXX:   (καὶ βούλεται κύριος ἀφελεῖν) ἀπὸ τοῦ πόνου τῆς ψυχῆς
       αὐτοῦ, δεῖξαι αυτῷ φῶς καὶ πλάσαι τῇ συνέσει, δικαιῶσαι
       δίκαιον εὖ δουλεύοντα πολλοῖς, καὶ τὰς ἁμαρτίας αὐτῶν
       αὐτὸς ἀνοίσει.

This verse, indeed the whole passage, 52:13-53:12, is
notorious for its difficulties (in addition to commentaries,
see Dahood, 1971; Driver; Gelston: 524-27; Orlinsky, 1967:
17-74, 92-94; Payne, 1971; Snaith, 1967: 194-97; and Thomas,
1968b). The textual tradition for this verse, however, is
amazingly consistent in both MT and LXX, the only variant of
note being אור after יראה in both of the Qumran scrolls (cf.
LXX: φῶς). We shall not discuss every proposal made in
interpreting the verse, but rather shall limit ourselves to
explicating יצדיק צדיק and δικαιῶσαι δίκαιον.

For grammatical and metrical reasons it is common to
delete צדיק as a dittograph of יצדיק (*BHK*; North, 1952, 1956;
McKenzie; and Gelston), or to reverse the order of these two
words and then treat צדיק as linked with ישבע בדעתו (*BHS*;
Thomas, 1968b; *NEB* and Driver further emend צדיק to צֶדֶק,
"vindication"). Others, on the basis of the almost unanimous
agreement of the Hebrew manuscripts and the Versions, retain
MT, although there is no agreement as to how this is to be
interpreted (*RSV*; North, 1964, reversing his earlier judgement;
Muilenburg; Westermann; Bonnard; Dahood, 1971; cf. GKC sect.
132b).

For those who retain צדיק the translation is generally
"righteous," sometimes more explicitly forensic, "innocent,"
although the syntactic relation to עבדי varies. Of note is
Dahood's suggestion that צדיק is a divine appellative (1971;
cf. 1966: xxxvii, and translation with commentary on Ps 11:3,
5, 7; 31:19; 75:11; 112:4; 141:5; also Rosenberg). He further

takes עבדי as direct object of the verb with the י - suffix
being 3rd person, as also in 52:13 (1971; cf. 1966: 10f).

הצדיק is given a forensic emphasis, "justify," in *AV*,
*RV*, Driver, North (1952) and Gelston, or more explicitly, "make
to be accounted righteous" in *RSV* and Muilenburg. A forensic
note, albeit with a different emphasis, is struck by *NEB* and
Snaith (1967: 197), "vindicate." Westermann's "show himself
righteous" (following Mowinckel: 199) is an unusual use of the
hiphil /4/. *RV*mg, Fahlgren (118), Ziesler (19) and Thomas
(1968b) all have "make righteous," though with varying
connotations. Bonnard moves in a different direction with
"dispenser la justice (au profit des foules)." (Compare TJ:
יזכי זכאין, overlooked by Bonnard.)

Linked with the salvific emphasis of צדק(ה) in deutero-
Isaiah, McKenzie has "deliver," although Fohrer's "Heil
schaffen" conveys this idea better. We must ask, however,
whether a salvific meaning does also apply to the verb.

The meaning seen is inseparably linked with the general
interpretation of the passage, especially the following phrase,
"he shall bear their iniquities/guilt." There is an exact
parallel in Lam 5:7, אנחנו עונתיהם סבלנו, which clearly means,
"we receive the penalty/punishment that was due to them"
(preceded by, "our fathers sinned and are no more"). In the
context of Lamentations the meaning is similar to Jer 31:29 and
Ezek 18:2: "The fathers have eaten sour grapes, and the
children's teeth are set on edge." A vicarious emphasis in
Isaiah is disputed especially by Orlinsky (1967: 51-59),
Bonnard and Ziesler (19). Ziesler believes that a vicarious
note could not be present at this early stage and therefore any
text which seems to have a vicarious connotation must have some
other meaning, but this seems to be exegesis on the basis of an
*a priori* decision. Bonnard's "il supporte leurs perversités
(sans se décourager et sans rendre le mal pour mal)" ignores
the setting of the verse and is contrary to the natural meaning
of סבל in v.4. To be preferred is the discussion in Westermann
and North. While the phrase in isolation could mean the same
as in Lamentations, that is, without any vicarious note (cf.
Orlinsky), references elsewhere in the chapter suggest that
"we" benefit (most clearly in v.5b and the end of v.12). V.9b

refers to the innocence of the sufferer. It seems difficult to avoid some vicarious note. In some way the "transgressors" benefit because of the servant's suffering which is linked with "the penalty of their guilt" (v.11, *NEB*). While these verses are concerned with the vindication of the servant, a vindication which includes various blessings so correcting past injustices, the "many" are also to enjoy certain blessings, not having to bear the penalty. The embracing translation of North (1964), "bring righteousness," seems most satisfactory, including both a forensic note and the idea of life in the covenant relationship. Perhaps one could also translate, "make many to have a just (or right) relationship."

The LXX of this "Servant Song" is discussed briefly by Ziegler who comments that it is not easy to form the *Vorlage* as there is a tendency to interpret and clarify by introducing certain favourite expressions (1934: 22-25; cf. Zimmerli and Jeremias: 676f). In v.11 two main points are of concern: the presence of φῶς and the translation δικαιῶσαι δίκαιον.

(1)  Although φῶς may be an interpretative addition (Ottley; Seeligmann; and *BHS*?), the presence of אור in both Q$^a$ and Q$^b$ suggests this was the LXX *Vorlage* (Ziegler, 1959: 42f). Whichever be the case the use of φῶς to refer to coming deliverance or vindication is natural. One may compare especially 62:1; also 9:2; 10:17; 13:10; 30:26; 42:16. (In 2:5; 4:5; 26:9; 50:10 allusion is probably to the Torah; see Appendix V.) While Seeligmann (108, 110) makes much use of φῶς as a pregnostic emphasis, comparing Hos 10:12, it is better to interpret the thought of the Isaiah translator in the light of the Isaiah LXX, especially as this provides a natural understanding. Thomas (1968b), on MT, includes אור as "prosperity," alluding to Ps 36:10. Significantly this is also a context of deliverance (this fact is not mentioned by Thomas).

(2)  In v.11b the LXX has interpreted the difficult syntax in light of the understanding of the whole passage. In the preceding verses the LXX, compared to MT, emphasizes the servant's vindication, minimizing the vicarious aspect. Of note are: the use of ἀπό twice in v.8b for מן, but, used with the verbs αἴρεται and ἤχθη, suggesting separation; the double use of ἀντί in v.9, the connotation being requittal [cf.

Zimmerli (677): there is "the distinctive assertion that
judgement is passed on the ungodly in retribution for putting
to death the παῖς (v.9), ... judgement ... executed by God
himself"]; the completely opposite meaning to MT in v.10a
(דכאו החלי /5//καθαρίσαι αὐτὸν τῆς πληγῆς); and the use of the
plural "you" in v.10b /6/.

δικαιοῦν δίκαιον in this context thus means to vindicate
or acquit one who has served well, so correcting the injustice
of v.8a /7/.

Thus δικαιοῦν is used here with God as subject and the
innocent sufferer as object. The connotation of correcting an
unjust situation by vindication is more narrowly forensic than
the probable meaning of הצדיק.

2.    QAL OF צדק.

In each of the three occurrences of the Qal of צדק
(43:9, 26; 45:25), LXX uses the passive of δικαιοῦν.

A.    43:9:

MT:    יחנו עדיהם ויצדקו וישמעו ויאמרו אמת

LXX:   Let them bring forth their witnesses and δικαιωθήτωσαν
       καὶ εἰπάτωσαν ἀληθῆ /8/.

This verse is in one of the five trial speeches
(*Gerichtsreden*) identified by Westermann: 41:1-5, 21-29;
43:8-15; 44:6-8, 21-22 (these 5 verses together); 45:20-25
(15-19, and commentary on these passages; cf. Bonnard: 30;
Schoors: chap. 3). It is a continuation of the controversy
between Yahweh and the gods with their devotees (thus different
from the distinctive form discussed by Huffmon and Harvey).
"They" in the first part of our quote are the "gods" (North,
1964; Westermann), or better the gods with their followers,
"the nations" (Bonnard; Schoors: 224). We might compare 41:23
where the gods are addressed directly, and other places where
the addressees are the coastlands and the peoples (41:1), the
nations and the peoples (43:9), and the survivors of the
nations (45:20).

The verbs in the second half (שמע, אמר) most aptly have
as their subject the court /9/. Thus there is a measure of
parallelism between ויצדקו and ויאמרו אמת (cf. 41:26: ונאמר
צדיק), suggesting that צָדַק here means "be shown to be in the

right," or "receive the verdict of being 'in the right'" (cf.
BDB, *RSV*, Westermann: "be justified"; North, 1964: "win the
verdict"; Schmid: 130, "Recht bekommen"; preferable to the less
dynamic KB, "im Recht sein, Recht haben").

The LXX translator regarded vv.8ff as continuing the
thought of the preceding verses. This is shown by the use in
v.8, of καί and of the first person, ἐξήγαγον /10/. Thus v.8
is seen to refer to the return of the exiles. In v.9 ἄρχοντες
translates לאמים and is regarded as syntacticly linked with
בהם (in MT, in the next phrase), this itself being rendered
ἐξ αὐτῶν. Accordingly "they" of the latter part of the verse
refer to "the rulers." Considering also the shift from the
aorist in the first verb of v.9 to the future in the second
verb, reference appears to be to a future judgement upon the
rulers of the nations who have ill-treated Israel.

Then follow three imperatives: "let them bring forth
their witnesses and δικαιωθήτωσαν and let them say true
things." As in MT there is the problem as to who are the
subjects of the last two verbs. The use of the accusative,
ἀληθῆ, links εἰπάτωσαν with either the witnesses or the rulers.
(In 41:26 ὅτι ἀληθῆ ἐστιν refers to a decision concerning the
truth of what has been said already.) The most natural sense
is to refer all imperatives to the "rulers."

δικαιωθήτωσαν is understood by Schrenk (1935: 213) as
"the vindication or right conduct of man (esp. the chosen
people) in relation to Yahweh," and Hill (108) refers to "the
confirmation of the man's 'in-the-right-ness' at some court of
appeal." This sense is possible, but unlikely in the LXX
context. The picture of the rulers being brought to judgement
for their treatment of Israel points rather to the usual Greek
meaning, "have justice done to one": they are being given a
chance to present their case so that they will not be punished
unfairly. This meaning fits in with the absence of καί
ἀκουσάτωσαν (included in some later manuscripts), so giving a
different connotation to "speak true things." The passage goes
on to speak, in v.14, of the judgement on the Chaldeans.
Indeed, although the word order is awkward, it is not
impossible for a Greek reader to see a meaning "punish," but
again being to "treat justly."

B.     43:26:

MT:   הזכירני נשפטה יחד ספר אתה למען תצדק

LXX:  σὺ δὲ μνήσθητι καὶ κριθῶμεν· λέγε σὺ τὰς ἀνομίας σου
      πρῶτος, ἵνα δικαιωθῆς.

Amongst modern scholars there is unanimous recognition
of this verse as being part of a disputation between God and
Israel, with הזכיר being used in a technical sense, "bring a
charge" (so especially North, Fohrer, Westermann and Schoors).
Within this context צָדַק has the clear connotation, "to be
proved to be in the right," i.e., the same meaning as in v.9.

Once again LXX interpretation is different. The two
uses of זכר in vv.25f (qal and hiphil) are both rendered by the
passive form, and the pronominal suffix of הזכירני is not
evident in LXX. Thus a possible MT word-play /11/ is interpreted simply as a contrast in subjects, the contrast being
suggested also by the inclusion of σὺ δέ. The general sense of
LXX is thus: "It is my practice never to remember sins (v.25),
but on this occasion you are to remember and let us enter into
dispute."

The addition of τὰς ἀνομίας σου in v.26b has been
interpreted by Ottley as referring to the need for confession,
followed by "being justified," i.e., quite a different sense
from MT.

The use of πρῶτος (πρῶτον in S) may signify that Israel
is the first one to speak in the dispute. But what she is to
speak about are her lawlessnesses, so that she may be punished.
This would be the meaning read by a Greek reader for this verse
in isolation.

Nevertheless, the whole tenor of the passage leads one
to expect a positive connotation for δικαιωθῆς. This is
suggested by the reference to past judgement in v.28, followed
by the adversative νῦν δέ in 44:1 (MT: ועתה) and the insertion
of ἔτι before βοηθηθήσῃ in 44:2 (MT: יעזרך). Also, in v.26,
τὰς ἀνομίας clearly looks back to v.25: ἐγώ εἰμι ἐγώ εἰμι ὁ
ἐξαλείφων τὰς ἀνομίας σου. V.24b points in the same direction.

As for v.9, Hill (108) refers to "the confirmation of
the man's 'in-the-right-ness'" and Schrenk is similar. This is
impossible in the LXX context. Following on from the
confession of sin, the meaning needs to be something like "to

be treated as righteous," i.e., "to be brought (again) into a
right relationship." It is as if confession of sin is
necessary before a state of justice and righteousness can be
restored.

C.    45:25 (45:18-25):

This verse also occurs in a trial speech. In this case
Yahweh challenges the "survivors of the nations," who trust in
another god (v.20b).

In vv.18-25 there are various uses of צדק which we shall
consider here. (The relationship between vv.18-19 and vv.20ff
need not concern us: vv.20ff contain the usual elements of the
genre; see North, 1964; Westermann; Schoors.)

*v.19*: The statement that Yahweh is the one who דבר צדק and
מגיד מישרים is the counterpart to the first part of the verse:
he does not "speak in secret, in darkness," and does not say to
his people, "seek me in chaos." As v.18 refers to his ordering
of creation, the meaning of צדק goes beyond "truth" or "what is
right" (*RSV*, *NEB*, Muilenburg), though it may include this (so
North; Schoors: 238; Fahlgren: 85, has "Wahrheit," with note 2,
"das Wort die Nebenbedeutung 'Heil' hat."). It seems rather to
embrace the idea of God's whole ordering of creation, which
includes his purpose of deliverance for Israel (vv.19a, 22-25;
cf. vv.12-13) (Westermann; Schmid: 131f; Schoors: 233, 238; and
Scullion, 1971: 340; Bonnard's "profere justice" and
McKenzie's "speak righteousness" are misleading, although
McKenzie comments, "Yahweh's word ... achieves the condition of
righteousness").

*v.21*: In the phrase, אל-צדיק ומושיע, we see clearly linked the
two attributives, which are explicated in the fact that God has
made known his plan to his people. *NEB* and North's
"victorious" (for צדיק) seems unsuitable in this context.
Westermann, followed by Schoors, has "righteous," linked with
"trustworthiness." While the disputation setting may at first
suggest a sense, "just," the nature of the disputation rather
suggests that God alone is צדיק: he alone acts or can act in
terms of the requirements of a relationship between a god and
his people - and when he says he will deliver he does deliver.
מושיע explicates the particular way in which he is צדיק (cf.
Schmidt: 131: "Gott ist nicht nur der, der das Richtige sagt,

sondern auch das Richtige tut"). Another possibility is that
צדיק is a divine name (Rosenberg), although, if so, reference
here is surely to the significance of that name.

*v.23:* יצע מפי צדקה. The meaning of צדקה is similar to that
noted for צדק in v.19, here including "vindication" and
"deliverance" of Israel (*NEB* has the narrower "victory").
*v.24:* צדקות ועז. The juxtaposition with עז and the use of the
plural lead most commentators to translate "salvation" (so
Westermann; Fohrer; Schoors; again preferable to "victory" used
by *NEB*; North, 1964; Snaith, 1967: 186). The plural refers to
specific acts, as in Judg 5:11, 1 Sam 12:7, and Ps 103:6. As
in v.21, the disputation setting suggests that Yahweh is the
only God who acts in accord with his responsibilities as God of
his people, indeed, of the world, for he alone has strength.
Therefore men shall be ashamed.
*v.25:* ביהוה יצדקו ויתהללו כל-זרע ישראל. Again צדק is linked
with another word. As for the noun forms, so here the verb is
commonly translated "find salvation." Westermann; Fohrer; cf.
Scullion, 1971: 340, "be prosperous"; earlier comments on
"victory" apply here to the translation "triumph" in North,
*RSV*, *NEB*). However, the disputation setting, together with the
opponents' being "ashamed" (v.24b; בוש often appears in
forensic settings with the connotation of "be shown to be in
the wrong," as shown by Olley, 1976), suggests that linked with
"find salvation" is the forensic idea, "be vindicated", "be
shown to have been right (to have trusted in Yahweh)" [so also
Snaith, 1967: 186, but see 160, n.3; Schoors: 237, comments
generally, without specific exegesis: "The prophet gives to
God's salvific acts a forensic overtone (because) what takes
place now is like a great legal context in which nations and
gods are involved".] At the same time the context and
description go beyond mere forensic language, with a strong
emphasis on God accomplishing his purposes of bringing about
order (e.g., vv.9-13, 16-17, 18-19).

The LXX translator in the whole passage  frequently uses
different syntax from MT, and occasionally uses words different
in meaning from MT. As in 43:8-15, the detailed imagery of the
disputation speech is completely absent. The assembling of
v.20 leads not to a disputation with and a verdict from God,

but to the hearing of an appeal from God.

Most of the important issues for our discussion arise from *vv.23b-25*:

> ἐμοὶ κάμψει πᾶν γόνυ καὶ ἐξομολογήσεται πᾶσα γλῶσσα τῷ
> θεῷ (24) λέγων Δικαιοσύνη καὶ δόξα πρὸς αὐτὸν ἥξουσιν,
> καὶ αἰσχυνθήσονται πάντες οἱ ἀφορίζοντες ἑαυτούς. (25)
> ἀπὸ κυρίου δικαιωθήσονται καὶ ἐν τῷ θεῷ ἐνδοξασθήσονται
> πᾶν τὸ σπέρμα τῶν υἱῶν Ισραηλ.

(1) ἐξομολογήσεται τῷ θεῷ, "confess to God," differs from the simple "swear" of MT. Elsewhere, throughout LXX, נשׁבע is translated with ὀμνύναι, but ὀμνύναι, used in v.23a, did not make sense here (Goshen-Gottstein, 1963: 156-58; Ottley's "swear by God" is a mistranslation).

(2) The use of δόξα in v.24 is obviously influenced by ἐνδοξασθήσονται in v.25 (cf. Δικαιοσύνη and δικαιωθήσονται). Brockington has demonstrated the fondness of the Isaiah translator for δόξα in salvation contexts.

(3) οἱ ἀφορίζοντες ἑαυτούς (MT: הנחרים בו) is of note. The only other occurrence in Isaiah of the Hebrew phrase is 41:11 (object, "you" = Israel), there translated οἱ ἀντικείμενοί σοι. It is this latter Greek expression which is used in 45:16: "All *who oppose him* shall be put to shame ..." Thus the use here of "those who set themselves apart" may be just a stylistic variation, but seems rather to be quite deliberate, referring more clearly to those who are unwilling to bow the knee. In the religious setting of the translator this could refer to those unwilling to become proselytes (so Seeligmann: 118). V.16 is a close parallel: "All who oppose him shall be ashamed and be put to shame and shall go in shame. Be renewed (ἐγκαινίζεσθε) to me, O islands." For the last phrase, compare 41:1a LXX. Here are two alternatives: shame, or becoming a worshipper. (See further discussion in Appendix V.)

The translator also has in view those who "know not" coming to "know": v.15: "For thou art God and we did not know" (MT: "thou art a god who hidest thyself"); vv.20f: "they did not know ... that they may know together" (MT: "they do not know ... let them take counsel together"). The last phrase is of note since the translator frequently uses βουλ-words (e.g., v.20a), but here seems to be taken up with the change, οὐκ ἔγνωσαν ... γνῶσιν ἅμα. The change carries through the purpose of God in using Cyrus to deliver Israel, "that they ... may know that there is no other beside me" (v.6).

(4) Instead of MT ביהוה followed by two verbs referring to Israel, LXX has one group who "*from* the Lord δικαιωθήσονται," and "the seed of Israel" who "will be glorified *in* God," i.e., probably, "share in God's glory" or "be glorified because of their relationship with God" (cf. LXX of 60:19; 62:2ff). The question is, who is the first group?

(a) Usually it is interpreted as also being Israel (as in MT). Accordingly Schrenk (1935: 212) contrasts MT, "they find righteousness with Yahweh," and LXX, "they are declared righteous by him." It is doubtful however whether the difference in prepositions alone warrants such a contrast in meaning. On the basis of our earlier discussion we must also disagree with his view that "the forensic element is even stronger in the LXX than the MT." The forensic setting is different (MT: trial speech; LXX: final judgement).

Hill (108) here again refers to "the confirmation of man's 'in-the-right-ness' at some court of appeal." Joachim Jeremias, while referring to Israel, interprets in the opposite direction:

> "In this saying Deutero-Isaiah clearly breaks
> through the bounds of forensic usage. The
> parallelism between 'to be justified' and 'to
> be glorified' demonstrates that δικαιοῦσθαι here
> assumes the meaning 'to find salvation'" /12/.

If Israel be the subject, the LXX context suggests a meaning somewhat in between: "have justice done, correcting injustices done to her." This sense is heightened in the reading of some later manuscripts, οἱ ἀφορίζοντες ἑαυτούς becoming οἱ διορίζοντες αὐτούς referring to those who ostracize the Jews (Rahlfs; Ziegler; cf. also Seeligmann: 113).

(b) Another possibility is suggested by the prescence in the second half of ἐν τῷ θεῷ and the position of "Israel" (at the end of the verse, as in MT), namely, that the subject of the first verb is distinct and is those who have confessed to God (cf. Ottley: "men shall be justified"). These shall "have justice done to them" in that they too will enjoy God's blessings because they have acknowledged him. This provides a parallel to the LXX understanding of 43:26 where the people of Israel δικαιωθήσονται following their confession of sin. There an appeal was addressed to Israel, here an appeal is addressed to "those being saved from the nations" (v.20).

(c)     Yet a third possibility is to take the syntactically
nearest group, namely, those who shut themselves from God and
who in the final judgement will be "ashamed." In this case
δικαιωθήσονται implies punishment, and further emphasises the
certainty of the fulfilment of God's δικαιοσύνη, which will go
forth from his mouth (v.23a) and issue in two results, the
humiliation of Israel's enemies and the glorification of
Israel. This duality appears also in vv.16f where MT reference
to God's activity through Cyrus in LXX refers to the final
judgement.

When we look at the whole tenor of the LXX context,
interpretation (a) is least likely as the main concern is the
future relation between the nations and Israel. We would
propose that the translator intended a combination of (b) and
(c): Israel is to be glorified and she will not be ashamed, but
the nations are going to "have justice done to them" from the
Lord - this is certain, and it is from him alone (in v.24 LXX
the subject of "shall come" is δικαιοσύνη καὶ δόξα). The
appeal is thus made to confess to God, be renewed, and so join
in Israel's glory, or else be ashamed when God's δικαιοσύνη
comes.

The general sense of these verses, and of v.25 in
particular, is thus quite different from MT. Whereas for MT it
is possible to see צדק and הלל as in some way parallel, for LXX
they appear antithetical.

With this understanding, we turn to the other occurrences of צדק in the passage.

Each of the three occurrences of the noun (ה)צדק (vv.19,
23, 24) is translated δικαιοσύνη. In v.19 the associated
מישרים is translated ἀλήθεια. Perhaps influenced by v.19, v.23
has δικαιοσύνη as subject of "shall go forth from my mouth,"
although this is an understandable interpretation of MT syntax.

צדיק (v.21) is translated unexceptionally by δίκαιος.
The general understanding of the passage leads one to see
primarily a general judicial connotation ("justice, just") for
all these occurences. Even the juxtaposition of δίκαιος and
σωτήρ (v.21, as in MT) can be compared with the contrast noted
in vv.24f.

3.   OTHER OCCURRENCES OF ΔIKAIOYN.

There are two other instances of δικαιοῦν, 1:17 and 42:21.

A.   1:17:

MT:            דרשו משפט אשרו חמוֹץ
               שפטו יתום ריבי אלמנה:

LXX:  ἐκζητήσατε κρίσιν, ῥύσασθε ἀδικούμενον, κρίνατε ὀρφανῷ
      καὶ δικαιώσατε χήραν.

In understanding MT there is little variation on *RSV*:
"Seek justice, correct oppression, defend the fatherless, plead
for the widow." Some would follow the sense of the Versions
and emend חָמוֹץ to חָמוּץ, translating "oppressed" (*BHK*; *BHS*, "?";
*NEB*; Kaiser; Fohrer), but the active "oppressor" fits the verb
(cf. Auvray; Eichrodt; Goshen-Gottstein, 1975; also 3:12;
9:16).

LXX follows the usual practice of translating שפט with
κρίσις/κρίνειν (see Appendix I), thereby probably limiting the
meaning of the word as compared with the Hebrew, the Greek
usage normally referring specifically to the "decision" or
"deciding." (The nouns, κρίσις, κρίμα, occur in non-Jewish
Greek mainly in legal settings, while κρίνειν has a wider
usage. Buchsel is very brief in discussing non-Jewish Greek
usage, and in his treatment of LXX assumes the Greek has same
meaning as the Hebrew; see LSJ and *Sup*.). The translator's use
of ῥύσασθε, "rescue," appears to be a result of the context (in
3:12 and 9:16, he has μακαρίζειν, "call blessed," confusing the
two homonyms, cf. KB). The unusual use of κρίνειν with the
dative is probably because κρίνειν with the accusative has the
idea of "deciding in favour of" or "choosing." The dative
suggests that one is not to neglect cases involving orphans,
but that one must "decide their cases." This sense also fits
perfectly with the very similar v.23 (cf. LXX Ps 9:39/MT
10:18).

Throughout Isaiah ריב is normally rendered by κρίσις/
κρίνειν (see Appendix I) /13/. As κρίνειν has already been
used in this verse, the translator here uses δικαιοῦν. In this
setting, and with the semantic association with κρίνειν, the
meaning is "treat justly," not, as Hill (106), "vindicate."
The general sense of the last half of the verse would be: "do

not neglect to judge the cases that are brought to you
concerning orphans and widows, decide their case and do so
justly." (See also our later discussion on 11:4.)

B.    42:21:

MT:   יהוה חפץ למען צדקו יגדיל תורה ויאדיר

LXX:  κύριος ὁ θεὸς ἐβούλετο ἵνα δικαιωθῇ καὶ μεγαλύνῃ
      αἴνεσιν. καὶ εἶδον, ...

The status of this verse is much discussed, as is also
the similar reference to תורה in v.24 (summary in Schoors:
204f). For example, Westermann speaks of a gloss by "a member
of a group which cultivated a legal piety that was absorbed in
admiring and abiding by God's word, the tōrāh," and North
(1964) of a "Deuteronomic in tone ... editorial revision." Be
that as it may, even as a gloss the editor saw its insertion
as being linked with the rest of the passage. As Schoors says,
"the verse links up nicely with what proceeds." He translates,
"Yahwe wished, because of his righteousness, to make his
teaching great and glorious" (so essentially RSV, Westermann,
North). Most commentators refer "righteousness" to God's
saving purpose as put into practice.

While the immediate context is Israel's disobedience and
Yahweh's judgement upon her, so suggesting a more strongly
ethical content for צדק, the thought of this verse closely
parallels v.4 and 51:4f which refer to God's rule over the
nations and the establishment of משפט and צדק. Thus again צדק
relates to God's ordering of the world, within which תורה has
an important role.

The LXX is of interest in various ways.

Surprising is αἴνεσιν, especially as in Alexandrian
Judaism there was much interest in νόμος (also in Isaiah LXX
according to Seeligmann: 104-08). It seems most likely that
the translator read תודה as there are no other occurrences of
either μεγαλύνειν or αἴνεσις which may have influenced the
translation here.

For ἐβούλετο, S, A and B read ἐβουλεύσατο ("he
deliberated"), but it is preferable to follow Rahlfs and
Ziegler in retaining ἐβούλετο, following Q and most cursives
and according with MT.

It seems probable that the translator read צדק וינדיל so

treating צדק as a Qal. This is supported by the translator's
practice elsewhere: למן followed by a noun or pronominal
suffix is translated ἕνεκεν (6 times) or διά (4 times) with the
noun or pronoun; למען with a verb is ἵνα and the verb (10
times) or the simple infinitive (30:1) or paraphrased (44:9).

The LXX meaning in the present context could be the same
as for צדק, i.e., "be shown to be righteous," in that God has
been just in his treatment of Israel as outlined in the
following verses. It is possible, however, that the sense here
is the same as elsewhere in Isaiah, i.e., "be treated justly."
The use with God as object of the act is unusual, but not
impossible. This sense is suggested further by the link with
μεγαλύνῃ αἴνεσιν: God is treated justly when he receives the
praise that is due to him as his right, over against the
blindness and deafness of Israel in vv.17-20. (LXX syntax in
v.17, including use of δέ, tenses and moods, shows that this
verse along with vv.18-20 refers to Israel; plurals are used
throughout vv.17-20.)

4.    SUMMARY AND CONCLUSIONS.

In every occurrence of δικαιοῦν in Isaiah, except 5:23,
there are indications in the immediate context that the
translator has, in varying degrees, understood MT differently
from modern exegetes. This fact has been overlooked in most
recent discussions.

A.    ACTIVE OF ΔΙΚΑΙΟΥΝ.

The three occurrences of הצדיק occur in settings which
strongly suggest forensic content, although the particular
meanings provided by the MT context range from the narrow
"acquit" (5:23) to "vindicate, show to be in the right" (50:8)
to a broader "bring righteousness, i.e., bring into the
benefits of the covenant relationship (because a penalty has
been borne)" (53:11).

Similarly, the four occurrences of the active δικαιοῦν
are also in forensic settings. The subject is either God
(50:8; 53:11) or leaders whose responsibility it is to give
judicial decisions (1:17; 5:23). In each case there appears to
be a general connotation of "to see that justice is done to a
person, to treat justly," the particular expression in a given

context being provided by the context itself. Thus in 5:23 the object τὸν ἀσεβῆ at first sight suggests "punish," but the addition of ἕνεκεν δώρων shows that in fact an *un*just situation is being envisaged, i.e., acquittal. In both 50:8 and 53:11 (here contrary to MT) the object is the servant who has suffered unjustly, but God is to correct the injustices. This is more explicitly forensic than MT usage.

B.   PASSIVE.

The three uses of the Qal of צדק occur in trial or disputation speeches. In each instance the meaning is clearly "be shown to be in the right" or "be vindicated." In 45:25 this seems to involve also enjoyment of the benefits of vindication, the blessings of "righteousness."

The four occurrences of the passive, δικαιοῦσθαι, are in contexts where LXX and MT differ. Although the LXX description is of judgement, the form of the passage is unlike the trial or disputation speech form seen by recent exegetes.

In 43:26 the most likely interpretation of LXX is that, if Israel comes to God and confesses her sins, then she will "be treated as righteous," i.e., enjoy the blessings of a harmonious relationship with God. Similarly, in 45:25, if the nations are willing to worship God they too will enjoy the covenant blessings with Israel, otherwise they will be punished.

For 43:9, "have justice done to one" (spoken of the rulers of the nations) is most likely. Perhaps this leads on to "be punished" for their treatment of Israel. Finally, 42:21 seems to refer to God being treated justly, i.e., obeyed and praised.

It should be stressed that only in 42:21 is it possible for δικαιοῦσθαι to have the same connotation as צדק, although here the Greek probably has a different connotation. Thus we cannot, for Isaiah, "assume that the Greek translators knew the force of the Qal of צדק" (against Hill: 108).

In 42:21; 43:9; and probably 45:25 (but not 43:26) the meaning is in accord with usual Greek usage, "to have justice done to one, be treated justly." Further, in 43:9 and 45:25 it is probable, although admittedly not necessary, that punishment is involved. In each of the four occurrences the action referred to is corrective, restoring a "just" situation.  In 43:26 restoration of a state of "righteousness" in the relationships between God, Israel and the nations is also in view, but here (and possibly also in 45:25) forgiveness is included: one will be "treated as being 'in the right'" if one (Israel or the nations) recognizes one's sins or failure to give God the allegiance due to him.

It may be countered that perhaps the translator has merely translated צדק with δικαιοῦν woodenly.  That he consistently and uniquely so translated cannot be gainsaid.  It is also apparent that he has used δικαιοῦν due to the presence of צדק in MT (perhaps under the influence of some tradition which he has inherited).  The fact, however, that his treatment of contexts varies from MT suggests that he believed his translation to be not inappropriate.

C.    GENERAL CONCLUSIONS.

(1)    The translator is often unaware of the specific connotation of MT and his usage seems to be much closer to classical Greek usage, "to do to a person what is necessary to correct an act or state of injustice," i.e., predominantly forensic.  All the uses in Isaiah come under this broad rubric, with a major qualification:-

(2)    While for the Greeks emphasis is placed upon the need for corrective punishment as perhaps being the major way injustice is corrected (this conclusion is on the basis of word frequency only), for the Isaiah translator the emphasis is upon vindication and also upon the possibility of forgiveness if the wrongdoer genuinely confesses his wrongdoing (this use is with God as subject).  Because the translation is a translation, the object of δικαιοῦν is usually not the wrongdoer, and so Hebrew emphasis is carried through into the Greek.  The interplay between Greek usage and Jewish faith is seen in the addition (to both MT meaning and Greek custom) of the thought of confession as a means of avoiding punishment, while still including the possibility of punishment (cf. the thought of the later Book of Baruch, Prayer of Manasseh and Prayer of Azariah).  This connotation is nowhere present in צדק.  (For "pity" to the wrongdoer in classical Greek, see Appendix III.)

(3)    What is evident in the Isaiah translation is a natural

consequence of the secular Greek forensic use of δικαιοῦν with
a personal object (including the passive).  It is unnecessary
to follow Ziesler (47f) in looking to the use of δικαιοῦν with
an impersonal object to understand LXX use.  The connotation is
chiefly, but not exclusively, the positive one of "vindicate,
acquit, restore to a right relationship."

# CHAPTER IV

THE BOOK OF ISAIAH: NOUN FORMS

1.    INTRODUCTION.

Although there may possibly be some distinction between
צדק and צדקה (see chapter I, note 12), there is no evidence
that LXX translators saw any difference and thus they shall be
treated together.

In the overwhelming majority of the 61 instances of
צדק(ה), LXX Isaiah uses δικαιοσύνη (45 times) or cognate words
(9 times; see Appendix I). Outside these occurrences
δικαιοσύνη is used only 5 times: 33:6, a LXX addition; 38:19
and 39:8, for אמת; 61:8, משפט; and 63:7, חסד /1/. This has led
to assumptions of semantic overlap between צדק(ה) and
δικαιοσύνη (especially Snaith, 1944: chap. 8), although Hill
adds the significant phrase, "in the estimation of the
translators" (104). This is a reminder of the need to look
beyond word statistics and to examine LXX contexts in detail.

On 4 occasions צדקה is translated by ἐλεημοσύνη (1:27;
28:17; 59:16) or τὸ ἔλεος (56:1). This has led to statements
such as that of Ziesler: "It is clear that δικαιοσύνη and
ἐλεημοσύνη can be used interchangeably for ts-d-q and ch-s-d"
[61, n. 3; so answering his earlier query (59) as to whether
"δίκαιος and δικαιοσύνη ... were not considered suitable for
this aspect (of 'benevolence')"]. Dodd goes to the other
extreme in concluding that "the two aspects of צדק are
polarized into δικαιοσύνη and ἐλεημοσύνη. In place of the
comprehensive virtue of צדקה, we have justice on the one hand,
mercy on the other" (56f). In between these Hill is ambivalent
(due to his failure to investigate LXX context?). At first he
states that "the usual rendering of צדקה by δικαιοσύνη would
not convey the idea of 'merciful action' ... therefore the
notion was introduced by the translation ἔλεος and ἐλεημοσύνη"
(104), but later in summarizing LXX usage he has, "through
being drawn into the covenant terminology the word δικαιοσύνη

was supplied from time to time with a content which is related
to that of 'mercy' (when translating חסד) and of 'loyalty' and
'trustworthiness' (when translating אמת)" (109).

In what follows we shall examine all departures from
צדק(ה)/δικαιοσύνη. In so doing we shall have cause to examine
several verses where this "usual" translation occurs.

2.      צדק(ה)/'ΕΛΕΗΜΟΣΥΝΗ, 'ΕΛΕΟΣ. /2/

A.      1:27 (1:21-28).

Here we quote in full vv.26b-27:

MT:     אחרי-כן יקרא לך עיר הצדק קריה נאמנה:
        ציון במשפט תפדה ושביה בצדקה:

LXX:    καὶ μετὰ ταῦτα κληθήσῃ Πόλις δικαιοσύνης, μητρόπολις
        πιστὴ Σιων. μετὰ γὰρ κρίματος σωθήσεται ἡ αἰχμαλωσία
        αὐτῆς καὶ μετὰ ἐλεημοσύνης.

Most commentators regard vv.27f as an addition, probably
exilic, to the speech, vv.21-26 (so, e.g., Duhm, Eichrodt,
Fohrer, Kaiser). Certainly the words of v.26 fittingly
conclude the lament of v.21, and there is also the use of פדה
in v.27. Even so, in v.27 the pointing of וְשָׁבֶיהָ is usually
retained, with a meaning such as "those who repent, Bekehrten"
(*RSV*; *NEB*; Duhm; Eichrodt, 1960; Fohrer; Kaiser; Auvray). LXX
suggests וְשִׁבְיָהּ, and others propose וְיֹשְׁבֶיהָ (*BHS*, KB) or וְשָׁבָה
(Tur-Sinai, on the basis of 10:21f). These emendations are
unnecessary as MT provides a straightforward contrast between
v.27 and v.28.

What is of concern to us is the connotation of צדק(ה) in
these verses. In vv.21-26 the attributing of צדק(ה) to Zion is
clearly linked with the presence of rulers and judges in her
who perform their task justly and righteously, in terms of the
covenant relationship (in opposition to the actions of
vv.21-23). Thus it is inadequate to see the meaning as simply
"that which is morally right in the sight of God" (Scott).
Schmid (115) has "Stadt der Ordnung (Jahwes)," alluding to the
state of well-being, well-orderedness and consequent prosperity
which follows when rulers perform their proper task, including
the punishing of evildoers (cf. Ps 72; Isa 9:7; 11:1-5). While
this may be so elsewhere, the parallelism with "faithful" in
both v.21 and v.26, and the counter-examples of vv.21d-23 place
emphasis on "justice" or "integrity" in social relationships,

in terms of the covenant. The common translation, "righteousness, Gerechtigkeit," is suitable, as long as this emphasis is
included.

While vv.21, 26 refer to attributes of Zion, צדקה in
v.27 refers to God's action in saving those who "turn" and
destroying those who rebel (so most, including the brief remark
by Bonnard: 542). It is possible that reference is to
qualities required by God (Auvray), so that a similar contrast
is seen in vv.27f to that in vv.19f, but the strong emphasis
upon the activity of God in the immediate context, vv.25f,
argues against this. What is of note is the duality of God's
action in both vv.25f and vv.27f: "So werden göttliches
Strafgericht und Umkehrforderung miteinander verbunden"
(Fohrer; similarly, Schmid: 137).

There are various items of significance in the LXX of
this passage:
(1)     As in MT, so in LXX there are the contrasts in vv.25f
and 27f. In vv.18-20, the prelude to this passage, is another
contrast, which is heightened in LXX by the use in v.18 of
διελεγχθῶμεν, with its note of disputation and testing, and by
the use of the same pair of verbs in v.19 and (with the
negative) in v.20.
(2)     The translation of the construct-absolute, עיר - הצדק
(v.26) quite literally as πόλις δικαιοσύνης is unusual as one
would expect δίκαια /3/. The translation may be influenced by
δικαιοσύνη in v.21. At the same time it is more likely that
the translator felt that to use δίκαια would be inappropriate,
as the emphasis in the passage is not upon the fact that Zion
will be "righteous," but rather that she will be a city "of
justice" because of the establishing (ἐπιστήσω for MT אשיבה) of
judges and counsellors.
(3)     LXX specifically sees the judgement of God as being
against the rulers by its rendering of vv.24f: the divine
title, אביר ישראל followed by הוי is made to refer to Israel's
leaders, Οὐαὶ οἱ ἰσχύοντες Ισραηλ, and the imagery of v.25 is
freely interpreted and expanded, including the phrase καὶ
πάντας ὑπερηφάνους ταπεινώσω /4/. In v.24 judgement is
described as κρίσιν ποιήσω (אנקמה).
(4)     Turning now to v.27, which LXX relates to the preceding

by the addition of γάρ, it is clear that the translator is
using κρῖμα to refer to the punishing, destroying action of
God. However, because of the "mercy" of God the body of
captives will be saved. (The use of σώζειν to translate פדה is
unusual, appearing elsewhere in LXX only in Job 33:28.
Seeligmann: 114 has argued that, for the Isaiah translator,
σώζειν and cognate words refer to "liberation from a powerful
political enemy, escape from a great political disaster." Its
use here is appropriate on the basis of the interpretation of
שביה.) If it is the translator's intention to contrast these
two aspects of God's dealings, δικαιοσύνη as "justice" (of God)
would be inappropriate. Further, δικαιοσύνη has already been
used in v.26 in a sense recognizable by a Greek reader, namely,
the state when everyone performs his proper function. Another
factor may be that the translator seems to avoid using
δικαιοσύνη *in the same context* to refer to both God and man (or
people). (Cf. later discussion on 56:1; 61:8, 10; and 51:1-8;
although 59:9-20 is a counter-example.)

B.      28:17a (CHAP. 28).

MT:     ושמתי משפט לקו וצדקה למשקלת

LXX:    καὶ θήσω κρίσιν εἰς ἐλπίδα, ἡ δὲ ἐλεημοσύνη μου εἰς
        σταθμούς.

The connotation of MT must be seen in the light of
vv.14ff. The main addressees are the rulers of Jerusalem who
have made a false alliance with "death" and "Sheol," relying on
this to save them when the "scourge" of Assyria comes.
Reference is either to a political alliance with the
Philistines and Egyptians (Duhm; Auvray) or to an adoption of
the religious practices of their neighbours (Kaiser; Mauchline;
Scott), or more likely to both of these together (Fohrer;
Eichrodt, 1967), Yahweh however is building Zion with a sure
foundation and those who rely on this foundation will be safe
(for יִסַּד, v.16, read יֹסֵד; cf. Qᵃ מיסד, Qᵇ יוסד; see BHS). It
is in this context of building that v.17 is placed.

Mauchline and, in a less emphatic sense, Kaiser refer
משפט and צדקה to the standards applied by God in his punishing
judgement (cf. Amos 7:7-9). It seems more in keeping with the
building metaphor, however, to say that only the city whose
characteristics are משפט and צדקה, resulting from a trust in

Yahweh's word (v.16) as opposed to "lies" and from a covenant
relationship with him rather than with "death" (v.15), will
stand the test when the Assyrians come (cf. vv.1-8, and 32:1f;
Duhm; Eichrodt, 1967; Fohrer; and Auvray).

Thus צדקה is again used to refer to a society in which
all, but rulers in particular, trust on Yahweh, acting
according to the covenant relationship.

The LXX of the whole chapter has many divergences from
MT and it is difficult to say where the translator has a
different *Vorlage*, where he misunderstood or guessed, and where
he has deliberately altered the sense for some theological
reason. While in the main, because of certain evident patterns
in translation, the LXX seems to be based on MT, there are
cases where a final answer cannot be given.

(1)      Of note is the frequency of ἐλπίς (10 times; Ottley:
1:50, and Ziegler, 1934: 14, refer to ἐλπίς as a favourite word
of the translator).   MT in vv.4f has צבי "beauty" /5/; in v.10
(twice), v.13 (twice) and v.17 קו /6/; in v.15 מחסה "refuge"
/7/; v.18 חזות "agreement" /8/; and in v.19 רק-זרעה "sheer-
terror" is ἐλπὶς πονηρά.

(2)      The translator appears to stress the two alternatives
facing the people, either a false "hope" in allies /9/ or a
"hope" based in the Lord (v.5).   The "strong and mighty one" of
MT (the Assyrians) is now "the strong and harsh wrath of the
Lord" (v.2).   However there will be a remnant (in both v.5 and
v.6 in LXX) which will enjoy the benefits of God's κρίσις and
ἰσχύς.   The two alternatives with their consequences have
influenced the rendering of vv.10, 13, where the MT קו is both
θλῖψις "affliction" (also reading צו as צר?) and ἐλπις, and of
v.12, with the contrast of τὸ ἀνάπαυμα "rest" and τὸ σύντριμμα
"affliction."   (The same MT parallelism, רגע/נוח, is in 34:14
translated ἀνάπαυσιν/ἀναπαύσονται, so רגע with the meaning
"rest" is known, as well as another meaning, "destruction."
What is significant is the meaning seen here; cf. Seeligmann:
52.)   Furthermore, the translator sees the rulers as already
being "afflicted" τεθλιμμένοι (v.14), perhaps interpreting
(reading?) לצון as צר(ל), but the rulers persist in their false
hope.

(3)      Therefore the Lord is to set up a new ruler (v.16), the

personal interpretation being implied in the inclusion of
ἐκλεκτόν /10/ amongst the epithets of the "stone" and of
ἐπ'αὐτῷ after ὁ πιστεύων (attested in all major texts except
B).

The LXX rendering of vv.19b, 20 fits into this context
with its reference to those who "of ourselves are weak" and so
need the help of God's appointed ruler.  There are many
striking parallels, in both words and thought, between vv.14-20
and 32:1-4 (which in LXX refers to the setting up of a
"righteous king").  This does not seem to be coincidental when
we note that neither passage is close to MT!

(4)    The translation of vv.17b, 18 is difficult (Ottley:
2:241) but seems to mean:

"and you who in vain trust in the lie that the
tempest will not come by you, take heed lest it
(in fact) take away your covenant of death; your
hope in Hades will not last."

The MT affirmation of coming destruction has become even more
explicitly a warning that Israel too may share in the
destruction that is to come upon her allies (see v.3 LXX).

(5)    Thus the context of v.17a is the dual emphasis of the
whole LXX chapter which affirms both the futility of false hope
and the certainty of hope in God.  The positive aspect is
stronger in LXX, particularly in its hope in the ruler whom God
will set up and who will rule with κρίσις.  Lest those,
particularly the rulers, who in the past have hoped in
"falsehood" fear that now there is no hope, there is given the
assurance of God's ἐλεημοσύνη.  While the "wrath of the Lord"
is "mighty and harsh" (v.2 LXX), "not for ever will I be angry
with you, nor shall the sound of my bitterness (πικρία /11/)
trample you" (v.28, LXX, freely interpreting MT metaphor) and
"you shall be taught by the judgement (κρῖμα) of your God"
(v.26 LXX, changing MT subject).

V.17 is thus in a context in which δικαιοσύνη could have
been used to translate הפדצ, in which case reference would have
been unambiguously to the rule of the king and the consequent
state of the city (κρίσις in v.17a would seem to refer to the
king's rule).  The translator, however, has interpreted הפדצ as
referring to God.  To have said ἡ δικαιοσύνη μου would have

been misleading as God's δικαιοσύνη may express itself in
punishment of the evildoer. The use of ἐλεημοσύνη unambiguously stresses the merciful action of God to those who have
trusted in a lie but are now willing to hope in God. This is
the emphasis of the whole chapter.

C.    56:1.

MT:   "Keep משפט and do צדקה, for soon my salvation will come
      and my צדקה be revealed."

LXX:  "Keep κρίσις, do δικαιοσύνη; for soon my salvation will
      come and τὸ ἔλεός μου be revealed."

Of note is the double use of צדקה. The second occurrence is usually seen as a deliberate reference back to chaps.
40-55, with meaning emphasising "salvation" as is apparent from
the parallelism. Thus Westermann sees a possible link with
46:13, while Bonnard refers to the different words but similar
idea of 40:5. D. R. Jones sees "the words but not the meaning
of II Isaiah," but this is improbable in light of other
instances of God's צדקה in chaps. 56-66.

The first occurrence is often seen to be related more to
the concern of chaps. 56-66 with the divine requirements (Duhm;
Jones; Westermann; Payne, 1967: 210, sees a deliberate use of
צדקה first in its "Proto-Isaianic" sense of "righteousness,"
then in its "Deutero-Isaianic" sense of "deliverance."). On
this understanding the announcement of salvation has become now
a means of admonition. The double use here, however, is in
keeping with the general emphasis of prophetic literature and
need not be post-exilic (Schmid: 136; and Scullion, 1971). The
link between the two halves of the verse is by no means a
contrast. One can see here reference to the covenant which
requires "righteousness" from Israel, but which is also linked
with "deliverance" from God. Kessler, after referring to the
"Gemeinschaft" aspect of צדקה says: "weil Gottes Wohlverhalten
sich bald erweisen wird, darum ist auch das Wohlverhalten des
Volkes Gott und seiner Ordnung gegenüber erforderlich."

The LXX use of τὸ ἔλεος in the second half may be purely
stylistic, from a desire to use another word, as is done
elsewhere in Isaiah with other words (particularly for words
relating to "wrongdoing," but not so prevalent otherwise).
Nevertheless, in 46:12f, צדקה also occurs twice, each time

being translated δικαιοσύνη. Further it is obvious that the
translator saw no incongruity in using δικαιοσύνη in contexts
of salvation. In v.1a δικαιοσύνη refers to "righteousness" in
terms of legal requirements (v.2b), and so it may be that he
hesitates to use in the same sentence the same word in
reference to God's "justice" (cf. our remarks at the end of
Section A, p. 68). Further τὸ ἔλεος fittingly recapitulates
ἐλεηθήσεται in 55:7: in both 55:6f and 56:1f there is a call to
life within the covenant relationship, linked with a promise of
merciful deliverance.

D.      59:16b (CHAP. 59)

צדק occurs once (v.4) and צדקה 4 times (vv.9, 14, 16,
17) in the whole chapter, which is rightly regarded as a unity
(see especially Westermann; Kessler has several dislocations
but still treats the chapter as a whole). The LXX also needs
to be considered on the basis of the whole chapter. Thus the
use of צדק(ה) throughout the chapter will be discussed.

Westermann regards the pattern as an interweaving of the
liturgy of the community lament (so Muilenburg, D. R. Jones)
and prophetic preaching (so Kessler). Of note is the threefold
expression of a lament contradicting the message of chaps.
40-55:

v.9a:   משפט is far away, צדקה does not reach us;
v.11b:  the hoped for משפט is not, ישועה is far away;
v.14a:  משפט is turned back, צדקה stands far away.

While D. R. Jones points out the connection with chaps. 40-55,
Scullion, 1971, emphasizes the value of the pattern in
interpreting the connotation of צדק(ה). Bonnard's conclusions
are similar.

*59:9*: There is general agreement that צדקה is used here in the
same sense as in chaps. 40-55, i.e., with a salvific emphasis.
Reference is to the deliverance and resulting harmony and
right-relationships that God will bring to his people, in
contrast to the description of vv.3-8.

*59:14a*: In contradistinction to v.9 almost all modern exegetes
regard משפט and צדקה here as being qualities lacking in Israel.
Westermann comments, "(The words) have a different frame of
reference from what they had in v.9. Here they refer to the
dealings of men one with another" (similarly Duhm, Muilenburg,

Kessler and Fohrer, although Scullion, 1971: 342, n. 27,
comments that in 1971 Fohrer verbally "stated that he would now
render צדק by *Heil* more often than in his commentary,
especially in chap. 59"). In this connection Westermann
regards vv.13-15a as a unit carrying on the description of
vv.5-8. However, the structure of v.14a, compared with the
statements of vv.9a, 11b and the reply in vv.15b-17, is such
that it is best to link v.13 with v.12 and to regard vv.14-15a
as providing a description of the consequences. This is
further supported by the parallelism of vv.14b-15a, so showing
v.14a to be a separate unit. It is thus clear that צדקה in
v.14a is to have the same salvific connotation as in v.9a.
*59:4*: The same roots, צדק, שפט, are used, though not in the
same pattern. The usual understanding is such as *RSV*: "No one
enters suit justly, no one goes to law honestly." This treats
קרא in the same technical sense as in Job 9:16 and 13:22,
rather than the different sense of Isa 42:6. Scullion, 1971,
strongly dissents and on the basis of an analysis of the use of
בצדק argues that here the sense is: "There is no-one to speak
or call בצדק, (i.e.) there is no king ... there is none to
recall the community's loyalty to Yahweh, to his covenant, to
each other." He contends that in Job 9:16 and Lev 19:15 it is
the context that provides the legal nuance. In reply it must
be said that: (1) the parallel use of the *niphal*, נשפט, in v.4a
/12/ is specifically judicial (as in 43:26; 66:16; etc.; see
KB); and (2) this verse is included in a description of their
sins and it is hardly likely that the absence of a leader would
be so regarded. It is typical of the prophetic tradition that
failure to be just is highlighted, along with the shedding of
innocent blood, e.g., Amos 5:7-15; Isa 1:17, 23; 5:23; 10:1f.
Thus we conclude that in v.4 בצדק means "justly," i.e., in
accord with what is required by the covenant relationship.
*59:16*: There is a close parallel between this verse and 63:5,
except that there חמתי is used in place of צדקתו. The
relationship is much discussed. Kessler and Westermann follow
Duhm in regarding vv.15b-20 as originally being a separate
section. There is, however, in the present setting a close
link in phraseology with that of the lament which strongly
suggests that צדקה is basic in the present context /13/:

"Yahweh saw" is a common introduction to an announcement of
God's action (cf. Exod 2:25; Isa 57:18; the opposite in a
lament as in Isa 40:27; 63:15; and the frequent use of סתר in
Psalms) and here links with the implied lament of v.2; "his
arm" that "saves" answers the complaint of v.1 (obscured in *RSV*
and *NEB*, "save" and "brought victory"); and the use of both ישע
and צדקה, together with Yahweh's displeasure that there is no
משפט, corresponds to the threefold lament noted previously.
Thus again צדקה refers to the saving act of Yahweh (or perhaps
"salvific will" as Kessler and Scullion): he is to restore
right order, where there is a lack of משפט in the human
situation.

*59:17*: This action (or will) of Yahweh has a dual aspect: on
the one hand, צדקה and ישוע, and, on the other, נקם and קנאה.
The latter is directed against Yahweh's foes. While at first
sight (and perhaps in the original use of the words) the "foes"
are the enemies of Israel as a nation, the inclusion of v.20
shows that salvation is limited to "those in Jacob who turn
from rebellion" (cf. 1:27). Thus "foes" refers to all who live
outside the covenant obligations. Therefore, in v.17, as in
v.16, צדקה refers to God's actions in terms of the covenant
relationship and there is no need to follow several modern
interpreters in using "salvation" in v.16 and "righteousness"
in v.17. (Although Kessler in his translation has this
difference, in his comment he describes "Gerechtigkeit" as "der
Wille, seinem Volk Recht zu schaffen," which actually corresponds to his use of "Heilswille" in v.16. *NEB* "integrity" is
inadequate, unless the reference, rather obscure, is to God's
intention to fulfil his covenant purposes.)

LXX throughout the book frequently diverges from MT in
its rendering of personal pronouns. This is so in chap. 59,
thus:

| Verses | 2-3 | 4-8 | 9-11a | 11b-14a | 14b-15a | 15b-21 |
|--------|------|-----------|--------|---------|---------|--------|
| MT | 2 pl. | 3 s. & pl. | 1 pl. | 1 pl. | - | same |
| LXX | " | " | 3 pl. | 1 pl. | 3 pl. | |

This may be of no significance since in several other

places no apparent reason for the changes is detectable, other
than that LXX seems to have a fluidity in person similar to
that in MT. In this chapter, however, it is possible to give a
consistent interpretation if one relates the translation to a
contemporary situation of the Jews suffering at the hands of
their rulers and those amongst whom they live (for hints of
this elsewhere in the Isaiah LXX, see Seeligmann: 88-91). Then
the 1st person refers to Israel and the 3rd person to her
enemies. The addressees of vv.2f may be either, but the
wording suggests Israel.

There is then observed a contrast between Israel, who
confesses (vv.11b-14a) because she "knows" her sins (v.12), and
her enemies, who "know not the way of peace" (v.8) and who
"turn away their mind from perceiving" (v.15a LXX). Israel is
suffering for her past sins (note tenses /14/), but repents.
The absence of Israel's "righteousness" (v.14) and "salvation"
(v.11) is described by the perfect tense, while "their (her
enemies') righteousness" (v.9) is described by use of the
common οὐ μή with subjunctive to refer to the future (Ottley:
1:37; in both vv.9, 14 MT has imperfect). There is no
possibility of the enemies enjoying a state of δικαιοσύνη, but
there is for Israel; "they" are still sinning, but Israel is
repentant. Accordingly, the duality which MT has in vv.17ff
is, in LXX, introduced much earlier.

It is recognized that any argument from changes in
person is to be used with caution (e.g., in v.16 "them" is used
of those being saved). Nevertheless the differences earlier in
the LXX chapter provide a consistent picture, and, in view of
changes of tenses and phrasing, are difficult to interpret if
applied solely to Israel (as in MT). Further, this heightening
by LXX of differences between groups is observed elsewhere,
e.g., 1:19ff, chap. 28, and 33:1-8.

With this general tenor of the passage we turn now to
specific verses:
*59:4*: λαλεῖ δίκαια, "speak just things," is the opposite of
v.3 which refers to the speaking of ἀνομία (שקר) and ἀδικία
(עולה) /15/.
*59:9*: "Therefore ἡ κρίσις went away from them and δικαιοσύνη
shall not overtake them." Apart from the change of person, LXX

is quite literal. In the context the verse is easily understood, whether one follows the Hebrew connotation of צְדָקָה and
מִשְׁפָּט or normal Greek usage.
*59:11b*: "We expected κρίσιν and there is none; σωτηρία is gone
away from us."
*59:14*: "And we caused to go away backwards τὴν κρίσιν and
ἡ δικαιοσύνη is gone away far (from us /16/)." The MT Hophal
יֻחַן is rendered actively in LXX, so placing the blame on "us"
rather than on Yahweh's apparent inactivity. The repeated use
of ἀφιστῆναι in various forms (v.9, 2 aorist; v.11, perfect;
v.14, 1 aorist and perfect) shows the continuity in the mind of
the translator, especially between v.11 and v.14, thus linking
the absence of σωτηρία and the absence of δικαιοσύνη. There is
further emphasis on "our" role in bringing about this state in
the use of ἀπέστημεν in v.13: "we have gone away from God." It
is possible that δικαιοσύνη in v.14 may be the same as in MT,
i.e., a salvific connotation. However, the whole structure
before and after suggests that v.14a continues the confession
of sin: "we went away from God ... and we removed (right)
judging from our community and δικαιοσύνη is missing because of
the absence of truth in the behaviour of our enemies." (The
last phrase is more literally, "truth is consumed in their ways
and through straight ways they are not able to pass." Both
ὁδός and εὐθεῖα are used metaphorically in a wisdom sense, cf.
33:15.) Thus δικαιοσύνη refers to the well-functioning,
harmonious society in which everyone does what is right. It is
absent both because of Israel's sins (which is the reason
salvation has not come) and because of the sins of those around
her.
*59:16-20*: "And (the Lord) saw that there was no man, and he
observed that there was none to help (ὁ ἀντιλημψόμενος) and he
came to aid (ἠμύνατο) them with his arm, and τῇ ἐλεημοσύνῃ he
was supported. (v.17) And he put on δικαιοσύνην as a breast-
plate and put a helmet σωτηρίου on his head and clothed himself
with a garment ἐκδικήσεως and the cloak (v.18) as repaying with
reproach to his adversaries (v.19) ... (v.20) and the deliverer
(ὁ ῥυόμενος) will come for the sake of Zion /17/ and shall
remove /18/ ungodliness from Jacob."
    The use of ἐλεημοσύνη (for צְדָקָה) reminds the LXX reader

of v.2: "Because of your sins he has turned his face from you
so as not to have mercy (ἐλεῆσαι/יִשְׁמָע)." Now in v.16 a change
in God's attitude is announced (in LXX, as in MT, by referring
to God's "seeing"), and it is appropriate to give emphasis by
the use of ἐλεημοσύνη. Indeed, δικαιοσύνη could here be
misleading as there has been so much emphasis on Israel's
ἀδικία which deserves God's judgement.

Why then, it may be asked, is δικαιοσύνη used in v.17?
Throughout Isaiah and heightened by LXX there runs a twofold
stream: (1) Israel's treatment at the hands of her enemies is
deserved because of her sins, and (2) this does not make the
nations' ill-treatment of her right, so they are to be punished
for their wrongs and Israel delivered. It would seem that,
having mentioned God's "merciful action," the translator can
now speak of God's δικαιοσύνη which, for him, involves both
punishment of evildoers and forgiveness of those who repent,
with deliverance of those being ill-treated. δικαιοσύνη here
is the attribute of a ruler or judge. Thus v.16 is directed
primarily to repentant, ill-treated Israel, and vv.17f to both
Israel and her foes /19/.

The imagery of v.17 may be influenced by Hellenic
imagery, especially amongst the Stoics, of life as a battle,
(cf. Brown). Such imagery is seen in the later Wisdom of
Solomon 5:18ff: δικαιοσύνη as θώραξ, and as helmet (κόρυς, in
Isaiah περικεφαλαία), κρίσις ἀνυπόκριτος. This influence may
have come through earlier Wisdom tradition in Alexandria of
which the Isaiah translator is aware, for certainly much in
Isa 59 reflects wisdom imagery (in both MT and LXX; there are
other parallels between Isa 59 and Wisd. Sol. 5: 59:19f and
5:2; 59:6-9 and 5:6f; 59:16 and 5:16, all common wisdom terms).
The wisdom influence is probably the reason for the repeated
use of ὁδός (4 times for 4 different Hebrew words in vv.7f and
14), and the surprising use of ἄφρων (v.7) and of συνιέναι
(v.15). At the very least, the translator's mind at this point
had wisdom imagery to the fore, so supporting our interpretation of δικαιοσύνη in v.17 as referring to the virtue
of "justice" appropriate to a ruler or judge (here God).

We may summarize our observations on (ה)צְדָק and its
translations in chap. 59 as follows:

(1)    In v.4, both MT בצדק and LXX δίκαια refer to what is
"just" or "right."

(2)    In the 4 occurrences of צדקה the contextual reference is
to the צדקה, משפט, and ישוע which chaps. 40-55 had promised
Yahweh would bring to his people. צדקה is thus closely linked
with "salvation," action in terms of the covenant relation
between Yahweh and his people and the consequent blessings.
Such blessings include a society in which Israel will fulfil
the requirements of the covenant. At the same time it is
clearly said that Israel has failed to fulfil her obligations
both in community life and towards Yahweh, and so does not now
enjoy משפט and צדקה.

(3)    The 3-fold lament and the response in MT (vv.9a, 11b,
14a and vv.15b, 16) do not have unity of reference in LXX.
V.9a now refers to Israel's enemies, v.11b to Israel's not
experiencing justice and salvation, and v.14b to Israel's own
life amongst the nations. The "judging" absent in v.15b now
leads on to help and pity to Israel and requittal to her
enemies. In these contexts δικαιοσύνη refers to a community
attribute (vv.9, 14), which is absent because of the ἀνομία and
ἀδικία of Israel or of the nations amongst whom she lives, or
to an attribute of God as ruler or judge (v.17). δικαιοσύνη
can be linked with salvation because of the context: Israel
needs to be delivered from her enemies and all ungodliness must
be removed (v.20) before Zion can enjoy δικαιοσύνη, which is
that well-ordered situation where everyone fulfils his proper
responsibility to man and God.

(4)    ἐλεημοσύνη is used in v.16 to refer to God's action
towards repentant Israel. δικαιοσύνη would be inappropriate in
this context without some other contextual indication of his
merciful action towards repentant sinners. δικαιοσύνη in v.17
is predominantly punishment of wrongdoers, but includes
deliverance of repentant, ill-treated Israel.

(5)    In most cases LXX translates the words being studied
quite literally, but a study of the context shows that the
translator has a different understanding to that seen today in
MT. His translation of other words and his syntax provide
important clues to his intended meaning.

3. ΔΙΚΑΙΟΣΥΝΗ TRANSLATING OTHER THAN (ה)צדק.

A. 33:6 (33:5-15)

Vv.6f have their difficulties in MT (cf. emendations proposed in the usually cautious *BHS*) and in both verses LXX differs considerably with quite different syntax as well as additions. That which arouses our attention is the addition of δικαιοσύνη at the end of v.6, but we turn first to *v.5* where δικαιοσύνη is used to translate צדקה:

MT: The Lord is exalted, for he dwells on high;
מָלֵא צִיּוֹן מִשְׁפָּט וּצְדָקָה׃

LXX: Holy is God who dwells on high, ἐνεπλήσθη Σιων κρίσεως καὶ δικαιοσύνης.

The idea in MT is clearly that because Yahweh is exalted, he is reigning and so causing Zion to be filled /20/ with the blessings of his מִשְׁפָּט and צֶדֶק (cf. 32:1, 15ff; 33:20-22). An allusion to moral qualities exercised by Zion is highly improbable, except in a secondary sense that one result of Yahweh's active rule will be the removal from Zion of all who are "unjust" (cf. vv.13-16) and of the oppressors (cf. v.19). On the other hand, LXX, by referring to the holiness of God and by using the passive in the second half, has shifted the emphasis. We shall return to this after considering *v.6*:

MT: וְהָיָה אֱמוּנַת עִתֶּיךָ, abundance of salvation, wisdom and knowledge, the fear of the Lord - such as his treasure.

LXX: ἐν νόμῳ παραδοθήσονται in treasures is our salvation; there is wisdom and knowledge and reverence of the Lord: these are the treasures of δικαιοσύνη.

Following basically *RSV*, the first phrase of MT may be translated: "and there will be security for all your times (cf. 32:17f)." As in v.5, emphasis is upon Yahweh's beneficence. We might compare Deut 28:12; 32:34, referring to Yahweh's "treasure" to be given to his covenant people, including material prosperity, vindication and deliverance. Here the result is his people's enjoyment of certain characteristics, characteristics which no doubt the prophet is calling on them to exercise.

The first phrase in LXX seems to refer to the punishment of Israel's enemies: παραδιδόναι is a favourite "stop-gap" word of the translator (Ottley: 1:50; Ziegler, 1934:14). It is used in v.1 also of those who seek to ill-treat and reject Israel.

The reason for using ἐν νόμῳ is unknown. It may be an attempt to translate a plural אמונות (Ottley) or a reading of עתיך as עדתיך "thy (Yahweh's) testimonies." More important is the meaning intended. Seeligmann (107) contends that, "Following on (v.1) ... this can only mean that the enemies of Zion will perish by (in the name of) the strict adherence to the Law by the inhabitants." He links this with a conception of the Law (found in 8:20) as "a protection extended by God to man during his lifetime." We can note further that v.7 LXX says that Zion's enemies will be afraid of her. At least it can be said that, for the translator, Israel's enemies will not be defeated by a battle, nor should Israel fear, rather her task is "in the law," trusting in God to deliver (vv.2, 10-13, etc.). The rendering of the rest of v.6 follows then naturally. We may paraphrase: "salvation is to be found in living a life of δικαιοσύνη, which includes wisdom, knowledge and the fear of the Lord." Here is δικαιοσύνη used in a classical sense of the sum total of all virtue, but with a Jewish emphasis ("reverence of the Lord" and obedience of the "law"). Seeligmann's "God's powerful aid" (98, 107) may be applicable elsewhere, but is most unlikely here.

The LXX emphasis on Zion's virtues in v.6, together with syntax of v.5b, strongly suggests that in v.5b Zion's virtue is also in view: v.5a affirms God's holiness, vv.5b-6, Zion's δικαιοσύνη. There is thereby an assurance that Zion's enemies will be "delivered up."

A similar use of δικαιοσύνη in an ethical sense, "uprightness," referring to one who is to be secure and who will announce the coming judgement (v.14b LXX; v.16), is found in v.15: הלך צדקות/πορευόμενος ἐν δικαιοσύνῃ.

In summary, the three uses of δικαιοσύνη in this chapter refer to an ethical virtue of the people of God (this is only so for MT in v.15), related to law-keeping and reverence of God.

B.    61:8 (CHAP. 61)

The whole chapter concerns an announcement of the salvation that God is bring to Zion, vv.1-3 leading naturally into vv.4-11. צדק(ה) occurs 3 times, two of these being translated by δικαιοσύνη (vv.3, 11), but in v.10 צדק is

surprisingly rendered by εὐφροσύνη. In LXX of v.8 there is use
of both δικαιοσύνη (MT: משפט) and δίκαιος (באמת). As the
overall interpretation of LXX is close to MT each verse shall
be treated in turn.

*61:3b*:

"They shall be called ...

אילי הצדק מטע יהוה להתפאר:

Γενεαὶ δικαιοσύνης, Φύτευμα κυρίου εἰς δόξαν.

Amongst modern exegetes there are 4 main lines of interpretation of צדק (with overlap):

(1) "Righteousness," referring to the character of
Israel, is most usual (Duhm; *RSV*; *NEB*; *JB*; Bonnard; D. R.
Jones). The comment of Jones is typical: "Righteousness which
in II Isaiah was the redemptive activity of God will now be
embodied in the character of Israel." This argument seems
however to be imposing a supposed legalism. More relevant is
the similar 60:21: "your people shall all be צדיקים."

(2) The imagery of vv.2b-3 favours a usage similar to
that in chaps. 40-55, i.e., "Heil" (Fohrer; Westermann;
Scullion, 1971).

(3) The enjoyment of צדק and the consequent prosperity
is suggested by the translation of Kessler (also Schmid: 103,
following KB), "immergrüne Baume," where "צדק = eine Sache, wie
sie sein soll" (Duhm suggests "immergrün" in his commentary,
though not in the translation, but refers to it as connoting
"Gesetztreue.").

(4) On the basis of the parallelism, "oaks of צדק,
planting of Yahweh," it is suggested that צדק is a divine name,
whether as צדק (Rosenberg /21/) or as a defective writing of
צדיק (Scullion, 1972: 117).

Of relevance is the use of פאר, a favourite root in
Isaiah, especially in chaps. 60-66 /22/. It is usually linked
with Yahweh's act of delivering Israel and is often associated
with צדק, especially in 60:21 which is similar in thought to
61:3b (cf. 61:10f, ישע, צדקה, פאר, and planting רתחלה). (צדקה ותהלה).
The "glorifying" of Zion is the "glorifying" of Yahweh: 61:3
begins and ends with פאר - Yahweh gives פאר that he himself
התפאר (cf. 60:7, 13; 63:14). The general usage of פאר
suggests strongly that here צדק refers to the full enjoyment of

the blessings of salvation. צדיק in 60:21 and צדק in 61:3
would seem to be much more than "righteous(ness)" in terms of
obeying God, although this would be included. Rather emphasis
is upon the full enjoyment of covenant blessings: freedom,
land, vindication, prosperity, admired by the nations, etc.

In LXX of v.3 there is a threefold use of the favourite
δόξα (for פאר, תהלה, התפאר; although not used for the similar
language of vv.10f). εἰς δόξα is ambiguous as to whose "glory"
is meant. The likelihood is that the translator intends Zion:
the Lord has planted, so glory will eventuate. Cf. 60:21: "And
all thy people (shall be) righteous, and they shall possess the
earth for ever, keeping the planting, the work of their (αὐτοῦ
referring to ὁ λαός σου) hands εἰς δόξα," continuing the
description of 60:15bff.

Γενεαί "generations" is probably a free rendering
linking v.3 with 60:21 ὁ λαός σου πᾶς δίκαιος (i.e., a stronger
link than in MT), although perhaps "oaks" suggested long-life
(cf. 65:22). The link with 60:21, together with the phrase,
"absence of ἀδικία (חמס)," in 60:18 (following ἐν δικαιοσύνη to
describe the actions of overseers in 60:17b) and the rendering
of 61:8 (see below), all suggest that uppermost in the use of
δικαιοσύνη is the state or quality (ethical, and as a result
harmonious) of Zion when all are "righteous."

*61:8:*

MT:     כי אני יהוה אהב משפט שנא גזל בעולה ונתתי פעלתם באמת
                                    וברית עולם אכרות להם:

LXX:    ἐγὼ γάρ εἰμι κύριος ὁ ἀγαπῶν δικαιοσύνην καὶ μισῶν
        ἀρπάγματα ἐξ ἀδικίας. καὶ δώσω τὸν μόχθον αὐτῶν
        δικαίοις /23/ καὶ διαθήκην αἰώνιον διαθήσομαι αὐτοῖς.

בָּעוֹלָה is unusual, but is adopted by RSVmg and also by
Scullion (1972: 119), who proposes ב as expressing equivalence:
"robbery as the equivalent of (i.e., in place of, instead of)
sacrifice." However, the interpretation of LXX and Targum,
supported by a few Hebrew Mss (so BHK, NEB) suggests בְּעַוְלָה to
give "robbery with violence," alluding to the capture of
Jerusalem. A similar meaning is obtained with MT pointing if,
with KB (cf. Scullion), עוֹי is regarded as a possible
contraction of עָוְי. This certainly fits the context. Yahweh
is concerned for משפט, to right injustice, so he will faith-
fully (באמת referring to Yahweh's actions) give recompense /24/

and will make an everlasting covenant.

LXX is unexpected in two related ways: the use of δικαιοσύνη and the translation of the second half of the verse. The use of δικαιοσύνη is evidently influenced by the opposite, ἁρπάγματα ἐξ ἀδικίας, rather than by any forensic note seen in משפט, and is related to the interpretative rendering of the verse as a whole. κρίσις (in the Greek sense) would be too weak a word to provide an antithesis. δικαιοσύνη here is a clear example of the definition given by Aristotle (see p. 27) with reference to "not taking more than one's due," and can be compared with the many Greek debates on "unjust" wars. ἁρπάγματα is used elsewhere in Isaiah only in 42:22, referring to the plundering of Israel by other nations. This context may also be a reason for the strong word, μόχθος /25/, referring to the hardship of those who love (and do) righteousness. The general sense of the verse, following on from preceding verses /26/, would be:

> "(You will inherit all these things) for I am the Lord, the one who loves righteousness (or fairness, i.e., ethical emphasis, human behaviour) and who hates those who try to gain wealth and prosperity by taking what is not theirs (referring to other nations); thus I will reward those who are righteous and persist in hard work (or perhaps better, those who suffer in being righteous) and with them I will make an everlasting covenant."

There is an implied exhortation to persist in doing "righteousness," no matter how difficult it seems and no matter how much the wicked prosper, for the Lord will reward those who are faithful. The translator sees באמת as referring not to Yahweh (as MT) but to Israel.

*61:10f*:

Although Fohrer, Kessler and Westermann follow Duhm in isolating v.10 as a response of praise to vv.1-9, 11, it is preferable to retain MT order, since vv.10f together form a fitting response. Together they return to the dual imagery of v.3, clothing and planting.

On the basis of their translations it appears that Kessler, Westermann and *NEB* see a difference in the connotation of צדקה in the two verses: v.10, "Gerechtigkeit" (*NEB*: "integrity"), v.11, "Heil" ("righteousness"). *NEB* seems loathe to use any connotation of "salvation" for צדקה in chaps. 56-66

(see Appendix II), and uses "integrity" only here and in 59:16f
(there referring to Yahweh), the reason being obscure, unless
it is simply a stylistic variant for "righteousness," but in
any case referring to a moral attribute. It is also unlikely
that Westermann and Kessler's use of "Gerechtigkeit" in v.10 is
due to the use of "Heil" for the parallel, ישע /27/. It
appears that both see צדקה in v.10 as referring to Israel and
in v.11 to the action of Israel. In fact, the parallelisms in
each verse suggest exactly the opposite!

In v.10 Yahweh provides צדקה and ישע for the redeemed
Israel. The picture of prosperity, joy, honour, and restored
relationship is conveyed also in the rest of the verse. The
result in Zion will then certainly /28/ be a state of harmony
and well-being (צדקה) which involves "praise" of the One who
makes this possible. The affirmation of v.11b is an obvious
parallel to v.9. In no way is there a connotation of
"righteousness" in an merely ethical sense in either v.10 or
v.11.

LXX translates reasonably literally, with some changes
in syntax that do not alter the general sense. The double
occurrence of שוש is rendered literally, εὐφροσύνῃ
εὐφρανθήσονται, with change of person in LXX, the subject now
being the "righteous" and their "seed" (vv.8f). It is no doubt
this occurence of εὐφροσύνη which has led to its unusual use
for צדקה in the phrase, χιτῶνα εὐφροσύνης. This translation
may be due to carelessness (so Ottley), or may be because again
the translator felt δικαιοσύνη to be inappropriate in this
context. In cases where δικαιοσύνη and σωτήριον are in close
parallel, reference is always to God's δικαιοσύνη — 46:13;
51:5-8; 59:17; 62:1 (MT refers to Zion's צדקה, LXX apparently
to God's); 63:1 /29/ — with a dual emphasis on vindication and
judgement, and with σωτήριον emphasizing God as saviour. In
v.10 however emphasis is more on Zion as the recipient of
salvation and so the translator in coming to צדקה also thought
primarily of that which Israel received. δικαιοσύνη with its
(Greek) ethical emphasis may have been deemed inappropriate and
so the translator chose the immediate εὐφροσύνη (cf. v.3). The
objection may be raised, that δικαιοσύνη is used in vv.3, 11.
The reply can be made that, in v.3, reference is back to the

state of Zion with "injustice" removed, and similarly in v.11 reference is to a general state of "justice" when the "righteous" are blessed. To use δικαιοσύνη in v.10 would suggest some virtue which God gives Israel, and that is not the point at issue: "I" am already one of the δίκαιοι, "I" do not need to be given the virtue of δικαιοσύνη, rather "I" need to see δικαιοσύνη as "justice" put into effect in Zion's experience amongst the nations (as in v.11).

This leads on to the likely understanding of δικαιοσύνη in v.11. The associated ἀγαλλίαμα (for חהלה /30/) is linked with and recapitulates ἀγαλλιάσθω in v.10 (חגל), i.e., Israel's response to God's action. The imagery reminds one of 45:8, where the Lord causes both הקדצ/δικαιοσύνη and עשי/ἔλεος to spring forth (ἀνατελλεῖν is used for יצמיח in both v.11 and 45:8, whereas LXX of 60:21 provides a different image). There δικαιοσύνη and ἔλεος probably refer to the accomplishment of God's purpose as being with justice, but showing pity to his own people who are being unjustly treated and to those who repent (see earlier discussion on 45:18-25; cf. also 1:27). The use in v.11 of σπέρματα (זרועים) is probably linked in the translator's mind with v.9, σπέρμα (זרע). Although both translations are correct, the association is closer in LXX because of use of the same noun. There is also, as in MT, the repeated reference to "the nations" (vv.9, 11). With these various links, as well as the emphasis in v.8, it is probable that in v.11, in using δικαιοσύνη, the translator is thinking of the time when the "righteous" will be rewarded, i.e., blessed (v.9), a time when justice will be done and seen to be done and hence when Zion will rejoice greatly (cf. 51:11; 25:9). In this way the song of praise (in LXX commencing the second phrase of v.9) fittingly recapitulates the preceding proclamation.

To summarize, for the occurrences of δικαιοσύνη in chap. 61 we have the following connotations: v.3: the quality of life in Zion when all are "righteous" and "wrong" is removed; v.8: that virtue which is opposite to seeking to take what is not rightfully one's own; and v.11: that state in the world when justice is done and seen to be done.

C.     63:7 (CHAPS. 63, 64).

63:1-6 forms a separate unit whose basic idea, the
annihilation of the nations, sets it apart from the rest of
chaps. 60-66. There are many similarities with chap. 34. At
the same time, as Bonnard points out, there are many points of
contact with surrounding chapters: "qui vient (62:6, 11), ...
au jour de la vengeance (61:2), rétablit la justice, apporte
salut (62:1, 11) et la rédemption (62:12), grâce à la puissance
de son bras (62:8)."

63:7 - 64:11(12) forms a separate prayer in the form of
a community lament, although with an expanded historical
section (see especially Westermann).

There are several textual and exegetical difficulties in
these chapters. Here we shall consider only those pertinent to
our main concern.

*63:1b:*

MT:     אני מדבר בצדקה רב להושיע

LXX:    ἐγὼ διαλέγομαι δικαιοσύνην καὶ κρίσιν σωτηρίου

The construction 'ל רַב is unusual, as is also רַב alone
meaning "mighty." Bonnard, citing LXX, emends רַב to רָב, "qui
querelle pour sauver," thus giving two participles in parallel,
as well as taking up the theme of 51:22f and 49:25f (cf. use of
ריב in 34:8). This is much more to be preferred than the
proposal of Duhm, אֲנִי רַב כֹּחַ (followed by Fohrer; Kessler; and
Westermann), and is more suitable in the context (cf. v.4) than
MT pointing.

מדבר צדקה has been variously understood (see Appendix
I). The use of 'ב argues against *RSV*, "announcing vindication"
(similarly, *JB*; *NEB*; McKenzie; Muilenburg; and Bonnard). Elsewhere 'ב following דבר has various meanings: (1) instrumental =
"through, by means of," usually a person, e.g., 20:2: Yahweh
spoke through Isaiah; and often in Pentateuch and Kings,
"Yahweh spoke by the hand of ..."; (2) describing source =
"from," though here the object is a place, e.g., Ps 60:8 and
108:8: "Yahweh spoke from his sanctuary" (*JB*, *NEB*), and 99:7:
"spoke from a pillar of cloud" (Dahood, 1968: 79); (3) manner,
e.g., 45:19 and 48:16, Yahweh has not spoken "in secret," and
several times in Ezekiel (5:13; 36:5f; 38:19; etc.) Yahweh
speaks "in my jealousy." The last seems most likely here,

although one must ask the connotation of the phrase, בצדקה (cf. literal rendering of Fohrer and Westermann, "in Gerechtigkeit"). The phrase is quite common, generally referring to actions in accordance with the demands of a relationship. See especially the discussion of Scullion (1971), leading to his conclusion, "It is I who speak; in (my) saving intention (Kessler: "in meinem Heilswillen") mighty ..." (note his change in syntax). The parallelism suggests a salvific emphasis (against Westermann), though including punishment of those who have oppressed Israel (vv.4f). Schmid (136, n. 294) also sees a dual aspect in צדקה: "richterliche Eingreifen Jahwes" and "sein heilbringendes Handeln." We can compare 42:6 and 45:13 where בצדקה probably means "because of my saving purpose" (North). We may note further that, in the semanticly similar passages in (3) above, דבר has far more the connotation of "act" (referring to what God has done). If one accepts Bonnard's emendation of רב, דבר may have a judicial sense (in 32:7 דבר is used of a plea for justice, and elsewhere it is used of a ruling made by a king).

Taking all of these observations into account, the most likely sense of MT is: "It is I, speaking (acting) with a saving, righteous purpose, entering into controversy in order to save."

The rest of 63:1-6 deals mainly with Yahweh's actions towards the nations as he "ransoms" his people. For the dual aspect of v.4, compare 61:2 and 34:8.

LXX highlights the judicial acting of God by its translation of the two occurrences of רב in this chapter, vv.1, 8. In vv.4-6 there are differences in person which emphasise the deliverance of God's people (secondary in MT). Vv.4-6 may be translated as follows (with significant differences in italics):

"For a day of repayment *came upon them* (Edom or Israel? /31/), and a year of ransoming /32/ is here. And I looked and there was no helper, and I perceived and no-one came to aid, and my arm *delivered them* (those who had no helper, i.e., Israel) and my wrath stood by and I trampled *them* (Edom) in my anger and I brought down their blood

to the earth."
Again we see a comparison between punishment of Israel's
enemies and deliverance of Israel. This duality is in v.1b
also:

> "I speak (or, present an argument concerning)
> δικαιοσύνη and a κρίσις σωτηρίου, i.e., justice
> and a decision relating to salvation."

The idea of deliverance as an act of God as just judge carries
on into the LXX of 63:7ff.

*63:7f:*

MT:     "I will remember חסדי of Yahweh, תהלת of Yahweh,
according to all which Yahweh has done for us,
וְרַב־טוּב to the house of Israel, which he has
done for us /33/ כרחמיו וכרב חסדיו; for he said,
'Surely they are my people, sons who will not
deal falsely,' and he became להם למושיע in all
their afflictions." /34/

The general understanding of MT is quite straightforward: the introduction leading to an accumulation of words
for God's gracious dealings with his people, here described as
"sons" (cf. 1:2-4 and 30:1, 9, likewise referring to their
disobedience and false dealings). Implicit is an expectation
that sons will be loyal. (McCarthy, extending Moran's study,
stresses the father-son relationship as one of respect and
obedience, and sees a tender aspect only in Hosea, denying its
existence in Isa 63:16. He concludes that this relationship is
essentially the same as the covenant relationship.)

LXX places more emphasis on deliverance as an act of
justice:

> "I remembered τὸν ἔλεον of the Lord, τὰς ἀρετὰς
> of the Lord in all things with which the Lord
> recompenses /35/ us. The Lord is κριτὴς ἀγαθός
> to the house of Israel; he brings upon us
> according to his ἔλεος and according to the
> abundance of his δικαιοσύνη. And he said, 'Are
> they not my people, children (who) will not set
> aside (my commandments)?' and he (it) became
> αὐτοῖς εἰς σωτηρίαν out of all afflictions."

This is the only occurrence in Isaiah of חסד rendered by

δικαιοσύνη. Here some other word than the usual ἔλεος was needed as ἔλεος had been used for חסדים. Given the context of God as a good judge, δικαιοσύνη is an appropriate choice: as a good judge he shows both justice and pity. This is far more likely to be the reason· than a translation on the basis of חסד being interpreted in a legalistic manner /36/.

The plural, ἀρεταί, seems to refer to God's marvellous acts. Elsewhere in Isaiah a singular noun is regularly used for MT plural when reference is to an abstract quality /37/. The plural here is best explained in terms of its Hellenistic usage, "manifestations of divine power" (for non-biblical instances, see LSJ, "ἀρετή. b"; BAG, "ἀρετή. 2"). So at the beginning of v.7 there is a link between God's mercy and his acts that bring judgement to the nations but deliverance to Israel. There is a note of hope throughout the passage in LXX: the present tense is used throughout v.7, so affirming a continuing aspect of God's dealings (rather than MT where the lament form gives a statement of the past situation which does not appear to be operative in Israel's present experience). This, together with v.8, suggests that if one obeys God now, he will also save out of the present affliction.

Similar is *64:2(3)f*. MT, "When you did *terrible things which we looked not for*, you came down, the mountains quaked at your presence," has in LXX become hope for Israel, "When you do *glorious things* (τὰ ἔνδοξα), trembling will take hold of the mountains," followed by "(We have not heard or seen ...) your works (ἔργα) which you will do for those who wait for ἔλεος (MT: him)."

Throughout LXX of chap. 63 there is thus emphasis upon God's "pity" which is going to issue in action to deliver his people. Their hope is certain because God is a "good judge" who acts according to "pity" and "justice" (δικαιοσύνη). Both characteristics are appropriate because Israel is obeying God's commandments as she lives among the nations, who are ill-treating her (vv.4-6). However, Israel has not always obeyed God. For this dimension, we need to continue further into chap. 64.

*64:4(5)f*:

These verses are full of difficulties and various

interpretations and emendations have been suggested. Nevertheless similar interpretations of (ה)צדק are given by most
scholars, irrespective of emendations used and import seen.

*RSV, JB, NEB,* Jones, McKenzie and Bonnard take v.4(5)a,
at least, as a general statement that God meets (so interpreting פגע; *JB,* "guides") those who do righteousness,
following God's ways. Muilenburg, Fohrer, Kessler and
Westermann are similar but follow *BHK* (and *BHS*) in inserting לו
at the beginning (haplography), "O that ..."

V.5(6) is then generally seen as a confession of sin,
צדקות being acts of Israel: "righteous deeds" (*RSV, NEB,*
Muilenburg), "Tugenden" (Kessler: "wörtlich: Frömmigkeits-
erweisungen"). Blank similarly has "virtues," but his general
interpretation is quite different. Starting from the order קצף
then חטא, he interprets as a grievance, akin to Job.
Similarly, but quite independently, based on an interpretation
of פגע as "du schlugst" (cf. 53:6), Fahlgren (95-97), followed
by Scullion (1971), sees all of vv.4(5)f as a complaint that
(quoting Scullion), "Yahweh seems to regard as worthless and to
visit with punishment all that they are doing in accordance
with what they think their community relationship with him
should be"; this is the unheard of act of v.3(4). Both צדק and
צדקות are thus interpreted mainly in terms of religious acts.
Such an interpretation does overcome some difficulties and has
both an inner cohesion and, particularly for Fahlgren and
Scullion, a link with preceding verses. Further, the same
emphasis can be carried on through vv.5b-6(6b-7): note the
order in v.6(7) with the use of כי.

Whichever interpretation one adopts, there is the same
appeal to Yahweh as Father, vv.7(8)f, and as the one to whom
belong Zion and the temple, "thy" in vv.9(10)f. Irrespective
of the overall interpretation, צדקה refers primarily to
religious acts, i.e., the people's understanding of what God
requires (cf. 58:2f; also 1:11ff and Ezek 18:24). צדק may be
more general as part of a standard phrase, עשה צדק. In both
cases reference is to the actions required by the relationship.

LXX, after v.4(3), "... your works which you will do for
those who wait for ἔλεος," (continues differences in italics),
"*for it* (mercy /38/) will meet with the doers of τὸ δίκαιον,

and they will *remember your ways*. Behold, you were angry and we sinned; *because of this we wandered*, and we all became as unclean men /39/, all our δικαιοσύνη as filthy /40/ rags."

This is one of 4 places where τὸ δίκαιον is used for צדק(ה) (צדק: 51:1; 59:4 and here; צדקה: 5:23). In 5:23 the reference is unambiguously to the "right" of an innocent person at law (see p. 45). 59:4 may be forensic referring to one's statements (see p. 75). Here and in 51:1 the connotation seems to be more generally "what is right, just" (as in classical Greek, when object of ποιεῖν), being further explained in terms of "God's ways." It seems that the use here is because the more abstract δικαιοσύνη is used in the following verse: the people's "righteousness" is of no value because they are not doing "what is right," they are "impure."

LXX, by its use of γάρ and the future tense, joins v.4(5)a to v.3(4). One can hope for pity because the Lord meets with pity those who do what is right, who will remember his ways. But, v.4(5)b, for the present, God was angry at the people's sins and so they wandered (both physically and morally? cf. 63:17), their virtue being nothing but a filthy rag. The Lord "*handed them over* (to their enemies; cf. Seeligmann: 112) *on account of* /41/ their sins," v.6(7). Thus the complaint (or confession of sin) of MT becomes in LXX more of a simple statement of fact. The plea of v.7(8) is also softer (omitting explicit reference to the potter): "And now, Lord, you are our Father, and we all are clay, the work of your hands;" and the plea of MT v.11(12) becomes a statement: "and in addition to all these things (regarding Zion) you forbore, O Lord, and kept silent and humbled us exceedingly" (all aorist tenses).

Thus throughout LXX of chaps. 63, 64 there runs the thought that God was "just" in punishing his people (there is no protest, nor agonizing plea), but there is hope of "pity" for those who do τὸ δίκαιον, conforming to God's ways, for apart from this they have no δικαιοσύνη (a virtue).

D.    38:19 AND 39:8 (CHAPS. 36-39).

The two occurrences in Isaiah of אמת translated by δικαιοσύνη are both in chaps. 36-39, as is also the only instance in whole LXX of אמת translated by ἐλεημοσύνη (38:18).

While it is now generally accepted that at least chaps. 1-35, 40-66 are by the one translator (see p. 8), there is a strong possibility that chaps. 36-39 is by a different hand. This is the conclusion of Hurwitz on the basis of the treatment of the few anthropomorphisms and other language differences. A further complication is the relationship of the MT and LXX texts of Isa 36-39 and 2(4) Kings 18-20 (Orlinsky, 1939; Deutsch). The unusual translation of אמת may be another indication (not observed by Hurwitz) that we are faced with a different translator.

It should be noted however that the context of אמת is different. Throughout chaps. 1-35, 40-66, wherever it is translated by ἀλήθεια (10:20; 16:5; 38:3; 42:3; 48:1; 59:14f) reference is to behaviour of people, but never of Yahweh. This of course reflects MT. (The only other instances of אמת are 43:9, ἀληθής, referring to a statement, and 61:8 where δικαίοις appears to be based on באמת.) The two unusual translations in 38:19f both describe Yahweh (39:8 will need further discussion), whereas אמת = ἀλήθεια is used in 38:3 of Hezekiah. Thus this may be another case of the translator (of the whole book) using a different word to describe God when he has already in the immediate context used the more usual word for man (see p. 68). We simply do not have any case of אמת applied to Yahweh in chaps. 1-35, 40-66 to provide a comparison. In Psalms (another translator) there is frequent reference to Yahweh's אמת = ἀλήθεια.

As a tentative conclusion, it appears unlikely that chaps. 36-39 are from the translator of the rest of the book. Nevertheless, because of uncertainty we shall still briefly examine these passages.

*38:18f.*

These verses are in the so-called "Psalm of Hezekiah" (vv.10-20), the actual form used being uncertain (MT: מכתב; LXX: προσευχή; see commentaries and Deutsch: 38-46). Vv.16-20 are both thanksgiving and praise for life, vv.18f taking up the motifs of vv.10f.

Some commentators regard the double use of אל־אמתך as suspect and, on basis of LXX ἐλεημοσύνη (but no Hebrew Mss support), emend the first אמתך to חסדך (so Duhm; *BHK*;

Seeligmann: 69; and Deutsch; but not Fohrer; Eichrodt; Kaiser;
*BHS*; or English versions). It is true that elsewhere in the
Bible there is no case of hoping in Yahweh's אמת while there
are cases of hoping in his חסד (Ps 33:18; 147:11; in each case
LXX ἔλεος); also חסד//אמת frequently occurs in Psalms referring
to Yahweh (17 cases noted, in each case LXX having ἔλεος and
ἀλήθεια). Nevertheless it is hard to see why then MT would
have אמת (the only possibilities are memory of Ps 30:10 and
homoioteleuton). Furthermore, ἐλεημοσύνη for חסד would itself
be uncommon (see Appendix III). In any case, MT refers to
God's faithfulness in providing what is necessary for life, and
for this both חסד and אמת are appropriate.

As to why the LXX translator used ἐλεημοσύνη and
δικαιοσύνη, there are two possibilities:
(1)    His *Vorlage* was different. Against this is the fact
that his treatment of vv.15-19 is full of difficulties. He
omits most of the difficult v.15 and v.17a, perhaps interprets
v.19b in light of a supposed childlessness of Hezekiah up to
his illness (so Ottley), and in v.17b seems to confuse חשׁק (MT)
with similarly sounding חשׂך, translating εἵλου "keep" (so KB,
*BHS*). Rather than using a different *Vorlage*, he seems instead
to have had genuine difficulty in understanding the text.
(2)    More likely he felt ἀλήθεια to be inadequate in the
context of deliverance. V.11 is given a soteriological
emphasis with MT יהיה (read יהוה) as τὸ σωτήριον τοῦ θεοῦ (so
avoiding saying "see God"). צדק and חסד occur frequently in
Psalms in contexts of the deliverance of a righteous sufferer,
particularly from death, often also associated with אמת. Here
likewise the "rightness" of Hezekiah's call to God is affirmed
(v.3). (At the same time, in many ways the Isaiah translator
is independent of LXX Psalms and the same may apply here, since
in Psalms ἔλεος is common.) Thus the use here of ἐλεημοσύνη
and δικαιοσύνη may well have arisen from the translator's
experience of Jewish worship, although the connotation may be
either Hebrew (covenant relationship) or Greek (qualities of
God in that he shows justice, delivering a righteous person).
The use of ἐλεημοσύνη rather than ἔλεος and of δικαιοσύνη
rather than the more restricted, subjective, but associated,
ἀλήθεια /42/ strongly suggests familiarity with Greek meaning.

*39:8b.*

MT:      כי יהיה שלום ואמת בימי:

LXX:    γενέσθω δὴ εἰρήνη καὶ δικαιοσύνη ἐν ταῖς ἡμέραις
         μου. /43/

Outside this verse the association of שלום and אמת is
rare, occurring in only Jer 33:6 (LXX 40:6), שלום ואמת/εἰρήνη
καὶ πίστις, and Ps 85(84):11f where צדק and חסד occur as well.
אמת may be however included in descriptions of a "שלום-type"
situation, e.g., Isa 16:3-5 and Ps 71:22. On the other hand
צדק(ה) and שלום occur frequently in association, e.g., Ps 72:3,
7; Isa 9:5; 32:17f; 54:13f; 59:8f; 60:17. (ה)צדק and אמת are
also frequently associated, e.g., Ps 31:1, 5; 40:11; 45:5;
85:11f; 89:15; 111:3, 8. It is probably this frequent word
association (at least in Hebrew usage, if not yet in Greek)
which has led to the translator here freely using δικαιοσύνη as
a broader term than ἀλήθεια when describing the whole nation.
Certainly neither Greek word conveys the meaning generally seen
in MT, i.e., "security," although δικαιοσύνη in its Greek
connotation is appropriate in the context of the absence of the
wrongdoing described in vv.6f, and of the LXX interpretation of
Hezekiah's statement (so MT) as a wish that the country may
enjoy peace and harmony, including freedom from attack.

We conclude (tentatively because of limited evidence)
that the translator of chaps. 36-39 in translating אמת shows
familiarity with the liturgical tradition (in Hebrew rather
than Greek). It is very doubtful whether this brings into
δικαιοσύνη the connotation of אמת (in opposition to Hill: 109),
but rather reflects the narrowness and inappropriateness of
ἀλήθεια for these two contexts as interpreted by the translator. That is, it is the textual context which affects the
translation rather than the word אמת itself - ἀλήθεια in its
Greek sense would be inappropriate. The narrow Greek understanding of ἀλήθεια may also be reflected in the translation of
61:8 where δικαίοις appears to correspond to באמה. Cf. Jer
33(40):6, πίστις.

In both cases the connotation of δικαιοσύνη is arguably
compatible with either Hebrew or Greek meanings. The balance
of evidence favours Greek meanings. Although the word choice
may have been influenced by Jewish liturgical usage, the

translator is not familiar with a translation tradition that could use ἀλήθεια with something of the full meaning of אמת (as is the case in Psalms). He uses ἐλεημοσύνη and δικαιοσύνη to refer to God's benevolent doing of what is just, and δικαιοσύνη along with εἰρήνη for a state of peace and harmony, free of unjust acts by others.

4. צדק/ΚΡΙΣΙΣ.

A. 11:4 (11:1-5).

The description of the rule of the "shoot from the stump of Jesse" has several similarities to other poetic descriptions of the rule of the Davidic king, especially Psalm 72, and may be compared with Isa 9:5(6)f; 16:5; 32:1ff; and the ministry of "my servant," 42:1-4.

Of particular concern to us is vv.3b-5. While v.4b refers to the consequent overthrow of evildoers /44/, vv.3b-4a is more narrowly judicial. The concern for the poor and meek is well known both in the Bible and in the ancient Near East (Kaiser, and references given there). בצדק is variously interpreted: JB seems to refer to the character of the ruler, "with integrity," while RSV, Kaiser, "with righteousness," and NEB, Auvray, "with justice," may refer more to the nature of the judging. The antithesis in v.3b and the parallel between v.4aα and v.4aβ suggest that in v.4aα reference is to justice, fairness and objectivity, to what is actually the "right" in that situation as opposed to hearsay or appearances (Scott: "according to what is right"; Fohrer: "wie es recht").

The description in v.5 concerning the wearing of צדק and אמונה alludes to common qualities required of a king (cf. Schmid: 114), referring in general to the faithful fulfilment of the covenant requirements. When he so rules there is harmony not only in the community but also in nature (vv.6-9). Eichrodt sees here also the qualities needed "für den täglichen Kampf um Gottes Recht." (Auvray misses the covenantal, relational emphasis in explaining צדק here as "conformité à la loi et à l'ideal de justice.")

LXX follows MT fairly closely. The endowment of the ruler (LXX v.2 and v.3a) is of note in that the difficult v.3a is interpreted as another endowment, "the spirit of the fear of

the Lord" (cf. Deist, who translates MT, "dadurch, dass er ihn
mit dem Gehorsam gegen Jahwe begeistern wird, so dass ...").
Apart from that, the Hebrew syntax and vocabulary is translated
literally.

In vv.3b-4a, however, LXX differs, giving an exact
parallelism:

οὐ κατὰ τὴν δόξαν κρινεῖ οὐδε κατὰ τὴν λαλιὰν
ἐλέγξει ἀλλὰ κρινεῖ ταπεινῷ κρίσιν καὶ ἐλέγξει /45/
τοὺς ταπεινοὺς /46/ τῆς γῆς.

This seems to mean: "He will not give decisions according to
appearances /47/ but he will decide the disputes /48/ of the
humble; he will not examine /49/ on the basis of the manner of
speaking /50/ but will examine the humble of the land." The
sense is thus similar to 1:17 LXX (see p. 59): he will not
concern himself only with the cases of those who are more
important or who can present a good case, but he will judge
also the cases involving the poor (as in 1:17, so here, the
dative is used). There is also contrast with 10:2, "shunning
the judging of the poor." The translator's concern is with the
*fact* that the lowly are not to be neglected, justice will be
done for them. He is not concerned with the *way* this is to be
done. This provides a consistent reason for the use of κρίσις
for בצדק, and does not imply that a narrow judicial meaning was
seen in צדק, but rather that the translator affirms that a just
ruler (v.5) will not neglect the cases of the poor.

In v.5 the Greek construction is different from MT, but
the meaning is unaltered: "he shall be girded with δικαιοσύνη
and wrapped around his sides with ἀλήθεια." Either the usual
Greek sense of "justice" and "truth" or the Hebrew connotation
are obviously both possible. Following on from LXX emphasis in
v.4, it seems most likely that the Greek sense of "justice" is
uppermost. This accords well with the hope seen elsewhere in
LXX that God (here through his king who has the "spirit of
God") will not neglect the case of his own people ("the poor of
the earth"), but that he will hear their plea for justice and
slay the ungodly.

B.      51:7 (51:1-8).

Within these eight verses צדק occurs three times (vv.1,
5, 7) and צדקה twice (vv.6, 8). In addition there are other

key words: מֹשׁפט (v.4) and שׁפֹט (v.5), תורה (vv.4, 7), ישׁועה (vv. 6, 8) and ישׁע (v.5), and a double reference to Yahweh's "arm" (v.5).

There are obvious parallelisms in structure:

"Hearken to me ... look ... look ... for ... for ..." (vv.1-3)
"Listen to me ... give ear to me ... for ..."      (vv.4, 5)
"Lift up your eyes ... look ... for ..."           (v.6)
"Hearken to me ... fear not ... for ..."           (vv.7, 8)

Nevertheless exegetes are divided in their understanding of the literary form. Westermann sees several dislocations and treats v.3 as a separate fragment, while Schoors regards vv. 1-3, 6-8 as "an artfully built, twofold proclamation of salvation" (167), treating vv.4f as a "composite interpolation" (156). Such difficulties in determining a "form," together with the vocabulary and structure links noted above, suggest that it is preferable to follow Muilenburg, North and Bonnard and treat vv.1-8 as a single oracle of salvation.

The translations of (ה)צדק vary amongst interpreters and from occurrence to occurence. Linked is the significance of משׁפֹט and תורה. The main issue is whether there is an ethical or a soteriological, eschatological emphasis. *JB* sees no soteriological emphasis in any of the five occurrences, while Fohrer and Westermann see all as soteriological. In between these two extremes, most interpreters see vv.5, 6, 8 as soteriological (// "salvation") and v.7 as ethical (// "in whose heart is my law"). For v.1, most regard as soteriological (including Fahlgren: 94, 101f), although North and *NEB* see an ethical emphasis (see Appendix II). Bonnard regularly uses "(la) justice," and interprets all in terms of the covenant, vv.1, 5, 6, 8 being primarily salvific but with an ethical note, and v.7 referring to practising the law (v.1 means "tendre vers un renoveau non seulement politique et social mais aussi religieux et moral," and vv.5, 6, 8, "le rétablissement de la vie droite ... sur la Terre Sainte où chacun respecte l'alliance avec Dieu et avec ses frères"). Schoors, like the German writers, sees a consistency of connotation and translates "salvific justice." We shall here examine each occurrence in turn.

*51:1*: The main hesitancy in seeing a salvific emphasis is due

to the verb, רדף "pursue" (so North, 1964). Also, the parallel
phrase, "seek Yahweh," has led Rosenberg to regard צדק as a
divine name. Both interpretations however seem unlikely
because of the close similarity to v.7. Further, if the people
were pursuing either "ethical righteousness" or simply Yahweh,
the answer of vv.2b-3 would be strange. The "rock" is most
likely Abraham (Schoors; North, 1964; and Westermann; against
de Boer: 58-67), along with v.2a, a significant reference.
There is no doubt the thought of his trust in God and of the
covenant relationship, and so the command to look to Abraham
implies the demand of similar obedient trust. Only then will
the experience of blessing be realized, i.e., צדק follows
trust. A salvific emphasis is thus dominant for צדק, referring
to the deliverance described in v.3. A salvific emphasis is
also seen if with Schoors (158f), and to a lesser extent
Muilenburg, we see in v.1a a reply to a lament.

*51:4, 5:* There are many similarities with the first Servant
Song, 42:1-4 (the association of משפט and תורה, the phrase יצא
משפט, "light" and involvement of the nations), although, as
North has well pointed out, the servant is not speaking here
but Yahweh. The use of לאמי referring to Israel is unusual and
many emend both עמי and לאמי to plurals, עמים and לאמים (*BHK*;
*BHS*; Westermann; cf. Syriac; cf. 49:1). Smith (60), followed
by Schoors, emends only לאמי (cf. LXX, see below): "Attend to
Me, O My people; O nations, give ear to Me." Both Israel and
the nations are then being addressed. Nevertheless, it seems
preferable to retain MT (as in *RSV*; *NEB*; Bonnard), לאמי being
used due to the need for a synonym for עמי.

In understanding תורה, *RSV* "a law" is inexcusable. *NEB*
"law" (cf. Muilenburg, "law," i.e., "revealed teaching") or
Westermann, "teaching," is an improvement but perhaps too much
bound by traditional understanding. Much better in the context
(God's eschatological acting) is Fohrer's "Weisung" or North's
"the voice of authority." The idea of a directive,
instruction, order, etc. from one in authority (a royal figure)
is most appropriate (cf. Orlinsky, 1967: 77). Schoors combines
this with the idea of "teaching" to give "the revelation of
God's salvific will in history." Similarly Jörg Jeremias sees
the joining here of משפט and תורה as "die umfassende Kundgabe

des göttlichen Willens, der als heilvolle Ordnung den Völkern heilvolles Handeln allerest ermoglicht" (38). The reference in the context to Yahweh's "arm" supports a salvific emphasis, here being also a ruling over the nations. שפט (v.5) is not subjugation, but a sharing in the benefits of God's saving will (Jörg Jeremias: 39; Berkovits: 193); this is what "the coastlands wait for." (See Appendix V.)

*51:6, 8*: There is general agreement that צדקה here is soteriological, referring to God's acting to deliver and restore his people. (For the parallelism with ישע, cf. 45:8; 46:12f; 56:1; 61:10; 62:1; also // שלום, 48:18; 60:17.)

*51:7*: One's interpretation of the phrase "knowers of צדק" will depend to a large extent upon how one interprets the parallel, "my תורה in their heart" /51/. An understanding of תורה as "law" or "teaching" has led many to a predominantly ethical connotation for צדק. If however, as well as referring to God's requirements, תורה includes the thought of "the revelation of God's salvific will" (to use Schoors' phrase), then צדק also has a broader connotation. To "know צדק" is to experience the blessings of God's saving purpose and to live accordingly (here, in expectation of those blessings). (In Jer 31:31-34 "תורה within them" is also in the context of enjoyment of blessings of the new covenant relationship, with the implied corollary that Israel on her part will obey.)

In summary, within these 8 verses there is brought together into one picture (a) Israel's salvation as an act of God, in terms of his relationship with his people and as an expression of his will, and (b) his "directive," which includes (a), but also embraces his requirements. The emphasis is soteriological, but with a secondary emphasis on Israel's need to continue in trusting obedience of Yahweh, knowing he will accomplish his saving purposes.

Within this context צדק(ה) is used five times with a soteriological emphasis, any ethical connotation being suggested by the implications of the context. That is, it is the context which reminds Israel of her responsibilities if she wishes to enjoy God's צדקה.

LXX has several differences, some of which appear to be linked with LXX of 42:1-6 and 60:1-14.

*51:1-3:*  (1) "Listen to me, you who pursue τὸ δίκαιον and seek
the Lord; look at the solid rock which you hewed and into the
hole of the pit which you dug, (2) ... (blessing of Abraham)...
(3) and you now will I comfort, O Zion ..."

De Boer's statement that in LXX the Rock is God is most
unlikely. Various reasons may be cited: (a) the description of
God as "Rock" in MT 26:4; 30:29 and 44:8 is omitted in LXX,
while the reference to "rock" in 8:14 is simply πέτρα, not
στερεὰ πέτρα as here; (b) LXX Exod 33:21f uses only πέτρα and
Deut 32:18 θέος; (c) στερεὰ πέτρα in 2:22 refers to the rocks
to which worshippers of false gods flee from God; and (d) in
50:7 symbolizes the servant's firm trust in God in face of
opposition Ottley (2:228) refers to the "evident repugnance" of
the whole LXX for the metaphor of God as Rock. It seems most
likely that for the translator, as for MT, reference is to
obedient trust in God in face of difficulties, similar to that
of Abraham, who though he was one became many. (Cf. vv.9b, 10
which refer to the accomplishments of Jerusalem when she
trusted in God.)  Thus v.1b is an exhortation to remember their
former trust in God and is related to pursuing "what is right,"
this being further defined in terms of the law of God which
Israel possesses (v.7).

*51:4f:* "Listen to me, listen, my people, and kings (οἱ
βασιλεῖς), give ear to me; for law (νόμος) will go forth and my
judgement (κρίσις) as a light to the nations (ἔθνη).  My
δικαιοσύνη is coming near swiftly, and my salvation will go
forth; and for my arm the nations will hope, the islands will
wait for me and for my arm they will hope."

לאמים is usually translated ἔθνη (17:12f; 49:1; 55:4;
60:5) or ἄρχοντες (34:1; 41:1; 43:4, 9; in each case, except
43:4, parallel to ἔθνη; cf. the usual Targum, מלכא; see also
Seeligmann: 51).  Only here is βασιλεῖς used for לאמים,
probably because of the close parallel, 60:3 LXX: "and kings
(MT: גוים) shall walk by your light" (cf. 60:10-12).  The going
forth of God's law and judgement (or judging) as a light to the
nations may be compared with 2:3f and 42:4, 6 /52/.  A
reference to "the nations hope" occurs similarly in 42:4 LXX —
"in his (Israel's) name," when judgement comes — while "the
islands wait" in 60:9 refers to the nations bringing back the

children of Jerusalem from afar and joining in service. 50:
9-11 and 60:11f also refer to the fact that the nations (or
kings) may share in Israel's blessings if they are willing to
walk in God's light and serve him and Israel, otherwise there
is punishment. (See discussion in Appendix V.)
*51:7*: "Listen to me, you who know κρίσις, may people, in whose
heart is my law."

The question must be asked, why was not δικαιοσύνη used
here? Certainly δικαιοσύνη does occur in this context in the
three similar statements, vv.5a, 6b, 8b, in each case parallel
to σωτήριον and in each case with the possessive "my"
(following MT). Although in these three instances δικαιοσύνη
could obviously be interpreted in MT sense, it seems more
likely that again the translator is thinking of the "justice"
of God which will bring salvation to Israel and wrath upon her
enemies. For the dual emphasis in this chapter, we may compare
LXX v.14, "for in your being saved, he (the one afflicting you)
will not stand nor linger, for I your God ...," and v.23, "I
will put it (the cup of my wrath) into the hands of those who
wronged you and who brought you low /53/" (cf. 60:14). There
is, of course, as noted earlier, a note of hope for those who
will follow God's law.

That the translator in v.7 uses κρίσις in parallel to
νόμος suggests a clear link with v.4: Israel already knows
God's law and so can be his agent in bringing κρίσις (but not
God's δικαιοσύνη /54/) to the nations. (This is preferable to
the interpretation that Israel has experienced God's "judging
in her favour" since that is still future, v.22a.)

Thus 51:1-8 is seen by the translator as an encouragement to Israel to continue in her obedience to the law among
the nations, for ultimately God will show that she is in the
right. This encouragement continues in LXX of vv.9f: "Awake,
awake, Jerusalem /55/, ... are not you (10) *she* who emptied the
sea ..."

5.    (ה)צדק/ΔΙΚΑΙΟΣ.

5:1:   ΤΟ ΔΙΚΑΙΟΝ.

The 4 instances where MT has צדקה and LXX τὸ δίκαιον
have already been discussed. Here we briefly summarize.

*5:23:* (pp. 45-46) Both צדקה and τὸ δίκαιον refer to "the right" of the innocent. δικαιοσύνη would be unusual Greek and too abstract.

*51:1:* (pp. 96-101) צדק probably has a salvific connotation, although some see an ethical concern. LXX τὸ δίκαιον is clearly an ethical interpretation, relating to the law. δικαιοσύνη is used in the following verses in reference to God's "justice" in saving his people.

*59:4:* (pp. 73, 75) קרא בצדק is generally interpreted as "enter suit justly." LXX λαλεῖ δίκαια interprets MT syntax loosely, the rendering being determined by the context. δίκαια is probably forensic, parallel to the opposites ἀνομία and ἀδικία.

*64:4(5):* (pp. 89-91) צדק is normally understood as "righteousness," i.e., "following God's ways," although some see a more narrow reference to religious acts. LXX has used τὸ δίκαιον in the general sense of doing "what is right," a standard Greek phrase, the emphasis being on deeds. In the following verse δικαιοσύνη is used in the general sense of "virtue."

τὸ δίκαιον also occurs in *47:3:*
MT for vv.3f may be translated: "... I will take vengeance (נקם) and I will spare no man. Our Redeemer - the Lord of hosts is his name - is the Holy One of Israel" (*RSV*; see North, 1964). LXX continues the address to the "virgin daughter of Babylon": "I will take τὸ δίκαιον out of you, no longer will I hand you over to men, said /56/ he who delivered you, the Lord Sabaoth is his name, the Holy One of Israel." There are some obvious difficulties in interpretation. παραδιδόναι, "hand over," is regularly used of being handed over to enemies: of Israel (25:5; 64:7/6), Tyre (23:7), and those who mistreat Israel (33:1, 6). Unless v.3b is an aside addressed to Israel (unlikely), the most natural interpretation is that God is here saying to Babylon: "In the past I let you be defeated by enemies and then rescued you, but that is to happen no longer: I will defeat you myself." Then we have for the first part: "Now is the time when I will exact 'justice' from you (for your merciless treatment of Israel, v.6)." τὸ δίκαιον, as in normal Greek usage, refers to the "just penalty."

Here is another instance where the translator has seen fit to emphasise the "justice" of God's future punishment of the nations for their ill-treatment of Israel.

5:2: OTHER INSTANCES OF ΔΙΚΑΙΟΣ.

There are four instances where צדק(ה) is translated by the adjective, δίκαιος. In 41:10 and 58:2 צדק follows a construct noun, while in 32:1 and 54:17 LXX is more paraphrastic.

A.    32:1 (CHAP. 32).

MT: "Behold, a king will reign לצדק,
            and princes will rule למשפט."

This is the only instance in the whole OT of לצדק. There are however cases of לצדקה: Isa 5:7, "(look) for 'צ"; Joel 2:23 and Hos 10:12, "bring forth 'צ"; and Ps 106:31, "(counted) as 'צ." למשפט occurs 22 times, 7 of these in Isaiah, the sense outside of 32:1 being "to perform 'מ" (34:5; 41:1; 54:17), or "(look) for 'מ" (5:7; 59:11; in 28:26 משפט refers to custom). This usage strongly suggests that the connotation here is not that of a quality of the rulers or their actions (against recent exegetes, e.g., *RSV*; Kaiser, "in righteousness ... in justice"; *NEB*, "with ... with ..."; Duhm; Fahlgren: 82, "nach ... nach ..."; Auvray, "en ... selon ..."). Rather reference is to the function of the rulers: a king will reign in such a way as to bring about צדק and rulers will perform properly their task of giving משפט /57/. This accords well with the rest of the chapter.

LXX: "For behold, a δίκαιος king will reign,
            and rulers will rule μετὰ κρίσεως."

The Isaiah translator tends to be quite free in rendering prepositions, using that Greek syntax which best suits his understanding. Thus for למשפט he translates: 34:5, μετὰ κρίσεως; 41:1, "(announce) κρίσις"; and 54:17, "(stand up against you) εἰς κρίσιν." Similarly for בצדק(ה), ἐν is used in 5:16; 42:6; and 54:14; μετά in 45:13 and 48:1; μετὰ ἐλεημοσύνης in 1:27; and more freely in 5:7; 11:4; 59:4 and 63:1.

Here in 32:1 the translator has seen in צדק reference to the character of the king, rather than the function of his rule. Also ἐν/μετά with δικαιοσύνη would have referred to the

fact that he reigns "justly" (i.e., legally) or "with
righteousness" (cf. other uses of these phrases in Isaiah).
The use of δίκαιος gives a thought similar to 11:5. The second
half of the verse appears to affirm that rulers will "give
judgement" (cf. 11:4). Thus while the second half is similar
to MT, the first half has been given a different emphasis by
LXX. At the same time his translation is closer to MT than if
he had used δικαιοσύνη — a "just" ruler will bring "justice"
and "harmony" to his people.

Later in the chapter, in the context of the description
of the coming Messianic age, there is triple use of צדקה in vv.
16f, each translated δικαιοσύνη.

MT:   "Then משפט will dwell in the wilderness,
           and צדקה in the fruitful land,
           and the yield of צדקה will be שלום,
           and the result of צדקה quietness and confidence
               forever."

LXX:   "And κρίμα will rest in the desert,
           and δικαιοσύνη will dwell in Carmel /58/,
           and the works (ἔργα) of δικαιοσύνη will be peace,
           and δικαιοσύνη will support (or attain) rest and (they)
               will be) trusting ones for ever."

The context is a time when the evildoers of vv.5-8 are
removed (cf. 9:6; 11:1-9; 33:5f) because of the rule of the
king upon whom God's spirit is poured as it is upon the people
(v.15a). צדקה has moral content (obedience of God's requirements), but goes beyond that to the total state of order,
harmony and prosperity.

δικαιοσύνη could have the same connotation as צדקה.
Indeed there is is any case an overlap between Hebrew and
classical Greek connotation (the latter being primarily
ethical, but referring also to that state of a society in which
everyone functions properly and in which there is no wickedness
or oppression by others). There is contextual indication that
the translator had both a forensic and a more general ethical
emphasis in mind: (a) κρίμα (rather than κρίσις) may refer to
the judgement of God in vv.9-14 - the sentence has ended
("rested") so now δικαιοσύνη has been restored to the total
situation; (b) the continuation of "works of righteousness"

will cause peace; (c) the use of πεποιϑότες (vv.17, 19) and
πεποιϑώς (v.18) places more emphasis than MT upon the people's
trust in God (although the translator has some difficulty with
some phrases); and (d) the use of κρατεῖν "take hold of,
support, attain" in the phrase, "δικαιοσύνη will support rest,"
also suggests that the people will enjoy rest if they continue
in the practice of δικαιοσύνη. It is most unlikely that there
is any allusion to God's "justice," as there is no thought here
of Israel being delivered from oppressors. In each case
δικαιοσύνη refers to the practice of the people, including
rulers, in a situation where evildoers have been removed.

B.      41:10 (41:1-13).

    MT:   "... I strengthen you, and I help you,
        I uphold you בימין צדקי."

    LXX:  "... who strengthens you and I have helped you,
        and I have secured you τῇ δεξιᾷ τῇ δικαίᾳ μου."

MT context is an oracle of salvation, vv.8-13 (so
especially, Fohrer, Westermann and Schoors). Thus צדק refers
to either "victory" or "salvation." There is some disagreement
as to which of these is most appropriate but Schoors'
conclusion seems most likely (53-55): on the basis of
comparisons with psalms of lament, reference is to Yahweh's
"world order," his "principle of salvation," a "characteristic
attitude." We note in addition that elsewhere Yahweh's "right
hand" refers to his rule of the world (48:13; 62:8) with "hand"
being symbolic of "power" (Wolff: 67f), the context of v.10
much emphasises the covenant relationship between Yahweh and
Israel (vv.8f), and legal terms are used in describing the
actions of her enemies (vv.11f; Beuken: 16-18). This could
suggest a translation, "my just right hand" (cf. LXX), but this
lacks the dynamic and covenant-related sense that seems to be
required by the context. Hence the best translation is "my
delivering right hand," deliverance being because of the
covenant.

If the translator saw in "right hand" a reference to
God's rule, then δίκαιος is appropriate in a context of the
rousing of "justice" (see below on LXX v.2), which leads to the
nations being afraid and looking to each other for help (v.5),
"but" (v.8, συ δέ) Israel is not to be afraid (v.10) for God's

rule is "just" and will lead to deliverance and victory for
Israel (vv.11-16a), in which she "will rejoice among the holy
things of Israel and the poor and needy will be glad" (vv.16b-
17a).

Chap. 41 begins with a trial speech (vv.1-5) in which is
the much discussed *v.2a*:

מי העיר ממזרח צדק יקראהו לרגלו

A commonly adopted translation is that of *RSV* (or
similar; so *NEB*; *JB*; North; Duhm; Fohrer; Westermann; Schoors;
Fahlgren: 103): "Who stirred up one from the east whom victory
meets at every step?" Of note is the comment in *JB*: "a victory
associated with the restoration of the world order willed by
God." Q$^a$ however reads ויקראהו (noted in *BHK* but not in *BHS*!)
and so some take צֶדֶק as object of the first verb (cf. LXX),
interpreting as "a righteous one" (Torrey; McKenzie and Bonnard
both see the abstract noun as being used for the person, and so
retain MT; cf. Vulgate, "iustum," and probably TJ, which
expands צדק in referring to Abraham). On either reading there
is still the question as to whether reference is to Cyrus or
Abraham. It is almost certain that Cyrus is the main subject,
although some of the language seems to be influenced by Abraham
(Gw. H. Jones). If we follow MT, "victory" is the most likely
connotation of צדק, although this is in the context of Yahweh's
plan to "save" his people.

LXX is of note, not only for its understanding of MT
syntax in v.2 /59/, but for its continuing reference in vv.2-4
to δικαιοσύνη by means of feminine pronouns (here "it"):

"Who aroused δικαιοσύνη from the east, called *it*
to his (God's) feet and it (or he) will go? He
shall set (it) before nations and he (or it) will
astound kings, and he will put their swords to the
earth and their bows as brushwood that is pushed
away; (3) and he will pursue them and the path of
*his* (masc.) feet shall go through in peace. (4)
Who produced and did these things? He who calls
*it* from the beginning of ages has called *it*. I
God am first, and to the coming times I am."

While ancient and modern exegesis has seen reference to
either Abraham or Cyrus, LXX refers solely to the action of

God, an action which results because God has called "justice"
to be with his feet as he goes. Initially this is God's
judgement of the nations (*their* swords and bows will be as
nothing in his path), but later leads on to deliverance for
Israel (vv.9ff). Seeligmann (98) says that in this context
δικαιοσύνη "surely means ... the powerful aid of God to Israel
which baffles kings and smites their weapons to earth." That
this is the effect is not doubted, but it is much more likely
that the translator is thinking of God's "justice." 41:1
reads:

> "Be renewed to me, O islands, for the rulers will
> exchange their strength; let them draw near and
> let them speak together, then let them announce
> κρίσις (= their matter for dispute)."

God then replies by announcing the calling of δικαιοσύνη, his
"justice."

C.    54:17 (54:11-17)

The description of the new state of Zion contains two
instances of צדקה, vv.14, 17. (For discussion of possible
divisions and rearrangements of the text, and for argument in
favour of present arrangement and unity, see Schoors: 140-46.)
*54:13b, 14* MT (following arrangement of *BHS*; also *NEB*):

> "And great shall be the שלום of your sons, בצדקה תכונני;
> You shall be far /60/ from oppression, for you need not
>     fear;
>   and from terror, for it shall not come near you."

תכונני seems to continue the building imagery of vv.11f,
and צדקה and שלום are parallel. Thus צדקה is something which
Yahweh is going to bring about (cf. v.17b, "from me").
Although there is both an ethical emphasis in "your sons will
be taught by Yahweh" (v.13a), and also freedom from oppression
and fear, these appear subsidiary to the major emphasis upon
Yahweh's action of accomplishing his saving purposes for his
people, of making Zion conform to his purposes for her (so
against *RSV*; *JB*; *NEB*mg; and North, 1964, who sees a reminis-
cence of 28:16f, see p. 68 above).
LXX:  "(And I will make all your sons taught by God) and in
      great peace your children. And ἐν δικαιοσύνη shall you
      be built. Abstain from wrong (ἀδίκου) and you will not

be afraid and trembling will not come near you."

The literal rendering of the imperative, רחק, but with
the middle, ἀπέχου "abstain," together with the simple καί for
כי and abridging of the last phrase, has given to v.14 a
different emphasis. One will only be unafraid if one abstains
from wrong. This then gives to the first half of the verse the
sense that Zion will be built by the doing of righteousness,
that is δικαιοσύνη has a strictly ethical connotation.

*54:15 MT* is basically a statement that any attack will
fail, irrespective of how it comes /61/ for God has his weapons
(v.16), therefore:

*54:17a*:  "no weapon that is fashioned against you shall
            prosper,
            and you will confute (תרישי) every tongue that rises
            against you in judgement (למשפט)."

The whole passage is then concluded with:

*54:17b*:  "this is the heritage of the servants of Yahweh,
            וצדקתם מאתי. Oracle of Yahweh."

Both North and Bonnard make much of the parallel between
"inheritance" (as in Deuteronomy referring to the land of
Canaan) and צדקה, and see in צדקה reference to their "right" to
live there in peace (North) or to the fact that in their life
in the land they will be a "peuple 'juste', c'est-à-dire
réhabilité, sauvé, paisable, droit et capable de vaincre les
difficultés" (Bonnard). *RSV* and *NEB* by their use of
"vindication" seem to regard v.17b as simply answering v.17aβγ,
but this is too narrow a conclusion. Duhm, Fohrer, Westermann
and Schoors have "Heil, salvation" which is more appropriate as
a conclusion to the type of difficulties which will be overcome
(vv.14b-17a), but which neglects the possible nuance in
"heritage," particularly as this passage is about the
restoration of Zion. Snaith (1944: 91) sees a composite
meaning: forensic, victory, general prosperity.

In the passage we can see a description of the "order"
which Yahweh has planned for his people: to live peacefully in
the land defended by Yahweh, taught by him, and consequently
serving him. צדקתם (ם' as objective suffix) is thus the
"harmonious, ordered life" which Yahweh is to give them.

*54:15f LXX*, although certainly based on MT, has quite a

different sense:

> "Behold proselytes will come (see Appendix V) to
> you (and dwell with you /62/) and take refuge
> (καταφεύξονται) with you. Behold, I create you,
> not as a blacksmith blowing charcoal and producing
> an instrument for work; but I have created you,
> not for destruction, ruining every perishable
> instrument."

*54:17* has various difficulties with variant readings.
In the middle of the verse is an addition with no MT
equivalent. We shall follow the majority of manuscripts as
does Rahlfs /63/. We may translate:

> "Against you I will not allow to prosper, even
> every voice (which) will stand against you for
> κρίσις; all of them you will defeat, and they
> who have sinned against you (so BAG, following
> Deissmann: 116) will be in it (feminine, i.e.,
> κρίσις /64/). There is an inheritance for those
> who serve the Lord, and you ἔσεσθέ μοι δίκαιοι,
> says the Lord."

Thus, compared with MT, LXX has reference to proselytes
finding refuge in Israel, and an assurance that God has a
permanent purpose for Israel. There is no reference to
physical attacks, but there is clear forensic content in v.17a.
In this setting δικαιοσύνη with a Greek sense would have been
either meaningless or misleading ("your righteousness" would be
irrelevant as a promise in this setting). As the LXX stands,
there are two possible senses: "you will be to me as innocent
ones," i.e., I will defend you when people rise unjustly
against you (cf. v.17a), or "I will regard you as righteous,"
i.e., Israel really is righteous. Most likely is a combination
of these: Israel, because she is serving the Lord (v.17bα, and
vv.13f) will be treated accordingly by God when people rise up
against her. δίκαιος is thus used in either a forensic sense
or a more general ethical sense, as is usual in Greek.

D.   58:2.

MT:  "Yet they seek me daily and delight to know my way,
        like a nation which does צדקה
             and does not forsake the משפט of its God;

    they ask of me צדק משפטי,
    they delight to draw near to God."
LXX:    "They seek me daily and desire to know my ways;
        like a nation having done δικαιοσύνη
            and not having forsaken the κρίσιν of its God;
        they ask of me now κρίσιν δικαιαν
        and they desire to draw near to God."

עשה צדקה is generally understood as "doing righteousness." There is frequent juxtaposition of צדקה and משפט, not
only in descriptions of Yahweh and of the king, but also in
describing the responsibilities of the people. Here, as for
example in Amos 5:7, 24, Jer 22:3, 15, and repeatedly in Ezek
18, they refer to the duties of the members of the covenant
community towards each other, including deliverance of the
oppressed and care of the poor.

    משפטי צדק is usually understood as "righteous (just)
judgements," referring to the rulings sought from God as ruler.
The same phrase in Ps 119:7, 62, 106, 164 (with the suffix ך' =
Yahweh) is in a context of praising Yahweh for his rulings and
of learning and observing them; the singular in Deut 16:18
refers to the responsibilities of judges. Here in 58:2 they
are the rulings, ordinances, etc. that are associated with
Yahweh's responsibility for צדק.

    The LXX, by its rendering of the two Hebrew perfect
verbs by Greek perfect participles and the imperfect by present
tenses, plus the addition of "now," has emphasised that
Israel's failure has a history and is not just a present
aberration. δικαιοσύνη as primarily a social virtue is quite
appropriate.

    κρίσις δικαία however may have a connotation quite
different to MT. κρίσις may refer to Israel's present
situation as she seeks deliverance from the nations: she
believes that she is innocent and hence being treated unjustly,
thus she asks God for a "just judging." The same Greek as in
58:2 is used in Deut 16:18, although in the later Ps 118(119)
τὰ κρίματα τῆς δικαιοσύνης σου is used. Certainly the
connotation of δίκαιος, when qualifying κρίσις, is "just."

6.    SUMMARY AND CONCLUSIONS.

In the course of the last two chapters not only have all
instances of departure from the use of δικαιοσύνη to translate
(ה)צדק been examined, but also more than half of the "usual"
translation, distributed evenly between chapters 1-39, 40-55
and 56-66, in a variety of contexts. Here we briefly summarize
our findings.

*6:1:    A Note on the translation.*

In several of the passages examined in detail it is
evident that the translator has given a different connotation
to a passage than that seen in MT by modern exegetes, or at
least has seen fit to emphasise one aspect. Sometimes he seems
caught up with one idea, frequently a contrast (often from one
verse, and usually present in MT), and carries on that emphasis
for several verses. For example, in 1:19ff; 33:1-8 and chapter
59 he emphasises the distinction between two groups of people,
and in chapter 28 he heightens the two alternatives of false
hope in allies, leading to destruction, or hope based in the
Lord. Similarly, ethical exhortation to Israel may be
strengthened, e.g., 32:16f; 54:13f; 51:1-8. Occasionally words
applied to Yahweh in MT are applied to Israel in LXX and vice
versa (e.g., 1:24f; 51:9f; 61:8; cf. 41:1-4; also 55:3, see
Appendix IV). In most of these cases MT is clear, with LXX
almost certainly based on MT, but differing in exact meaning.

There may be some reflections of the translator's
historical background in his emphasis upon Israel's being ill-
treated and oppressed (see also next chapter, on ἀδικ-words),
and also in LXX reference to proselytes (54:15f; also 14:1f, as
in MT, and perhaps 50:9b-11 and 45:15-25; cf. 56:8), together
with the appeal to the "islands" to "be renewed" (42:1; 45:16).
Through Israel's obedience God's law or the knowledge of his
ways are made known to the nations (42:1-9 LXX; 51:4-7 LXX;
2:4; cf. 50:9-11 LXX). Especially in view of the references to
proselytes and LXX 42:1-9, together with the implied call to
become proselytes in the midst of warnings of judgement (LXX
50:9b-11; 45:15-25), it is apparent that for at least the
translator, if not for MT, this refers to present responsibilities as well as to the results of a restored Zion (see
further in Appendix V).

*6:2*   צדק(ה)

It has not been our purpose to make a new, extensive investigation of the connotation of צדק(ה) in Isaiah. Rather we have sought to examine the understanding of several modern exegetes in the passages chosen. Nevertheless, contextual exegetical study has caused us often to disagree with certain scholars and interpretations, especially in chaps. 56-66. In general, exegesis supports the understanding of Schmid which allows for a variety of concrete meanings, including, in chaps. 40-55, God's saving action. This meaning continues in chaps. 56-66 (especially chap. 59) and is also present in chaps. 1-39 (e.g., 1:27; 5:16). We would, however, place more emphasis upon God's action as being in terms of the covenant relationship and resulting in harmony and right-relationships.

צדק(ה) frequently occurs in contexts referring to a society where all, but rulers in particular, perform their tasks justly and righteously in fulfilment of covenant requirements and where evildoers are punished (e.g., 1:21-26; 5:7; 9:7; 11:1-7; 28:17; 32:1, 16; 33:15; 54:11-17; 56:1; 61:10). Reference is to a "just and harmonious society." Sometimes it is the ruler's responsibility to bring this situation about (16:5; 32:1), although more often it is Yahweh who accomplishes this - this is his "saving action," the "salvation" he brings (especially in chaps. 40-66). Only in a couple of instances is reference more narrowly forensic (5:23; 59:4; and perhaps 33:15), this sometimes being the function of a ruler as judge (11:3b-4a).

*6:3:*   δικαιοσύνη.

Two uses of δικαιοσύνη should be distinguished, that referring to men (usually the community, Zion or Israel), and that referring to God.

*(1)   Use for community or individuals.*

In several places δικαιοσύνη describes the state or quality of a community (Zion, Israel, the redeemed Israel) where there is harmonious good order, everyone doing what is right (32:16f; 59:9, 14), injustices corrected (61:11), and evildoers removed (61:3; 32:16f).

Often there is explicit contextual reference to this "just harmony" including rulers (1:21, 26) or to the rulers or

leaders either having this virtue themselves or having
responsibility to bring it about in the community (9:6; 11:5;
16:5; 60:17).

At times it is clearly an ethical virtue, related to
law-keeping and reverence of God [33:5, 6, 15; 56:1a; 58:2;
61:11; 64:5(6)], and contrasted with taking what is not one's
own (61:8) or with "wrongdoing" (τὸ ἄδικον, 54:14; ἀνομία,
5:7).

In these uses there is evident much overlap between
(ה)צדק referring to man and society and δικαιοσύνη in the
classical Greek sense. While in Hebrew "what is right" is
described in terms of the covenant relationship, a Jewish
reader of the LXX would probably think in terms of God's law,
but in both cases this is from the social context of the word,
rather than the word itself. In some instances the translator
appears to place more emphasis on ethical aspects than does MT
(e.g., 1:27; 32:16f; 33:5f; 54:13f; 59:14; 60:17), occasionally
referring to Israel (or Zion) where MT refers to Yahweh's
action which is either his (ה)צדק or his bringing about (ה)צדק
(33:5f; chap. 51; 54:13f; 59:14). (In 51:1-8 LXX also
emphasises Israel's ethical responsibilities, but δικαιοσύνη is
not used.)

In several instances (ה)צדק referring to man or society
is not rendered by δικαιοσύνη:
(a)    τὸ δίκαιον is used in 5:23, the "right" of the innocent,
and 64:4(5), the standard Greek phrase, ποιεῖν τὸ δίκαιον (in
the following verse δικαιοσύνη is used as general virtue).
Both follow normal Greek usage where δικαιοσύνη would be
unusual.
(b)    The adjective δίκαιος is used in 32:1 to describe the
ethical quality of the ruler rather than, as in MT, his task
and in 54:17 to assert that God will treat the Jews as
"righteous" or "innocent" when others rise against them
(δικαιοσύνη would be most inappropriate).
(c)    In 51:1, τὸ δίκαιον "what is right," and 51:7, κρίσις as
now Israel's responsibility since she has God's "law" (cf. LXX
51:4; 2:4; 42:1-4), the translator seems also to be avoiding
using δικαιοσύνη of man when it is used in the immediate
context of God's "justice" bringing deliverance to Israel and

wrath to her enemies.

(d)     δίκαια as object of "speaking" (59:4) is a natural
antonym of άνομία and άδικία.

(e)     κρινεῖν κρίσιν (MT: בצדק משפ) (11:4) is the result of
the translator emphasising the fact that the cases of the
"lowly" will be heard, rather than the manner of judging (cf.
1:17).

(f)     εύφροσύνη in 61:10 is surprising, but, as we have
argued, δικαιοσύνη as a virtue (as in 61:3, 11) would have been
inappropriate here.

(g)     In addition, τὸ δίκαιον occurs in 47:3 (MT: נקם) in the
Greek sense of "just penalty," imposed on Babylon.

It will be noted that in each case the translator's
rendering follows Greek usage, usually following a possible MT
sense.

There are no instances of δικαιοσύνη rendering man's
חסד, although there is just one instance of δίκαιος: 57:1,
חסד ׳אנש/άνδρες δίκαιοι, parallel to הצדיק/ὁ δίκαιος (twice).
It is hard to see this as introducing any covenant idea into
δίκαιος (and thereby into δικαιοσύνη).

In 39:8, possibly from another translator, δικαιοσύνη
translates אמת in describing the continuing situation of Judah
promised to Hezekiah.  It is most unlikely that this introduces
any idea of "security" into δικαιοσύνη, but rather reflects the
utter inadequacy of άλήθεια (in its Greek connotation) in the
context.  The translator has chosen a word which is
contextually appropriate: a word to describe absence of
wrongdoing and freedom from attack with consequent peace and
harmony.

The only other noteworthy instance of δικαιοσύνη is its
use to translate משפט in 61:8.  MT refers to Yahweh's concern,
while LXX uses δικαιοσύνη to describe the human virtue opposite
to άρπάγματα ἐξ άδικίας, a common Greek usage (κρίσις, in Greek
connotation, is inappropriate).

Thus, in reference to man and society, the Isaiah LXX
usage is indistinguishable from classical Greek usage, except
perhaps in that he uses δικαιοσύνη more commonly than τὸ
δίκαιον.  While there is considerable semantic overlap with
(ה)צדק in any case, our examination of departures from (ה)צדק =

δικαιοσύνη leads to the conclusion that the translator is in fact thinking of Greek connotation. The contribution of Jewish faith and the biblical context is in further explication of the kinds of actions or situations which may be referred to as "righteousness," "justice" or "what is right." (This will be further supported by the brief discussion in the following chapter of some other related Greek words.)

*(2)    Use in reference to God.*

There are many instances where LXX refers to God's δικαιοσύνη or to his concern that δικαιοσύνη be brought about. Our examination of LXX contexts has shown that in an overwhelming number reference is clearly to God's "justice" which expresses itself in:

(a)    deliverance of Israel because she is being unjustly illtreated by the nations amongst whom she dwells (46:12f; 59:17), Israel occasionally being described as righteous (63:7f);

(b)    punishment of evildoers (59:17; 45:23);

(c)    or more commonly a combination of these (41:1-13; 45:23f; 46:12f; 59:17; 61:11; 63:1).

(d)    In 51:4f there is also the fact that if the nations are willing to follow God's law, they too will share in the blessings; otherwise there is punishment (cf. 45:22f, and the thought of 42:4 and 54:15f).

The duality of deliverance (or vindication) and punishment is also reflected in (ה)צדק, and to this extent there is semantic overlap between (ה)צדק and δικαιοσύνη. However, cases where (ה)צדק is not rendered by δικαιοσύνη point to δικαιοσύνη, in the translator's mind, as being more narrowly "justice."

Although ἐλεεῖν and ἔλεος are favourite words for the translator (see Appendices I and III), only in 56:1 is τὸ ἔλεος used for צדקה, perhaps because δικαιοσύνη is used in the same verse to refer to Israel's ethical behaviour and also there is clear parallel in thought with 55:7 which includes ἐλεεῖν and speaks of pardon for sins. On the other hand τὸ ἔλεος *is* used in 4 of the 5 instances of Yahweh's חסד (LXX interpretation; see Appendix IV). Only in 63:7 does δικαιοσύνη translate חסד, ἔλεος having just been used for רחמים, and here the choice of δικαιοσύνη is appropriate in a context of God being a "good judge" (63:7f), rather than being due to any connotation introduced into δικαιοσύνη from חסד.

What is of note are the instances of צדקה being translated by ἐλεημοσύνη (following Pentateuchal precedent for cases where δικαιοσύνη as "justice" would be erroneous; see Appendix III, note 2). In 1:27; 28:17 and 59:16 the context has emphasised Israel's sin and God's punishing of evildoers, so Israel can only look to his "benevolent action" - in each case reference to God's "justice" would be inappropriate. (On the other hand, δικαιοσύνη in 59:17 refers to God's "justice" in punishing evildoers who ill-treat repentant Israel.) The use of δικαιοσύνη and ἐλεημοσύνη to translate אמת in 38:18f (a different translator?) seems to reflect a feeling on the part of the translator that ἀλήθεια is inappropriate in the context and so other related words have been chosen to express God's benevolent justice.

In view of the overwhelming opinion of modern exegetes (including the present writer, with some qualifications) that (ה)צדק, especially in chaps. 40-66, is often best translated "salvation," it is of particular note that nowhere is there any translation overlap with ישע /65/.

For the Isaiah translator it thus appears that δικαιοσύνη (of God) refers to God's actions and character as ruler or judge (63:7f expresses many of the emphases of the translator): he delivers Israel from unjust ill-treatment by her enemies and punishes evildoers. He was also "just" in punishing Israel by exile (chaps. 63f), but is willing to "pity" her when she repents and does what is right [cf. 64:3(4)f] - he is a "judge" who shows "pity" (e.g., 30:18; see Appendix III). Such mercy is also extended to proselytes (54:15f). Where the context has not referred to Israel's sins, but rather her being unjustly oppressed or her doing what is right, then δικαιοσύνη is used unambiguously to refer to deliverance of Israel and punishment of evildoers; but where the context has emphasised Israel's sins then the translator uses ἐλεημοσύνη for (ה)צדק referring to God's delivering act.

With regard to the various views of Dodd, Hill and Ziesler summarized at the start of this chapter and also in Chapter I. 4, the following can be said concerning the usage of the Isaiah translator:

(a)     There is considerable but certainly not complete
semantic overlap between (ה)צדק and δικαιοσύνη with reference
to God.  δικαιοσύνη is usually "justice," although as a good
judge, the practice of justice may include the wise use of
mercy.

(b)     Over against previous writers, it is noted that
δικαιοσύνη and ἐλεημοσύνη cannot be used interchangeably for
צדק and חסד (so Ziesler), nor in fact is there evidence that
the translator saw in חסד and אמת any covenantal association or
connotation of faithfulness (so Hill).  Nor, on the other hand
are the two aspects of צדק polarized into δικαιοσύνη and
ἐλεημοσύνη (as Dodd).

(c)     Nowhere does δικαιοσύνη mean "victory," "salvation" or
"deliverance" (so Hill); rather the translation emphasises
salvation of Israel as being an act of God's justice.

(d)     The idea of the "righteousness (or justice) of God"
comes straightforwardly from the classical Greek ideal of the
just ruler or judge.  The contribution of the Jewish context is
to enable this analogy to be applied to God, but δικαιοσύνη
itself has Greek connotation.

(e)     Nevertheless it must be said that, because of the
contexts of (ה)צדק in MT, the translator uses δικαιοσύνη
predominantly in contexts of God's saving action.  This
involves "mercy" to those who repent and who are willing to
obey God's law.  It is incorrect to say that the content of
"mercy" is thus "supplied" (so Hill) to δικαιοσύνη, as it has
been noted that mercy to the wrongdoer who can be cured is
commendable in Plato, Lg. 731b-d as part of the act of justice
(see Appendix III).  The Isaiah context rather serves to
emphasise this possible (albeit sometimes misused and
neglected) content of δικαιοσύνη in Greek usage.

        In summary, God is a good judge, who in his justice
shows mercy to the genuinely repentant and delivers them from
oppression, punishing evildoers, so correcting injustice.

# CHAPTER V

SOME OTHER RELATED GREEK WORDS IN ISAIAH

Some other insights on the translator's word usage and
theology can be seen in his usage of other words in the wider
semantic field. Here we summarize his use of δίκαιος and
positive σεβ-words, and of ἀδικ-, ἀνομ - and ἀσεβ-words.

A.   ΔΙΚΑΙΟΣ.

In the previous chapter various instances of δίκαιος
were discussed. Apart from the instances of τὸ δίκαιον,
δίκαιος is used in 41:10 of God's "just" rule and in 58:2 of
his "just" judging; in 32:1 reference is to the "just" king who
will rule, while in 54:17 God is to treat Israel as being "in
the right" or "innocent" (when unjustly treated by others).

In addition, δίκαιος is used 8 times for צדיק. In 45:21
it is an epithet of God, probably meaning "just." In 3:10;
5:23; 29:21; 53:11 and 57:1 (twice, plus being used for חסד)
reference is to "righteous" individuals who are being or have
been treated unjustly, while in 60:21 it is all the people of
Israel who shall be "righteous" in the restored state.

All of these occurrences are thus in situations familiar
to Greek readers, except the clear description of God as ruler-
judge.

B.   POSITIVE ΣΕΒ-WORDS.

As in much of the LXX, the positive σεβ-words are
comparatively rare in Isaiah.

εὐσεβεῖν occurs nowhere, while εὐσεβής is only used 4
times. 3 times are for צדיק: once in 24:16, in contrast to
those who "despise the law" or who have "transgressed the law
and changed the ordinances, the eternal covenant" (v.5); and
twice in 26:7, where the context emphasizes obedience of and
trust in God. Once is for נדיר: in 32:8, in contrast to רע/
πονηρός (v.7), in a context of trust in God.

Unlike Psalms and Proverbs where the phrase יראת-יהוה is

119

translated φόβος κυρίου (Foerster does not take account of
variations between translators; see also Seeligmann: 103), the
Greek phrase occurs in Isaiah mainly in the sense of being
afraid of God, so 2:10, 19, 21 and probably 26:17(18).  The
good sense of reverence and awe is conveyed, as is usual in
Greek, by εὐσέβεια in 11:2 (φόβος θεοῦ in v.3 is probably in a
literal rather than religious sense, appropriately for a ruler
who is involved in judging others) and 33:6 (φοβ-words are
used 4 times in v.7 referring to fear of men).  The verb usage
is similar: σέβεσθαι is used in 29:13; while φοβεῖσθαι with God
as object occurs in the sense of "be afraid of" in 59:19
(although in 57:11 and 63:17 it is open to either sense, "be
afraid" or "revere").  φοβεῖσθαι occurs very frequently with a
human object, often in the imperative, "do not be afraid."

The only other instance of a σεβ-word is σεβόμενος in
66:14 for עבד (B and some mss have φοβούμενος).

It can be seen that the Isaiah translator's usage is
more akin to Hellenistic practice than to the later Jewish
usage in Psalms and Proverbs.

C.    ᾽ΑΔΙΚ-, ᾽ΑΝΟΜ- AND ᾽ΑΣΕΒ-WORDS.

These words are used in Isaiah for a great variety of
Hebrew roots.  Certain tendencies and patterns are more clearly
seen by means of diagrams.  (Although one may occasionally
question the LXX *Vorlage*, the link with MT is almost always
clear.)  /1/

*Nouns*:

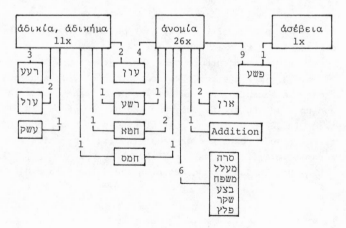

*Adjectives*:

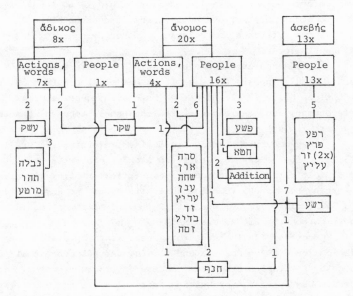

*Verbs*:

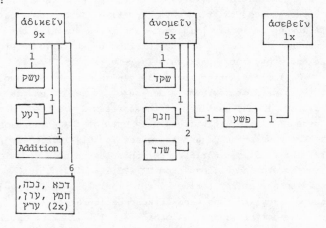

This information, together with investigation of the contexts, leads to the following observations:

(a)     While the translator follows the Pentateuch practice of using ἀσεβής for עָשֵׁק /2/, he also uses ἀσεβής for other roots when reference is to Israel's enemies. This is so for 5 of the other 6 occurrences of ἀσεβής, the only exception being 33:14 (חֲנֵף) where reference is to Israel, ἄνομος being used adjacently for חָטָא.

(b)     ἀνομία and ἄνομος are used mainly in reference to Israel. This appears to be so in 38 out of 42 occurrences, the exceptions being 13:11 and 24:20 (both being general references), and possibly 59:4, 6 (the people amongst whom the Jews are living).

(c)     ἀδικία occurs with ἀνομία 5 times referring to Israel (33:15, twice; 43:24, 25, twice in A only, otherwise once; 59:3). It is used of actions within Israel in 58:6, clearly referring to oppressive and unjust situations, as also in 33:15 and 59:3. In 57:1; 60:18 and 61:8 it applies to oppression of the righteous by wicked enemies.

(d)     Foerster (187) states that there is no apparent distinction between ἀσέβεια and ἀδικία. Actual contextual usage by the Isaiah translator however strongly suggests that for him there is an overwhelming preference for the use of ἀδικία and ἄδικα for *actions*, particularly when reference is to the oppression of the righteous (sometimes Israel as a nation), while ἀσεβής (adjective) is preferred for describing the oppress*ors*. ἀνομία and ἄνομος refer more generally to wrongdoing and wrongdoers, particularly referring to Israel.

(e)     A similar distinction is seen with ἀδικεῖν and ἀνομεῖν. ἀδικεῖν is used of oppressive action by Israel's leaders (3:15), or, in the passive, of the oppressed who need to be delivered (1:17). It is frequently used of the actions of those who have attacked and oppressed Israel (10:20; 21:3; 23:12; 25:3f; 51:23; 65:25). For this latter use, occasionally LXX interpretation differs from MT (23:12; 21:3; 25:3f) or ἀδικεῖν is an interpretative addition (51:23), so it appears that the translator has used ἀδικεῖν deliberately.

(f)     The only instance of ἀσεβεῖν (59:13) is in an explicit description of Israel's disobedience of God.

The question must be asked whether there is any theological reason for these linguistic preferences, for he certainly goes beyond the Pentateuchal precedent. An interpretation that is consistent with his understanding of the contexts is that:

(1)     Acts of oppression by rulers and judges and attacks on other nations are, as in secular Greek understanding, "unjust." ἀσέβεια or ἀσεβεῖν would not convey this significance as that refers to actions towards the gods, not to other people.

(2)     Nevertheless, these acts are done, not merely because the oppressors are by nature "wrongdoers," but more basically because of their failure to serve the Lord. ἀσεβής most appropriately conveys this emphasis.

(3)     For Israel's disobedience of the law of God ἀνομ-words are appropriate.

It can also be seen that this usage is further evidence that the translator viewed Israel's treatment by the nations as being "unjust." Hence God's acting to right this is an act of "justice."

CHAPTER VI

CONCLUSIONS

It is not intended here to repeat the summaries given at
the end of each chapter. Rather some further general comments
shall be made related to issues raised in the first chapter.

1.   METHODOLOGY.

This investigation of one small word group has demonstrated the necessity of contextual exegetical study of the LXX,
taking into account variety between translators. One cannot
assume that, because a particular Hebrew word is "usually"
rendered by a particular Greek word, therefore there is
considerable semantic overlap. Much can be learned by looking
at possible contextual reasons for "unusual" renderings, on the
initial heuristic assumption that the translator intended his
reading to make sense. In the case of our study this
assumption has been seen to lead to a consistent picture of
some aspects of the translator's theology and technique.

2.   JEWISH GREEK?

Examination of the literary contexts of δικαιοῦν,
δικαιοσύνη and related words has shown that for the Isaiah
translator the understanding of these contexts often differs
from that of MT (as seen by modern exegetes). Further, LXX
contexts show that he has not interpreted words with root צדק
according to Hebrew connotation, but rather in a sense more
closely linked with Greek usage. While the fact that he uses
δικαιο-words is due to צדק in MT, this is not simply a case of
"automatic response translation" since no instance has been
found where this leads to a meaning unrecognizable on the basis
of secular Greek usage.

For both the verb and the noun it seems evident that the
translator begins with the usual secular, non-Jewish Greek
meanings. These meanings do however undergo slight semantic
expansion due to their usage within a Jewish theological

125

framework, being used in contexts which are recognizable but
perhaps uncommon in secular Greek:-

(a)     The use of δικαιοῦν chiefly, but not exclusively, in a
positive sense, "do justice to, acquit, vindicate, restore to a
right relationship," is an extension of the Greek forensic use
with a personal object, "do to a person what is necessary to
correct an act or state of injustice."

(b)     δικαιοσύνη and δικαιοῦν in contexts of deliverance from
unjust oppression or of pardon for those who show genuine
repentance and desire to follow God's law (Jews and proselytes)
is a straightforward extension to God of similar attitudes and
actions by a good and wise secular ruler or judge (including,
e.g., remission of a sentence for one who shows he can be
corrected).

It can be seen that these extensions can be readily
understood by anyone familiar with Greek usage, on the basis of
the literary contexts in which they appear.  There is no
"Jewish Greek" but rather Greek words with some new
associations added due to the Jewish context.  Thus for
δικαιοσύνη referring to man the Jewish context links
"righteousness" with God's requirements but does not alter the
basic Greek connotation of "righteousness."  δικαιοσύνη
ascribed to God refers to his concern to act on behalf of his
people - he is "just" and acts according to "justice" to bring
about a state of "justice."  That God is like this is added by
Jewish faith, but the translator believes that "justice" is an
appropriate word to use.  The historical situation of the Jews
and the translator's reading of MT lead to emphasis on God's
"justice" as being seen in both deliverance and punishment.
The use in such new contexts may influence the later semantic
development of the Greek words, but the translator clearly
starts with Greek meanings.

It is here strongly suggested that the translator
translates as he does because he sees God's actions and
attitudes to Israel in terms of "justice" - salvation is an act
of justice, correcting injustices, bringing about a just
situation in regard to the life of the Jews amongst their
neighbours and in their relationship with God himself.

3.    SIGNIFICANCE FOR THE REST OF LXX AND THE NT.

Our work has dealt with the Isaiah translator.  It is
not possible to make comments about the use of δικαιοσύνη,
etc., in the rest of LXX, except that in passing it has been
suggested that in at least a few places LXX Pentateuch seems to
reflect Greek usage of δικαιοῦν (Exod 23:7, see p. 45) and
δικαιοσύνη (Deut 6:25; 24:13; see Appendix III, note 2).  More
investigation is needed along the lines of this work.

Regarding NT (and later Christian) usage only brief
remarks can be made.  While it is true that LXX Isaiah has its
inadequacies as a translation, yet for most early Christians
this was the version in which Isaiah was read!  As the Book of
Isaiah is a major source for the view that צדקת־יהוה is
salvific, it is significant that this meaning is not conveyed
in LXX.  Rather there is the image of God as the just
deliverer - salvation is an act of justice.

The question must be raised as to the extent to which NT
writers were affected by LXX words in LXX context.  Of course
many other factors affect NT usage of Greek words, including
inter-testamental literature and the NT writers' familiarity
with both Aramaic and Greek.  The point being made here, as
throughout, is that Greek words in the LXX must be understood
in their separate LXX contexts.

## APPENDIX I

### FREQUENCY AND DISTRIBUTION OF HEBREW WORDS
### AND THEIR GREEK TRANSLATION EQUIVALENTS

| Hebrew word and Greek translation | No. of occurrences | | | | |
|---|---|---|---|---|---|
| | chaps. 1-35 | 36-39 | 40-55 | 56-66 | Total |
| צדק Qal | – | – | 3 | – | 3 |
| Hiphil | 1 | – | 2 | – | 3 |
| δικαιοῦν | 1 | – | 5 | – | 6 |
| צֶדֶק | 8 | – | 10 | 7 | 25 |
| δικαιοσύνη | 6 | – | 6 | 4 | 16 |
| τὸ δίκαιον | – | – | 1 | 2 | 3 |
| δίκαιος | 1 | – | 1 | 1 | 3 |
| κρίσις | 1 | – | 1 | – | 2 |
| δικαιοῦν | – | – | 1 | – | 1 |
| צְדָקָה | 12 | – | 11 | 13 | 36 |
| δικαιοσύνη | 9 | – | 10 | 10 | 29 |
| τὸ δίκαιον | 1 | – | – | – | 1 |
| δίκαιος | – | – | 1 | – | 1 |
| ἐλεημοσύνη | 2 | – | – | 1 | 3 |
| ἔλεος | – | – | – | 1 | 1 |
| εὐφροσύνη | – | – | – | 1 | 1 |
| צַדִּיק | 7 | – | 4 | 3 | 14 |
| δίκαιος | 3 | – | 2 | 3 | 8 |
| εὐσεβής | 3 | – | – | – | 3 |
| φυλάσσων δικαιοσύνη | 1 | – | – | – | 1 |
| ἀληθής | – | – | 1 | – | 1 |
| ἀδικῶς | – | – | 1 | – | 1 |
| אֱמֶת | 2 | 4 | 3 | 2 | 11 |
| ἀλήθεια | 2 | 1 | 2 | 2 | 7 |
| ἀληθής | – | – | 1 | – | 1 |
| δικαιοσύνη | – | 2 | – | – | 2 |
| ἐλεημοσύνη | – | 1 | – | – | 1 |

| Hebrew word and Greek translation | 1-35 | 36-39 | 40-55 | 56-66 | Total |
|---|---|---|---|---|---|
| חָסֶד | 1 | - | 4 | 3 | 8 |
| ἔλεος | 1 | | 2 | 1 | 4 |
| δικαιοσύνη | - | | - | 1 | 1 |
| δίκαιος | - | | - | 1 | 1 |
| δόξα | - | | 1 | - | 1 |
| (plural) τὰ ὅσια | - | | 1 | - | 1 |
| שׁפט Qal | 10 | - | 3 | - | 13 |
| Niphal | - | - | - | 2 | 2 |
| κρίνειν | 7 | | 1 | 1 | 9 |
| κριτής | 2 | | - | - | 2 |
| δικαστής | 1 | | - | - | 1 |
| ἄρχειν | - | | 1 | - | 1 |
| κρίσις | - | | - | 1 | 1 |
| Not translated | - | | 1 | - | 1 |
| משׁפט | 22 | - | 11 | 9 | 42 |
| κρίσις | 13 | | 10 | 8 | 31 |
| κρίμα | 7 | | - | - | 7 |
| κριτής | 1 | | - | - | 1 |
| κρίνειν | - | | 1 | - | 1 |
| δικαιοσύνη | - | | - | 1 | 1 |
| (plural) προστάγματα | 1 | | - | - | 1 |
| ריב (verb, noun) | 6 | - | 7 | 4* | 17 |
| κρίσις | 3 | | 2 | 2 | 7 |
| κρίνειν | 1 | | 3 | - | 4 |
| κριτής | - | | - | 1 | 1 |
| δικαιοῦν | 1 | | - | - | 1 |
| ἀντίδικος | - | | 1 | - | 1 |
| ἐκδικεῖν | - | | - | 1 | 1 |
| Mistranslated? | 1 | | 1 | - | 2 |

\*  Including 63:1, 7 where LXX has interpreted רָב־ as
   from ריב.

| Hebrew word and Greek translation | 1-35 | 36-39 | 40-55 | 56-66 | Total |
|---|---|---|---|---|---|
| ישע Verb | 5 | 3 | 12 | 8 | 28 |
| Noun forms | 9 | - | 11 | 7 | 27 |
| σῴζειν | 5 | 2 | 8 | 3 | 18 |
| σωτήρ | 2 | - | 2 | 1 | 5 |
| σωτηρία | 5 | 1 | 8 | 2 | 16 |
| σωτήριον | 2 | - | 3 | 6 | 11 |
| ῥύεσθαι | - | - | 1 | 1 | 2 |
| ἔλεος | - | - | 1 | - | 1 |
| ἀμύνειν | - | - | - | 1 | 1 |
| πλανᾶν | - | - | - | 1 | 1 |

*Additional occurrences of significant Greek words:*

| Greek word and Hebrew equivalent | 1-35 | 36-39 | 40-55 | 56-66 | Total |
|---|---|---|---|---|---|
| δικαιοσύνη (no equiv.) | 1 | - | - | - | 1 |
| τὸ δίκαιον (נקם) | - | - | 1 | - | 1 |
| κρίσις (נקם) | 2 | - | - | - | 2 |
| " (דין) | 2 | - | - | - | 2 |
| κρίνειν (עזר) | - | - | 1 | - | 1 |
| ἔλεος (רחם, רצון, and 2 free translations) | - | - | 2 | 4 | 6 |
| ἐλεεῖν (חנן, חמל, נחם, רחם, and 3 free translations) | 10 | - | 9 | 1 | 20 |
| σῴζειν (נצל, פלט, מלט) | 6 | 2 | 5 | 1 | 14 |
| (פתח, חסה, שׁוב, פדה, עשׂה?) | 4 | - | 1 | - | 5 |
| σωτήριον (תהלות) | - | - | - | 1 | 1 |
| " (מעוד) | 1 | - | - | - | 1 |
| " (addition) | - | 1 | 1 | - | 2 |

APPENDIX II

A COMPARISON OF MODERN TRANSLATIONS OF ALL
OCCURRENCES OF THE ROOT צדק IN ISAIAH

1.    THE NOUN צדק(ה).

A.    CHAPTERS 1-39:

RSV:    always has "righteousness," except 5:23, "(his) right,"
        and 33:15, "righteously."
JB:     always uses "integrity," except 5:23, "due."
        "Integrity" is defined in a note on 1:21 as "judicial
        equity" and also a "'justness' characterising a
        dispensation in which Yahweh the king grants his
        subjects some share in his own sanctity."
NEB:    has "righteousness" 12 times, "justice" 6 (5:23; 10:22,
        margin: "righteousness"; 11:4f; 26:9f), "(do) right" in
        16:5 and "upright (life)" in 33:15.
Duhm:   has "Gerechtigkeit" 14 times, "Recht" 5 (1:26; 5:23;
        26:9f; 32:17b), with "Rechtsprechung" in 5:7.
Fohrer: always uses "Gerechtigkeit," except 5:23 and 32:17b,
        "Recht," and 11:4, "wie es recht ist."
Eichrodt: has "Gerechtigkeit," except 1:26, "Rechts-," 5:23,
        "gute Sache," 11:4, "gerecht," and 32:17b, "Recht."
Kaiser: always has "Gerechtigkeit," except 5:23, "Recht."
Auvray: always uses "(la) justice."

        It is seen that, for all, צדק(ה) is interpreted
exclusively in terms of ethical "righteousness" or forensic
"justice, right."  One notable exception is Bonnard who says
concerning the salvific aspect of צדק that "ne paraît presque
pas en Isaïe (1-39): 1:26f and 5:16" (542).

133

134

B.    CHAPTERS 40-55.

| | *RSV* | *JB* | *NEB* | North |
|---|---|---|---|---|
| 41:2 | victory | victory | victory | victory |
| 41:10 | victorious | victorious | victorious | victorious |
| 42:6 | righteousness | serve the cause of right | righteous purpose | saving purpose |
| 42:21 | " | integrity | justice | righteousness |
| 45:8a | " | victory | righteousness | victory |
| 45:8b | " | deliverance | " | salvation |
| 45:13 | " | victory | " | saving purpose |
| 45:19 | truth | with directness | what is right | truth |
| 45:23 | righteousness | truth | victory | truth |
| 45:24 | " | victory | " | victory |
| 46:12 | deliverance | " | " | deliverance |
| 46:13 | " | " | " | " |
| 48:1 | right | uprightness | sincerity | sincerity |
| 48:18 | righteousness | integrity | just success | prosperity |
| 51:1 | deliverance | " | the right | right |
| 51:5 | " | " | victory | victory |
| 51:6 | " | justice | saving power | triumph |
| 51:7 | righteousness | integrity | what is right | what is right |
| 51:8 | deliverance | " | saving power | triumph |
| 54:14 | righteousness | " | triumph Mg: righteousness | righteousness |
| 54:17 | vindication | triumphs | vindication | right |

* "Manifester sa justice, c'est, pour le Seigneur, ... surtout déployer fidèlement son dessein de salut" (108).

| Duhm | Fohrer | Westermann | Bonnard |
|---|---|---|---|
| Sieg | Sieg | Heil | Justice* |
| treu | heilvoll | heilsam | qui fait justice |
| Gerechtigkeit | Gnade | Gerechtigkeit | la justice |
| Treue | " | Treue | justice |
| Recht | Heil | Heil | la justice |
| Gerechtigkeit | " | Gerechtigkeit | " |
| " | Gnade | Gnade | " |
| Recht | Recht | Heil | justice |
| Wahrheit | Wahrheit | Wahrheit | la justice |
| Sieg | Heil | Heil | justice |
| Heil | " | " | la justice |
| " | " | " | (ma) justice |
| Recht | wahrhaftig | Gerechtigkeit | droiture |
| Heil | Gedeihen | Heil | (ta) justice |
| " | Heil | " | justice |
| " | " | " | (ma) justice |
| " | " | " | " |
| Recht | " | " | la justice |
| Heil | " | " | (ma) justice |
| " | " | " | la justice |
| " | " | " | (leur) justice |

C.    CHAPTERS 56-66.

| | RSV | JB | NEB | Duhm |
|---|---|---|---|---|
| 56:1a | righteousness | integrity | the right | Gerechtigkeit |
| 56:1b | deliverance | " | righteousness shows itself victorious | " |
| 57:12 | righteousness | " | righteous | " |
| 58:2a | " | " | rightly | " |
| 58:2b | righteous | just | righteous | " |
| 58:8 | righteousness | integrity | righteousness | Recht |
| 59:4 | justly | just | with just cause | mit Recht |
| 59:9 | righteousness | integrity | right | Gerechtigkeit |
| 59:14 | " | " | righteousness | " |
| 59:16 | " | " | integrity | " |
| 59:17 | " | " | " | " |
| 60:17 | " | " | righteousness | " |
| 61:3 | " | " | " | " |
| 61:10 | " | " | integrity | " |
| 61:11 | " | " | righteousness | " |
| 62:1 | vindication | " | right | Recht |
| 62:2 | " | " | triumph of your right | " |
| 63:1 | " | " | right has won the day | " |
| 64:4 | righteousness | " | what is right | recht |
| 64:5 | righteous deeds | " | righteous deeds | Tugenden |

*   Scullion (1971: 342, n. 27) reports a verbal comment by
    Fohrer (January, 1971) that "he would now render *ṣedeq* by
    *Heil* more often than in his commentary, especially in
    c. 59."

137

| Fohrer | Westermann | Kessler |
|---|---|---|
| Gerechtigkeit | Gerechtigkeit | Gerechtigkeit |
| Heil | " | Heil |
| Gerechtigkeit | " | Gerechtigkeit |
| Recht | " | " |
| gerecht | recht | gerecht |
| Heil | Heil | Heil |
| mit Recht* | gerecht | mit gerechtem Grund |
| Gerechtigkeit | Heil | Heil |
| " | Gerechtigkeit | Gerechtigkeit |
| Heilswille | Heil | Heilswille |
| Gerechtigkeit | Gerechtigkeit | Gerechtigkeit |
| " | " | " |
| Heil | Heil | immergrün |
| " | Gerechtigkeit | Gerechtigkeit |
| " | Heil | Heil |
| " | " | " |
| " | " | " |
| Gerechtigkeit | Gerechtigkeit | Heilswille |
| " | recht | Gerechtigkeit |
| " | " | Tugenden |

It is obvious that *JB* and Duhm entirely, and *RSV* and *NEB* in most cases (only 4 and 3 exceptions respectively), do not continue on into chaps. 56-66 the emphasis on "victory" and "deliverance" seen in chaps. 40-55. On the other hand, the three later German commentators uniformly continue the emphasis on "Heil." (It should be noted that "Heil" is more comprehensive in meaning than the usual English equivalents. Thus, e.g., Stalker in ET of Westermann uses "salvation" 15 times, "victory" once and "deliverance" 3 times.) The justification for the difference in the English translations seems to be a presupposed legalism inherent in chaps. 56-66. The actual language used (parallelisms, etc.) argues strongly for the German understanding.

Bonnard in chaps. 56-66 uses "(la) justice" throughout.

2.    THE ADJECTIVE, צדיק.

The translations surveyed do not depart from the basic meaning of "righteous" (including here "innocent, being in the right"), except:

45:21: "victorious" (*NEB*, North), "heilvoll" (Fohrer);
60:21: "Heilsgenossen" (Westermann, following Volz),
       "lauter Fromme" (Kessler, rejecting
           "Heilsgenossen").

Of particular note is the use as a divine appellative in 24:16 in *RSV* and *JB*.

3.    THE VERB.

A.    QAL:

In 43:9, 26 the verb is unanimously translated in a forensic sense, such as "be proved right."

In 45:25 all translations contain some salvific emphasis (e.g., "triumph"), except Bonnard "obtiendra justice" and Duhm "singen."

B.    HIPHIL:

There is unanimously the idea of "acquit", in 5:23, and "vindicate" in 50:8.

For 53:11 the translations are quite varied:

*RSV*:        "make to be accounted righteous";
*JB*:         "justify";

139

| *NEB*: | "vindicate"; |
|--------|--------------|
| North: | "bring righteousness"; |
| Fohrer: | "Heil schaffen"; |
| Westermann: | "als gerecht bestehen"; |
| Bonnard: | "dispenser la justice." |

# APPENDIX III

## ΤΟ 'ΕΛΕΟΣ, 'Η 'ΕΛΕΗΜΟΣΥΝΗ IN NON-JEWISH GREEK AND LXX

1. NON-JEWISH GREEK.

The variety of situations in which ἔλεος occurs has been
well described by Bultmann (cf. LSJ). Aristotle (EN II.1105b)
includes it in the category of πάθος, not ἀρετή, and describes
the tendency to this emotion as a weakness of both young men
and old, for differing reasons (Rh. II.1389b-1390a). Plato in
his discussion of poetry and drama in the ideal state also
describes "pity" as a weakness (R. X.605-6; Lg. XI.936). This
attitude is carried even further by the Stoics (see Schwer).

Bultmann uses such statements to show the dangers of a
judge being partial due to "pity," contrasting this with LXX
usage in relation to God. Similarly, Hill refers to the lack
of semantic development "away from strict justice" for
δικαιοσύνη (103). Closer examination, however, suggests
qualifications. Plato, Lg. 731b-d, does point out the danger
of showing pity to the "utterly corrupt person," using very
strong words to describe this type of person. For such,
"wrath" is commendable. Yet the same passage just as much
stresses the need for pity to the wrongdoer who can be cured.
In a similar vein Demosthenes 25:81, 83 argues that pity should
not be shown to Aristogeiton because he has not shown pity when
he should have, and in 21:99, 100 "pity" is to be shown to
those who show pity when in authority. It would appear that
the criticisms of Plato and Aristotle are of a pity that
overrules reason.

The later noun form ἐλεημοσύνη, first known in the 3rd
century B.C. /1/, refers more to benevolent activity.
Chantraine puts its derivation as through ἐλεήμων (e.g.,
Odyssey 5:191, Demosthenes 21:101), which has a dual sense as
subject or object, "qui a pitié, pitoyable" (2:336; similarly,
LSJ: "pitiful, merciful").

141

2.    LXX IN GENERAL.

ἔλεος occurs quite frequently, predominantly translating
חסד. In the Pentateuch it is used 15 times, 11 of these for
חסד, and in Psalms more than 80 times, exclusively for חסד. It
is used for a variety of roots in Isaiah (12 times, 4 of these
for חסד; see Appendix I) and in Jeremiah. In the whole OT it
translates צדקה only in Isa 56:1 and Ezek 18:19f.

Over against this, ἐλεημοσύνη is used for חסד only in
Proverbs (7 times) and in Gen 47:29. Only in Isa 38:18 does it
appear to render אמת (see p. 91). Elsewhere it renders צדקה:
twice in Pentateuch /2/, three times in Psalms /3/, three times
in Isaiah and twice in Daniel.

Although one must be cautious in using word statistics
without more detailed contextual investigation, there is a
strong suggestion that for the translators of the Pentateuch
and Psalms חסד and צדקה were associated, although distinguished, חסד connoting mainly the feeling and צדקה the outward
acting, usually of God. In Isaiah the same distinction is
seen, although ἔλεος is not used for man's חסד (see further in
Appendix IV).

APPENDIX IV

THE TRANSLATION OF חסד IN ISAIAH

חסד occurs 8 times in Isaiah. The LXX interprets 5
occasions with reference to God and 3 times to man. There are
no instances of חסיד.

1. GOD AS SUBJECT.

*16:5*: "A throne will be established בחסד/μετὰ ἐλέους."
The Hebrew would seem to refer to the character of the
Messianic rule (*NEB* and Fohrer see reference to an alliance
between Israel and Moab "in David's tent"), while the Greek
connects ἔλεος to the action of establishing or setting right,
i.e., to an action of God.

*54:7b, 8b*: ברחמים גדלים/μετὰ ἐλέους μεγάλου אקבצך/
ἐλεήσω σε ... עולם רחמתיך בחסד/ἐν ἐλέει αἰωνίῳ ἐλεήσω σε
(or ἠλέησά σε).

*54:10b*: מרחמך יהוה ... וחסדי מאתך לא־ימוש/οὕτως οὐδὲ τὸ
παρ'ἐμοῦ σοι ἔλεος ἐκλείψει ... κύριος Ἵλεώς σοι.
LXX clearly emphasizes the "mercy" of God, using ἔλεος-words
for both רחם (twice) and חסד (twice), and ἐλεῖν in the
rendering of v.7b.

*63:7*: Refer to discussion on pp. 88-89. MT emphasises
God's saving deeds associated with the covenant relationship,
but LXX is far more concerned with the qualities of the Lord as
judge. This is the only occasion in Isaiah where חסד is
translated δικαιοσύνη, no doubt because ἔλεος has already been
used.

2. MAN AS SUBJECT.

*40:6*: "All flesh is grass, וכל־חסדו/καὶ πᾶσα δόξα
ἀνθρώπου like the flower of the field."
חסד has caused trouble to exegetes and it is common to
translate such as "beauty" (*RSV*), either on the basis of
emendation (Duhm, *BHS*) or possible Aramaic meaning (Volz).

143

Both North and Bonnard retain the normal sense of חסד (cf. Hos 6:4), the suffix referring to "flesh." This then provides a fitting contrast to the sure, faithful word of Yahweh (v.8b): man's "steadfast love" is like the flower of the field, but God's "steadfast love" (implied) is forever.

It appears that LXX had difficulty with the verse and translated according to sense, using δόξα in contrast to ἡ δόξα κυρίου in v.5. This contrast explains the addition of ἀνθρώπου (cf. Ziegler, 1934: 150).

*57:1:* הצדיק/ὁ δίκαιος in parallel with אנשי חסד/ ἄνδρες δίκαιοι.

LXX seems to have interpreted as the killing of "righteous" men, as is seen by the addition of ἡ ταφή in v.2.

*55:3* חסדי דוד הנאמנים/τὰ ὅσια Δαυιδ τὰ πιστά

Most exegetes refer MT to God's actions towards David, e.g., North (1964), "the manifestations of my love for David," and Westermann, "the steadfast, sure promises of grace to David." Bonnard, however, argues for deeds done by David (as agent, the ultimate source being still Yahweh), namely, the establishing of Jerusalem and the setting up of the temple. Bonnard's exegesis of this verse and of several parallels he uses for support (2 Chr 6:42; Lam 4:20 and Ps 89:39f; but not Ps 89:50) seems rather forced and we must conclude that this meaning is improbable for MT. Nevertheless, something like this appears to have been LXX understanding.

Bonnard translates LXX as "les actes saints de David" /1/. Dodd is similar, although without reference to divine origin: "'The trustworthy religious ordinances of David', i.e., presumably the religious institutions which he was supposed to have founded" (63). The phrase is quoted, with a different verb, in Acts 13:34 where the common interpretation follows MT original and is such as *NEB*: "the blessings promised to David, sure and true." In a major study Dupont argues on the basis of the use of the plural ὅσια in inscriptions /2/, together with Deut 29:18 LXX, that in Isa 55:3 reference is to "les bienfaits qu'on peut attendre de Dieu" /3/. While he, correctly in our view, criticizes BAG (following Bauer) for referring τὰ ὅσια to divine decrees /4/, he still sees τὰ ὅσια as originating from God.

Further investigation of the inscriptions shows the
following aspects of the form: (a) the use is an imprecatory
formula addressed to the gods, (b) the article is never used,
(c) ὅσια is frequently followed by καὶ ἐλεύθερα, (d) there
commonly follows some explicit phrase, such as reference to a
reward for the return of a lost bracelet (*SIG* 1184), and (e)
there is no instance of ὅσια with the name of a person in the
genitive, although the pronoun in the dative occurs. The
meaning seems to be that someone's actions are to be regarded
as ὅσια by the gods, who treat that person accordingly. (Cf.
LSJ which places the usage under the general rubric, τὸ ὅσιον =
εὐσέβεια.) That is to say, the context is laws relating to
one's obligations in the presence of the gods and the expected
consequences in terms of the god's attitudes towards one.
Perhaps there is a parallel between τὸ δίκαιον used to refer to
the decision of a human judge concerning disputes in societal
relationships, and ὅσια referring to the attitude of the gods
to human actions related to the gods. Be that as it may, it
cannot be doubted that in the inscriptions, as in other uses,
it is *human* actions that are primary.

Thus non-Jewish Greek usage, together with the preceding
phrase in Isa 55:3, which LXX translates straightforwardly as
διαθήσομαι ὑμῖν διαθήκην αἰώνιον, suggests that reference is
either to "decrees concerning worship of God as made by David"
or "religious acts such as performed by David," in either case
narrowly explicating the contents of the διαθήκη.

3.    CONCLUSION.

For the Isaiah translator חסד is translated differently
depending upon whether reference is to God or man. It seems
that he saw no general semantic reference to either the
covenant or to faithfulness. The use of ὅσια in 55:3, in a
context of both covenant and faithfulness, supports this
contention. Nevertheless his translation is understandable
although a narrowing and changing of emphasis of the rich
Hebrew word (for Hebrew usage, see Glueck and Larue). For God
the emphasis is upon his "mercy," which is one dimension of חסד
/5/, while for man it is upon his responsibilities in obeying
the law of God. Unlike other translators (cf. Jer 2:2; Hos
6:4), the Isaiah translator does not use ἔλεος when referring

to man's חסד, although admittedly statistics are limited.

## ISRAEL AND THE NATIONS

The question of universalism in Isaiah 40-66 and of the nature of the ministry of "my servant" has been much debated. Blauw gives a useful summary (29-43). Recently Orlinsky (1967, 1970) and Snaith (1967) have argued persuasively for a strong nationalistic emphasis, highlighting the many passages where the nations are to be punished for their treatment of Israel and are to serve the restored Israel. For them the ministry of "my servant" is only to Israel, with "a light of nations" (42:6; 49:6; cf. chap. 60) either being "a light throughout all the gentile world, in order that God's salvation of Israel may reach the end of the world" (Snaith, 1967: 155f, 180, 188f), or describing the situation when "Israel will dazzle the nations with her God-given triumph and restoration" (Orlinsky, 1970: 117). Both deny any "mission to the nations."

At the same time there are passages throughout the Book of Isaiah which refer to the restored Zion as a place from which "teaching" and "light" will go out for the guidance of the nations, and which affirm that any Gentile, who is willing to enter the covenant people of Israel, performing the covenant obligations, is able to enjoy the covenant blessings (2:1-4; 14:1-2; chap. 19; 26:9; 42:4; 51:4, 5; 56:1-8; 60:3; cf. Orlinsky, 1970: 218-28). Thus, while any active mission is questionable, there is no doubt of the possibility of proselytes and of the nations enjoying peace if they are willing to serve Israel (the alternative being destruction). Israel's task (avoiding "mission" with its idea of being sent) is to be obedient to her God in terms of the covenant relationship.

Clearly the debate concerning MT can also be carried into LXX. Here we consider those passages or word translations which differ from MT and so may point to any different emphasis.

148

1.    PROSELYTES

*54:15 LXX*:  "Behold proselytes will come (προσήλυτοι
προσελεύσονται) to you and take refuge (καταφεύξονται) with
you."

MT has certain difficulties but it seems LXX translator
has read the root גור as גֵּר ("resident alien," in biblical
period).  Tov (1967b: 37) and BAG point out the technical use
of προσήλυτος.  Seeligmann comments:

> "It was apparently obvious to him to read into
> the difficult text 54:15 ... a reference to
> proselytes ...  It should be noted that the
> term καταφύγειν is known, from the Hellenistic
> Greek of the papyri, as a more or less standard
> expression for seeking or finding asylum.
> Apparently, the translator regarded the conversion
> of the Gentiles to Judaism as their safeguard
> against the wrath of God."  (117f)

*41:25 LXX*:  "I have raised up one from the north and one from
the rising of the sun: they shall be called by my name" (MT:
"he shall call on my name").

Seeligmann sees reference to inhabitants of those lands
(117), although it should be observed that v.25b goes on to
speak of the defeat of rulers and v.27 reads: "I will give
dominion to Zion and will encourage Jerusalem in the way."
Perhaps here one has reference to two groups, proselytes and
others.  This distinction appears in *14:1f* where LXX and MT are
similar: in a promise of Israel's return to her own land we
read "הגר ('aliens')/ὁ γειώρας (from Aramaic, גיירא,
'proselyte') will join them," followed by reference to
"peoples" who will bring Israel back to the land and be her
servants.  In both MT and LXX a distinction is made between
those who join Israel and "the peoples."

Elsewhere we have argued that there a various passages
where in LXX there are the two alternatives, recognizing God
and entering the covenant people or suffering humiliation or
even destruction: 45:15-25 (pp. 54-58), 51:4-6 (pp. 100-101),
and perhaps 50:9b-11 (p. 47; see further below).  To these can
be added *66:5*: "Hear the words of the Lord, you who tremble at
his word; speak, our brothers, to those who hate and despise
you, that the name of the Lord may be glorified and be seen in
their joy and those shall be ashamed."  This translation can be
understood if one sees here yet another reference to two

groups, those who join Israel and so experience joy and those who will be ashamed. This interpretation of these passages is consistent with the explicit reference to proselytes in 54:15 and 14:1.

Finally we observe *56:8*. MT " ... I will gather yet others to him besides those already gathered" may refer simply to dispersed people of Israel, although the context of vv.6f leaves open the possibility that reference is to "foreigners who join themselves to the Lord." The LXX begins v.8, "says the Lord." While a natural translation of נאם יהוה, this gives a closer link between v.7 and v.8, as does also the use of ὅτι to commence v.8b: "for my house shall be called a house of prayer for all nations, says the Lord who gathers the dispersed of Israel, for I will gather to him a congregation (συναγωγή)." (Cf. Seeligmann: 117)

2.    CALL TO THE "ISLANDS."

Linked closely with the thought of proselytes are the references to the "islands."

*41:1* and *45:16 LXX* both have the phrase, ἐγκαινίζεσθε πρός με νῆσοι "be renewed to me, O islands." In 41:1 it is possible to see in LXX an etymologizing of החדישו for MT (איים) החרישו (Ottley; Seeligmann: 117), and similarly in 45:16 where MT has (צירים) חרשי. The LXX contexts of both are significant. In 41:1f the "rulers" are to announce their matter for dispute, followed by God's calling forth of his "justice" (see pp. 106-107). In 45:14f Egyptians, Ethiopians and Sabeans are to be Israel's servants "because God is in you and they will say there is no God beside you, for you are God and we did not know, O God of Israel, Saviour." Then follows vv.16f: "all that are opposed to him (not in MT) shall be ashamed and shall be put to shame and shall go in shame. Be renewed to me, O islands. Israel is saved ... they shall not be ashamed ..." It seems most likely that the call is to be renewed now, i.e., join Israel, or be put to shame in the future (see p. 56).

An interesting feature of LXX is that when איים is translated with νῆσοι a positive relationship with God is usually involved: 24:15f; 41:1; 42:10, 12 (in 42:17 LXX those who trust in idols are to be ashamed); 49:1; 51:5; 60:9; and

66:19.  Instances where the אִיִּים stand in a negative relationship are either not translated or another word used: 40:15;
41:5; and 59:18.  The only exception is 42:4 ("on his name the
ἔθνη hope").  While in 60:9 and 66:19 the "islands" are to
serve Israel or to see a glorified Israel (their "hope" is a
restored Israel: 51:5), at the same time there is some evidence
of a call to a response now (24:15 LXX; 41:1 LXX; 45:16 LXX and
49:1).

3.    LIGHT, LAW AND THE PEOPLES.

We have already noted above several verses in MT which
refer to "teaching" and "light" going out from Zion to guide
the nations.  Here are noted some significant LXX verses.

*26:8f*:    MT: "In the path of מִשְׁפָּטֶיךָ, Yahweh, we wait for you...
            when מִשְׁפָּטֶיךָ are in the earth, the inhabitants of
            the earth learn צֶדֶק."

            LXX: "... for the way of the Lord is κρίσις; we have
            hoped ...; because your προστάγματα are a light
            upon the earth, learn δικαιοσύνη you who dwell on
            the earth."

This provides a contrast to *24:1-5*: God is going to lay waste
the whole world (οἰκουμένη) (vv.1-4), because "her inhabitants
... have transgressed the law and changed the προστάγματα, the
eternal covenant" (v.5).

In looking at the phrase, "light of nations" φῶς ἐθνῶν,
we observe first the significant difference in LXX of *60:3*:
"Kings shall walk by (MT: to) your light and nations by your
brightness."  A similar reference to "kings" and "nations" is
*51:4f LXX*: "Listen to me, listen, my people, and kings (MT
לְאֻמִּי; see p. 98), give ear to me; for νόμος will go forth from
me and my κρίσις as a light of nations."  It should be noted
that immediately preceding is *50:10f LXX*: "Who among you fears
the Lord?  Let him hear the voice of his servant.  You who walk
in darkness with no light, trust in the name of the Lord and
stand on God.  Behold, you all kindle a fire and feed a flame:
walk by the light of your fire and by the flame you have
kindled.  These things have happened to you because of me, you
will lie down in sorrow."  While MT is addressed to Israel, LXX
seems to be addressed to the nations, especially in view of the
last sentence.  Here are linked a call to "trust in the name of

the Lord," "light (of nations)," "law" and "judging." Then in
*51:7 LXX* Israel, who "knows κρίσις, in whose heart is my law,"
is not to fear the reproaches of others, and so Jerusalem is to
awake (v.9). Finally, in *42:1-9 LXX* "Jacob, my servant" (v.1)
is to bring κρίσις to the nations (vv.1b, 3, 4), and the
nations (ἔθνη/איים) will hope in his name (ὄνομα/תורה), he is
to be a "light of nations" (ἔθνη/גוים). The repeated use of
ἔθνη is significant.

4.    CONCLUSION.

It can be seen that, when compared with MT, LXX has a
stronger emphasis upon the going forth from the restored Zion
of "law" and "judging" as a "light" for kings and nations.
Because this is going to happen, Israel is called to be
faithful in her obedience of the covenant despite present
difficulties and others are called to become proselytes now or
else face punishment later. Such ideas appear explicitly in
several LXX passages, where MT allows, but does not explicitly
require, such meanings. The interpretation of "light" in terms
of "law" is quite evident.

NOTES

# CHAPTER I

/1/     Sections of this chapter, together with some
conclusions, have previously appeared in Olley, 1975.

/2/     Especially by Bowman. For the Sapir-Whorf hypothesis
see Carroll. A critical summary and discussion of this
hypothesis is given by Henle: 1-24.

/3/     See Sawyer, especially ch. III and references given
there. It should be noted that Sawyer himself has tended to
etymologize and neglects contrastive elements (see Wernberg-
Møller).

/4/     He quotes from C. F. Hockett, in H. Hoijer, ed.,
*Language in Culture* (Chicago, 1954): 122.

/5/     In J. Hermann and F. Baumgärtel, *Beiträge zur
Entstehungsgeschichte der Septuaginta* (Berlin, 1923). I have
been unable to see this work.

/6/     Cf. Seeligmann's comments on Isaiah (48), and Brock,
1972: 31-36. These characteristics may provide another
explanation of the few instances, mentioned by Gehman, 1954:
337-48, where ἅγιος seems to be understandable only if one
reverts to the MT.

/7/     A verbal remark reported by Kraft, 1971: 488-90.

/8/     Particular reference should be made to the summaries of
previous discussions and new contributions in Hill: 82-162;
Ziesler; and Stuhlmacher; also Dodd: 42-59; and Seeligmann: 98,
103f (Isaiah only).

Several references are given by these writers, out of which we
may highlight and to which add: Achtemeier, P. J.; Cranfield:
92-103; Cronbach (does not discuss LXX); Descamps and Cerfaux;
Fielder; Käsemann; Klein; Morris: 224-74; Reicke; Reumann;
Sanday and Headlam: 24-39; Schrenk, 1935; Snaith, 1944: 51-93,
159-166; and Watson.

/9/     Works consulted include: the monographs and articles of
Cazelles, Dünner, Fahlgren, Jepsen, Justesen, Lofthouse,
Reventlow (1971), and Schmid; dictionary and encyclopaedia
articles by E. R. Achtemeier, Horst, Schwarzchild, Skinner, and
Szubin and Jacobs; and sections in various theologies of the
OT, Eichrodt, 1961: 239-49; Jacob: 94-102; Knight: 245f;
Pedersen: 336-77; and von Rad, 1962: 370-83 (also 1966: 125-30,
243-66).

/10/    Beginning with E. Kautzsch, *Die Derivate des Stammes*
צדק *in alttestamentlichen Sprachgebrauch* (Tübingen, 1881), and
followed, with varying emphases, by Skinner, Quell, Snaith
(1944), Morris, Jacob, Knight, and Hill amongst others. I have
not seen a copy of Kautzch.

/11/    H. Cremer, *Die paulinische Rechtfertigungslehre* (Gütersloh, 1899; I have been unable to see a copy) and Fahlgren. This emphasis, with variations, is followed by Pedersen, Eichrodt (1961), von Rad, Cazelles, E. R. Achtemeier, Stuhlmacher, Ziesler, and Szubin.

/12/    Although Schmid (67, 133), following Jepsen (80, 87; cf. Jacob: 98; Knight: 245, n. 1), sees an original distinction between צדק and צדקה, both he and Jepsen recognize that this distinction is not always evident in Biblical Hebrew. In particular, Schmid refers to deutero-Isaiah as one place where the distinction is disappearing.

/13/    Orlinsky (1974: 169, n. 1) argues that "$y^e shu^c ah$ is best rendered 'triumph, victory, vindication.' Traditional 'salvation' has become quite misleading with its almost wholly post-biblical theological overtones and associations." We shall however continue to use "salvation," including here ideas of freedom, victory, deliverance, prosperity (cf. Sawyer).

CHAPTER II

/1/    The limitations of the English word are recognized. We refer to those passages where δικαιοσύνη and related words are discussed.

/2/    Rodgers, in a discussion on use before Plato, argues that δίκη "has nothing to do ... with a 'moral sense of right and wrong', and everything to do with power ... Being δίκαιος thus depends on knowing where one stands in society" (299). This view, while a corrective, is overstated. See especially Frisch.

/3/    ἀδικεῖν here clearly denotes both "harm" and "injustice" as βία is used elsewhere in the context.

/4/    So Shorey (Loeb), 1:415, note g: on the basis of the use of ὀνομάζειν.

/5/    ET by Treddennick. Cf. Xenophon, *Mem.* I.1.1. Schrenk suggests a meaning here for ἀδικεῖ of "have an unjust cause in the eyes of the law" (1933: 159). However the link with περιεργάζεται suggests rather "do wrong," including a connotation that such action is unjust.

/6/    Hill's comment is unwarranted: "The verb has the sense of 'to set right,' or possibly 'to recognise as right': but this meaning is unusual" (101, n. 2).

/7/    So Rackam (Loeb). Vlastos discusses possible English renderings of πλεονεξία, but despairs of finding an adequate rendering, concluding that "greed" or "covetousness" would seem best in most contexts, though neither are exactly right (71, n. 17).

/8/    For "corrective" justice τὸ διορθωτικόν is usually used, though τὸ ἐπανορθωτικὸν δίκαιον occurs in 1132a19, apparently without any difference in meaning.

/9/    For lexica and indices consulted as the basis of this investigation, see Bibliography. I have been unable to find other relevant uses of δικαιοῦν beyond those given below.

/10/    LSJ, "pronounce judgement," is inappropriate. Reference is to something granted or regarded as a right for valour shown in fighting with Pausanias.

/11/ Schrenk (1935: 211) "desire," and C. F. Smith (Loeb), "demand," weaken the argument of the Athenians.

/12/ In a footnote (I have been unable to see copies of the whole inscriptions).

/13/ 3rd Cent. B.C.: *PCair. Zen.* 59351.1; 59443.2; *PHib.* 34.1; 235.1; 236.1; *PMich. Zen.* 71.1; *PMerton* 4.9; 2nd Cent. B.C.: *PMerton* 5.3; *PTeb.* 23.3; 42.5; *et passim.*

/14/ *PCair. Zen.* 59236.21; 59351.5; 59443.16; *PMich. Zen.* 71.8.

/15/ *PCair. Zen.* 59199.10; 59228.2; 59362.11; 59368.11; *PTeb.* 5.213-16, 263; *PMerton* 5.30.

/16/ *PCair. Zen.* 59132.7; *PHib.* 91.2; *PTeb.* 105.41; 109.21; and the opposite, "ἄδικον ... οὐ δίκαιον," *POxy.* 717.10.

/17/ An impersonal object is rare. The only instance noted is in *OGI* I.90.27. This is in contrast with δικαιοῦν which is frequently used with an impersonal object.

/18/ Ziesler (47-48) is concerned only to find whether δικαιοῦν in secular Greek is declaratory ("declare righteous") or ethical ("make righteous") and so misses this dynamic sense. Schrenk [1935: 212; followed by Hill: 109; cf. BDF 148(4)] overstates in saying "outside the LXX and NT δικαιοῦν is never found in this sense (to secure someone justice) with a personal object," as this neglects Aristotle's passive use. Dodd is more cautious in recognizing a neutral sense, "to do a person justice" (50). His statement, "but the lexica cite no examples from Greek literature or papyri," would seem to need correcting in light of our discussion of Aristotle and Polybius.

CHAPTER III

/1/ Snaith (1944:87) is alone in translating "cause to triumph," without any moral significance.

/2/ This is also the only instance of הצדיק in Proverbs; there are no instances of δικαιδυν.

/3/ The question of the origin of the songs and their relationship to surrounding verses need not concern us. The isolation of 50:4-9 is generally adopted, although with a growing awareness of links with surrounding verses, cf. Westermann and North. Bonnard is alone in denying separate existence of the Songs (37-39). The LXX translator apparently saw no break between v.9 and v.10, using "you" in both verses.

/4/ Note that Westermann, ET: 255, has the translation "justify," where the German: 206, has "Als Gerechter wird mein Knecht vor vielen bestehen." There is no discrepancy in the commentary proper (ET: 267).

/5/ For various meanings of this, see Driver: 96-101.

/6/ Although the 2nd person probably comes from the verbal prefix, 'ח, suggested by his use of ψυχή, this does not explain the plural ὑμῶν for the suffix in נפשו.

/7/ It may be observed that TJ removes any idea of the

suffering of the Messiah and also regards צדיק as object, using the plural זכאין.

/8/   In general partial translation of MT and LXX will be given when it is not necessary to draw attention to the original, either because of unambiguous translation or because it is not needed for our discussion.

/9/   So North, 1964; Westermann; Bonnard; and Schoors: 223. *RSV* has simply "they," interpreted by Muilenburg as being the witnesses who "will confirm what the gods have had to declare." Fohrer is similar, while *NEB* makes the second half antithetical to the first, using "or."

/10/   Schoors (223), in emending MT הוציא to הוציאו, quotes LXX for support. However, ἐξήγαγον follows on without interruption from a succession of three verbs, all in 1st person. Orlinsky in a private communication has suggested a possible LXX *Vorlage* for the first word of v.8: ואוציא (including dittography of ו at the end of v.7). While one cannot rule out this possibility, instances elsewhere in Isaiah of changes in person seem to make it possible that here the translator is using MT. Of course, this does not affect our understanding of LXX.

/11/   For a critical discussion of word-play, see Payne (1967). He does not include these verses.

/12/   He goes on to quote from 4 Ezra 12:7 where "to find grace," "to be justified" and "to be heard in prayer" are used as synonyms: "The idea of a trial in court has been abandoned." It must be countered that v.9 continues, "for thou hast judged me worthy," and 6:32 and 10:39 refer to Ezra's righteous conduct.

/13/   In 57:16 ἐκδικεῖν is no doubt used because of the inappropriateness in the context of κρίνειν (with classical Greek sense). A similar reason explains the use of ἀντίδικος in 41:11.

CHAPTER IV

/1/   In 49:13a, S* and most of L and C add a phrase from Ps 71 (72):3, καὶ οἱ βουνοὶ δικαιοσύνην.

/2/   See Appendix III for a brief discussion of ἔλεος and ἐλεημοσύνη in non-Jewish Greek and the LXX.

/3/   The only other occurrences of a noun in construct followed by צדק are 41:10 and 58:2 where δίκαιος is used. There is the similar use of חסד in 57:1, also δίκαιος. עיר in the construct is generally translated with the absolute noun rendered by an adjective: 26:1 (עז/ὀχυρά); 48:2 and 52:1 (קדש/ἁγία); and 61:4 (חרב/ἔρημος). The only exception is 64:9(10): ערי קדשך/πόλις τοῦ ἁγίου σου where LXX gives a different interpretation.

/4/   This phrase is not in B, but is in the other major uncials and cursives. The verb is omitted in S* and V. See Ziegler, 1939.

/5/   Also translated ἐλπίς in 24:16; elsewhere ὁ ἔνδοξος (23:9), βουλή (4:2), or not rendered (13:19; 28:1).

/6/   Understood as from קוה? In 34:11 σπαρτίον γεωμετρίας is
used, so the other sense is known to the translator.

/7/   The similar MT of v.17b is rendered πεποιθότες; cf.
πεποιθόσιν for חסות in 30:3.

/8/   In the similar expression in v.15, חזה = συνθήκας.

/9/   Vv.1, 3: μισθωτοί "hirelings" for MT שֹׁכְרֵי "drunkards."
Perhaps LXX read as שֹׂכְרֵי; cf. the reverse in 7:20.

/10/   There is no textual support for Seeligmann's contention
(36) that this word has come into LXX from a different source
used in 1 Peter 2:6.

/11/   This reflects the double use of πικρία in v.21, where
again LXX seems to shift the MT emphasis.

/12/   Misprinted as "*mishpaṭ*" in Scullion, 1971.

/13/   Mauchline observes that "in a liturgical lament the
priest would offer an oracle of assurance or a sign (cf.
Ps 86:17) of God's favour."

/14/   Ottley: 1:43f, suggests that the LXX translators often
used a "representation" method, using the aorist for the Hebrew
perfect and the future for the imperfect "when the context did
not absolutely forbid." In this chapter, the variety shows
that this method was not adopted here.

/15/   The translator seems to use various words for wrongdoing
almost interchangeably. In this chapter alone there are: פשע
(noun): ἀνομία (v.12, twice), ἀσεβεία (v.20); (verb): ἀσεβεῖν
(v.13); און: ἀνομία (vv.4, 6), ἄφρων (!) (v.7); שקר: ἀνομία
(v.3), ἄδικα (v.13); עון: ἀμάρτημα (v.2), ἀδίκημα (v.12); עולה:
ἀδικία (v.3); רשע: ἄδικος (v.13); חטא: ἀμαρτία (vv.2, 12).
There appears to be a decided preference for ἀνομία (5x) and
ἀδικ-words (4x). See further discussion in Chapter V.

/16/   Added in most of the Alexandrian and Lucianic texts, but
otherwise implied.

/17/   Reading ἕνεκεν Σιων as in majority of texts (MT לֹו).
The reading ἐκ Σ' (cf. Rom 11:26) which Duhm regards as
original is only known in a few late texts and is inappropriate
in this context.

/18/   Probably reading וישיב for ולשבי.

/19/   Note the (surely coincidental) parallel between the
three verbs in Polybius III. 31.9, ἐλεήσων, συνοργιούμενος,
δικαιώσων, and the cognate nouns in vv.16, 17, 19, ἐλεημοσύνη,
δικαιοσύνη, ὀργή. It thus seems not unnatural in Greek thought
for these three ideas to be linked.

/20/   *NEB* is alone in emending to מָלְאָ and translating: "if you
(i.e., Israel) fill Zion with justice and righteousness, ..."
This is contextually unwarranted as these 2 verses are an
affirmation of praise, not an admonition.

/21/   He compares Ps 4:6; 17:1; and Isa 51:1, and suggests
that צדק has become a hypostasis of Yahweh.

/22/   Piel 4 times (3 in chaps. 60-66), Hithp. 5 (2), פָּאַר 3
(2), תִּפְאָרָה and תִּפְאֶרֶת 18 (7).

/23/   So Rahlfs. Ziegler's δικαίως has the support of only

158

one late Ms. (544).

/24/ פעלה as something due as compensation (cf. KB, "Verdienst") is also used in 40:10; 49:4; and 62:11; another vocabulary link between chaps. 40-55 and 56-66. The negative sense, recompense for evil done, is in 65:7.

/25/ μόχθος is used for פעלה only here; elsewhere, 40:10; 62:11; 65:7: ἔργον, and 49:4: πόνος.

/26/ V.7a MT has no equivalent in LXX, although v.7b is a close parallel.

/27/ For the same parallelism elsewhere they use "Heil" for (ה)צדק, and "Hilfe, Rettung, Heil" for ישע (45:8; 46:13; 51:5-8; 56:1).

/28/ Certainty is conveyed by the familiar imagery of seed springing forth into flower: 42:9; 43:19; 44:4; 45:8; 55:10f; 58:11; 60:21f.

/29/ In 45:8, MT (ה)צדק//ישע, LXX δικαιοσύνη//ἔλεος, appears also to refer to God's judgement.

/30/ The translator's rendering of תהלה is quite varied.

/31/ ἀνταπόδοσις is used with enemies as object in 59:18 and with Israel as object in 35:4 and 63:7.

/32/ The verb is used in v.9 (MT גאל). Cf. Payne, 1967: 227.

/33/ There is no need of emendation. In Ugaritic an enclitic *mem* is used to balance a parallel pronominal suffix. Dahood, 1970: 408, gives examples in Psalms. See also Scullion, 1972: 123, and references given there.

/34/ Reading v.9a with v.8 as do LXX and most modern translators (except *RSV* and McKenzie).

/35/ ἀνταποδίδωσι (MT: גמל, "render"). The noun גמול is rendered by ἀνταποδο-words in 35:4 and 59:18, but not 3:11.

/36/ Against Hill: 106, n. 2: "The translation of חסד by δικαιοσύνη may be evidence of the growing legalism of the period in which the LXX translation was made"; similarly, Dodd: 65. Hanhart, 1970, while commending Hill's statement of methodology, criticizes him at this point and elsewhere for using an assumed background to elucidate the text rather than vice versa.

/37/ צדקות, δικαιοσύνη (33:5; 45:24; 64:5); גבורת, ἰσχύς (63:15); משפטים, κρίσις (26:8; 58:2; but προστάγματα in 26:9); and in this verse, חסדים, ἔλεος and δικαιοσυνη, and רחמים, ἔλεος.

/38/ Ottley's "he" is meaningless. Elsewhere in these verses God is spoken of in 2nd person. LXX's 3rd person seems deliberate.

/39/ ἀκάθαρτοι may have a moral connotation (LSJ; BAG).

/40/ Same word as in Lev 20:18, i.e., same connotation as MT.

/41/ δία with accusative. MT has ביד "into the hand of," although Dahood, 1963, suggests "because of," followed by Westermann and Scullion, 1972.

/42/ Hommel discusses the relationship between these words in

Greek and other languages.

/43/ In 2 (4) Kg 20:19 MT has both שלום and אמת, but all LXX texts have only εἰρήνη, except B which does not include v.19b and Lucianic texts which add δικαιοσύνη, perhaps on the basis of Isaiah.

/44/ With most modern exegetes (not *RSV* or Auvray), we read עָרְץ "tyrants" for עָרֶץ "earth" (2nd occurrence).

/45/ Goshen-Gottstein (1965) comments that the omission of במישור is a "change based on the translator's desire to achieve a more perfect parallelism with exegetical change in beginning of verse." In 1975 edn, he says simply "condensed rendering."

/46/ Several Greek Mss have ἐνδόξους. Goshen-Gottstein (1965, 1975) compares with Targum variants חשיכי/חשיבי ("poor/ notable"), and (1975) also compares with 26:15 LXX.

/47/ While δόξα can mean "mere opinion, appearance" (LSJ), similar to MT, there may be a connotation of "fame, honour," especially as it is antithetical to the "humble."

/48/ Cf. use of κρῖναι ... κρίσιν in Plato, *R.* II. 360e, "make a decision," although not a forensic situation.

/49/ ἐλέγχειν usually has a negative sense, "disgrace, convince, refute," but may be neutral, "examine, question," as is the case here (cf. LSJ).

/50/ λαλιά has two possible connotations, "speaking" (including "gossip, common talk") and "manner of speaking" (cf. LSJ, BAG). Even if the sense is "gossip," this would still be to the detriment of the lowly person.

/51/ Westermann's dislocations make v.1a refer to the nations and v.7a to Israel, followed by vv.1b-2, but this has no other warrant than an assumed exegesis.

/52/ In 42:4, however, νόμῳ (so Ziegler) occurs in no Greek codices, instead ὀνόματι (so Rahlfs) occurs (= Matt 12:21).

/53/ Q^a has מיגיך ומעניך. Ziegler, 1959: 42f, regards LXX and Q^a as original. Cf. *BHS*.

/54/ δικαιοσυνη would have suggested the meaning, "you who know (my) justice." We have noted elsewhere the translator's tendency to avoid using the same word in reference to both God and man in the same context. The same tendency also gives a reason for the use of τὸ δίκαιον rather than δικαιοσύνη in v.1.

/55/ It is possible that the translator inserted "Jerusalem" unthinkingly on the basis of the similar v.17, 52:1 and 60:1. But it is more likely that it is deliberate as he continues to apply vv.9-11a to Jerusalem.

/56/ Omitted in some codices, conforming to MT.

/57/ In the similar 11:4 'ב, not 'ל, is used. It is significant that although Dahood, 1970, suggests many possible meanings of prepositions, he gives no instance of ל meaning "with" or "in," and no instance of ל and ב being interchanged.

/58/ ὁ Κάρμηλος as in 35:2; ὁ Κερμελ in v.15 and 29:17. LXX has translated כרמל as a common noun in 10:18; 16:10 and 37:24.

/59/ It is unlikely that LXX had a different Vorlage, such as

160

Q^a, as there is no καί, except in the single ms. 309. In several places in Isaiah LXX has different punctuation and syntax.

/60/ The imperative is used to express a promise (so North, 1964; GKC sect. 110c), especially of blessing (Schoors: 143).

/61/ MT of v.15 has certain difficulties, although most commentators agree with a sense something like *RSV*.

/62/ Added in B and some mss., but omitted in most major texts. See Ziegler.

/63/ Ziegler follows a small part of the Lucianic tradition, while Seeligmann (10) follows "only two mediaeval codices, representing a Lucianic text" (Ziegler's 147, 233).

/64/ Ziegler: ἐν λύπῃ "in grief"; so also Seeligmann.

/65/ In 1 instance (45:8) ἔλεος is used for יַשׁע (out of 55 occurrences of יַשׁע) and in 1 instance (56:1) for צֶדֶק (out of 61 occurrences of צֶדֶק)!

CHAPTER V

/1/ For further details, see Hatch and Redpath. Instances listed there have been checked.

/2/ In the Pentateuch ἀσεβής is used only for רָשָׁע, and that for 11 of the 14 occurrences of רָשָׁע.

APPENDIX III

/1/ Callimachus, *Del*. 152. Bickerman quotes another 3rd century B.C. use in *PCair. Zen*. 59495 (183, note 41).

/2/ Deut 6:25; 24:13. It is of note that of the 16 occurrences of the nouns (ה)צדק in the Pentateuch, it is only these two verses in which δικαιοσύνη with the usual Greek connotation would give an erroneous meaning. The LXX sense is quite unambiguous: "If you obey God's commandments, he will treat you with ἐλεημοσύνη" (cf. 7:9f).

/3/ Only in 23 (24):5 is δικαιοσύνη inappropriate: "he who has clean hands ... will receive ἐλεημοσύνη from God."

APPENDIX IV

/1/ He similarly translates the Targum, טבות דויד, "les bienfaits (opérés par) David."

/2/ *SIG* 1184:4, 10, 12; 1199:5f; 1179:16; also Moulton and Milligan: 460.

/3/ He also contends that LXX misread MT חֲסָדָי as חֲסִידָי, especially as elsewhere the plural of חסד is τὰ ἐλέη, in 2 Chr 6:42 (of David), Ps 17:7; 107:43; Lam 3:23; or ἔλεος as in Isa 63:7; Ps 89:2; 106:7. This is unnecessary when one recognizes the different translators, and also the different subject.

/4/ The references given by BAG to support this meaning of τὰ ὅσια, in contrast to τὰ δίκαια, including Plato, *Plt*. 301d, and Xenophon, *HG* IV.1:33, actually refer to laws relating to one's religious duties.

/5/    F. Asensio, *Misericordia et Veritas* (Rome: Gregorian University, 1949), as summarized in Larue, (10-14) has in fact started from this early understanding to argue that the meaning "mercy-feeling" and "mercy-work" is also dominant in Hebrew.

# ABBREVIATIONS

| | |
|---|---|
| ATD | Das Alte Testament Deutsch. |
| BAG | Arndt, W. F. and Gingrich, F. W., *A Greek-English Lexicon of the New Testament* (ET and adaptation of Bauer, W., *Griechisch - Deutsches Wörterbuch*) |
| BAT | Die Botschaft des Alten Testaments. |
| BDB | Brown, F., Driver, S. R., and Briggs, C. A., *Hebrew and English Lexicon of the Old Testament* |
| BDF | Blass, F. and Debrunner, A., *A Greek Grammar of the New Testament*, ET by Funk, R. W. |
| BHK | *Biblia Hebraica*, ed. Kittel, R., 7th ed. |
| BHS | *Biblia Hebraica Stuttgartensia*, ed. Elliger, K. and Rudolph, W. |
| Bib | *Biblica* |
| BIOSCS | *Bulletin of the International Organization for Septuagint and Cognate Studies* |
| BZAW | Beihefte zur *Zeitschrift für die alttestamentliche Wissenschaft* |
| CBQ | *Catholic Biblical Quarterly* |
| DBSup | Pirot, L. and Robert, A., ed., *Supplément* to *Dictionnaire de la Bible*. Paris: Letouzey & Ané, 1928- . |
| ed. | editor(s), edited by; edition |
| EncJud | *Encyclopaedia Judaica*, 16 vols. Jerusalem: Keter, 1972. |
| ET | English translation |
| EvQ | *Evangelical Quarterly* |
| ExpT | *Expository Times* |
| f, ff | following page(s), verse(s), etc. |
| GKC | Kautzsch, E., ed., *Gesenius' Hebrew Grammar*, 2nd English ed. by Cowley, A. E. |
| HUCA | *Hebrew Union College Annual* |
| IB | Buttrick, G. A., ed., *The Interpreter's Bible*, 12 vols. New York & Nashville: Abingdon, 1956. |
| ICC | International Critical Commentary |
| IDB | Buttrick, G. A., ed., *The Interpreter's Dictionary of the Bible*, 4 vols. New York & Nashville: Abingdon, 1962. |
| IDBSup | Crim, K. ed., *Supplementary Volume to IDB*. New York & Nashville: Abingdon, 1976. |

| | |
|---|---|
| *Int* | *Interpretation* |
| *JB* | *The Jerusalem Bible* |
| *JBL* | *Journal of Biblical Literature* |
| *JSJ* | *Journal for the Study of Judaism* |
| *JSS* | *Journal of Semitic Studies* |
| *JTS* | *Journal of Theological Studies* |
| KB | Koehler, L. and Baumgartner, W., *Lexicon in Veteris Testamenti Libros* |
| Loeb | Loeb Classical Library series |
| LSJ, *Sup* | Liddell, H. G. and Scott, R., *A Greek-English Lexicon*, revd. Jones, H. S., (1940); *Supplement* Barber, E. A., ed. (1968). |
| LXX | The Septuagint Greek Version of the OT (following the editions of Rahlfs and Ziegler, specifying further by name of editor where their editions differ). |
| MT | Massoretic Text, as given by *BHK* and *BHS*. |
| *NEB* | *New English Bible*, together with Brockington, L. H., ed., *The Hebrew Text of the OT: The Readings adopted by the Translators of the New English Bible*. Oxford University and Cambridge University, 1973. |
| NT | New Testament |
| *NTS* | *New Testament Studies* |
| OT | Old Testament |
| *OTS* | *Oudtestamentische Studiën* |
| $Q^a$ | (= 1QIsa$^a$) Burrows, M., ed., *The Dead Sea Scrolls of St. Mark's Monastery, Vol. I*. New Haven: American Schools of Oriental Research, 1950. Also *Scrolls from Qumran Cave I* (from photographs by J. C. Trever). Jerusalem: The Albright Institute of Archaeological Research, and The Shrine of the Book, 1972. |
| $Q^b$ | (= 1QIsa$^b$) Sukenik, E. L., *The Dead Sea Scrolls of the Hebrew University*. Jerusalem: Magnes, 1955. |
| *RB* | *Revue Biblique* |
| *RGG* | *Die Religion in Geschichte und Gegenwart*, 3rd ed., Galling, K., *et al.*, ed., 7 vols. Tübingen: Mohr, 1957-65. |
| *RSV* | *Revised Standard Version* |
| SBT | Studies in Biblical Theology |
| *TDNT, TWNT* | *Theological Dictionary of the New Testament* (Grand Rapids: Eerdmans, 1964-74), ET of *Theologisches Wörterbuch zum Neuen Testamentum*, Kittel, G., and Friedrich, G., ed., 9 vols. (Stuttgart: Kohlhammer, 1932-73). In the bibliography dates are for *TWNT*. |

| | |
|---|---|
| *TR* | *Theologische Rundschau* |
| TJ | Targum Jonathan of Isaiah, as in Sperber, A., *The Bible in Aramaic*, Vol. III |
| *UF* | *Ugarit-Forschungen* |
| *VT* | *Vetus Testamentum* |
| *VT Sup* | *Vetus Testamentum Supplements* |

Abbreviations for Greek material (classical authors, papyri, inscriptions) follow those listed in LSJ and *Sup*.

Throughout citations follow the "social sciences format" similar to that described in *Journal of the American Academy of Religion* 45 (1977): 139-40. For commentaries, the absence of page numbers means that reference is to the section where the relevant verse or passage is discussed.

BIBLIOGRAPHY

I.   BIBLICAL MATERIAL

A.   *Texts*

GOSHEN-GOTTSTEIN, M. H.
1965          ed., *The Book of Isaiah: Sample Edition with
              Introduction*. Jerusalem: Magnes. Text of chaps.
              2, 5, 11 and 51.
1975          ed., *The Hebrew University Bible: The Book of
              Isaiah, Parts One and Two*. Jerusalem: Magnes.
              Text of 1:1 - 22:10.

KITTEL, R.
1937          ed., *Biblia Hebraica*, 7th ed. revised by ALT, A.
              and EISSFELDT, O. Stuttgart: Württembergische
              Bibelanstalt.

RAHLFS, A.
1935          ed., *Septuaginta*, 2 vols. Stuttgart: Württem-
              bergische Bibelanstalt.

SPERBER, A.
1962          ed., *The Bible in Aramaic, Vol. III: Targum
              Jonathan, Latter Prophets*. Leiden: Brill.

THOMAS, D. W.
1968a         ed., *Liber Jesaiae*, Fasc. 7 of *Biblia Hebraica
              Stuttgartensia*, ed. ELLIGER, K. and RUDOLPH, W.
              Stuttgart: Württembergische Bibelanstalt.

ZIEGLER, J.
1939          ed., *Isaias. Septuaginta: Vetus Testamentum
              Graecum Auctoritate Societatis Litterarum
              Gottingensis editum, vol. xiv*. Göttingen:
              Vandenhoeck & Ruprecht.

B.   *Lexica, Concordances and Grammars**

ARNDT, W. F. and GINGRICH, F. W.
1957          *A Greek-English Lexicon of the New Testament and
              Other Early Christian Literature*, ET and
              adaptation of BAUER, W., *Griechisch - Deutsches
              Wörterbuch zu den Schriften des Neuen Testaments
              und der übrigen urchristlichen Literatur*, 4th
              ed., 1952. Chicago: University of Chicago.

---

* I have been unable to see SCHLEUSNER, J. F., *Novus Thesaurus
philologico-criticus sive lexicon in LXX et reliquos
interpretes graecos ac scriptores apocryphos Veteris
Testamenti*, 1820-21.

168

BLASS, F. and DEBRUNNER, A.
1961        *A Greek Grammar of the New Testament and Other
            Early Christian Literature*, ET and revision by
            FUNK, R. W. Chicago: University of Chicago.

BROWN, F., DRIVER, S. R. and BRIGGS, C. A.
1906        *Hebrew and English Lexicon of the Old Testament.*
            Oxford: Clarendon.

HATCH, E. and REDPATH, H. A.
1897, 1906  *A Concordance to the Septuagint and the Other
            Greek Versions of the Old Testament*, 2 vols. with
            *Supplement.* Oxford: Clarendon. Reprinted Graz:
            Akademische Druck-U., 1954.

JASTROW, M.
1903        *A Dictionary of the Targumim, the Talmud Babli
            and Yerushalmi and the Midrashic Literature.*
            Reprinted New York: Judaica, 1971.

KAUTZSCH, E.
1910        ed., *Gesenius' Hebrew Grammar*, 2nd English ed. by
            COWLEY, A. E. Oxford: Clarendon.

KOEHLER, L. and BAUMGARTNER, W.
1958        *Lexicon in Veteris Testamenti Libros* with
            *Supplementum.* Leiden: Brill.

LISOWSKY, G.
1958        *Konkordanz zum Hebräischen Alten Testament.*
            Stuttgart: Württembergische Bibelanstalt.

MANDELKERN, S.
1967        *Veteris Testamenti Concordantiae Hebraicae atque
            Chaldaicae.* Tel Aviv: Schocken.

II.   CLASSICAL AND HELLENISTIC GREEK

A.    *Texts*

Unless otherwise stated all texts are as edited and translated
in the appropriate volumes of the *Loeb Classical Library*,
London: Heinemann; and Cambridge, Mass.: Harvard University,
1912- .

Published volumes of papyri and inscriptions.

B.    *Lexica and Indices*

AST, D. F.
1835        *Lexicon Platonicum.* Leipzig: Libraria
            Weidmanniana.

BÉTANT, E.-A.
1843        *Lexicon Thucydideum.* Reprinted Hildersheim:
            Olms, 1961.

BONITZ, H.
1870        *Index Aristotelicus.* Reprinted Graz: Akademische
            Druck-U., 1955.

CHANTRAINE, P.
1968, 1970  *Dictionnaire Étymologique de la Langue Grecque.
            Vol. I, A-D; Vol. II, E-K.* Paris: Klincksieck.

DES PLACES, E.
1964        *Platon: Oeuvres Complètes, Tome XIV: Lexique de*
            *la langue philosophique et religieuse de Platon.*
            Paris: Société d'Édition "Les Belles Lettres."

ELLENDT, F.
1872        *Lexicon Sophocleum.* Reprinted Hildesheim: Olms,
            1958.

ITALIE, G.
1955        *Index Aeschyleus.* Leiden: Brill.

LIDDELL, H. G. and SCOTT, R.
1940        *A Greek-English Lexicon,* 9th ed. revised by
            JONES, H. S. Oxford: Clarendon, reprinted 1968,
            together with
1968        *Supplement,* ed. BARBER, E. A.

MOULTON, J. H. and MILLIGAN, G.
1930        *The Vocabulary of the Greek Testament.* London:
            Hodder & Stoughton.

POWELL, J. E.
1938        *A Lexicon of Herodotus.* Cambridge: Cambridge
            University.

PREISIGKE, F.
1925-31     *Wörterbuch der griechischen Papyrusurkunden,* 3
            vols., ed. KIESSLING, E. Berlin: Selbverlag der
            Erben.

STURTZ, F. W.
1801        *Lexicon Xenophonteum,* 4 vols. Reprinted
            Hildersheim: Olms, 1964.

TODD, O. J.
1932        *Index Aristophanes.* Cambridge, Mass.: Harvard
            University.

WYTTENBACH, D.
1830        *Lexicon Plutarcheum.* Reprinted Hildersheim:
            Olms, 1962.

III.   OTHER WORKS

ACHTEMEIER, E. R.
1962        "Righteousness in the OT," *IDB* 4: 80-85.

ACHTEMEIER, P. J.
1962        "Righteousness in the NT," *IDB* 4: 91-99.

AUVRAY, P.
1972        *Isaïe 1-39.* Sources Biblique. Paris: Gabalda.

BARR, J.
1961        *The Semantics of Biblical Language.* London:
            Oxford University.
1968a       *Comparative Philology and the Text of the Old*
            *Testament.* London: Oxford University.
1968b       "Common Sense and Biblical Language," *Bib* 49:
            377-87 (review of Hill).
1969        *Biblical Words for Time.* SBT 33. Revision of
            1962 ed., with "Postscript and Retroscript."
            London: S.C.M.
1972        "Semantics and Biblical Theology - a contribution

to the discussion," *VTSup* 22: 11-19.

BAUER, W.
1957    "An Introduction to the Lexicon of the Greek New Testament," BAG: ix-xxv.

BERKOVITZ, E.
1969    "The Biblical Meaning of Justice," *Judaism* 18: 188-209.

BERTRAMM, G.
1954    "παιδεύω," *TDNT* 5: 596-625.

BEUKEN, W. A. M.
1972    "Mišpāṭ: The First Servant Song and its Context," *VT* 22: 1-30.

BICKERMAN, E.
1976    *Studies in Jewish and Christian History, Part One*. Leiden: Brill. Includes (167-200) reprint with revisions of "The Septuagint as Translation," *Proceedings of the American Academy for Jewish Research* 28 (1959): 1-39.

BLANK, S. H.
1952    "'And all our virtues' - an interpretation of Isaiah 64 4b-5a," *JBL* 71: 149-54.

BLAUW, J.
1962    *The Missionary Nature of the Church*. New York: McGraw-Hill.

BONNARD, P.-E.
1972    *Le Seconde Isaïe, son disciple et leurs éditeurs: Isaïe 40-66*. Etudes Bibliques. Paris: Gabalda.

BOWMAN, Th.
1960    *Hebrew Thought compared with Greek*. London: S.C.M.

BROCK, S. P.
1969    "The Rhenomenon of Biblical Translation in Antiquity," *Alta: the University of Birmingham Review* 2/8, reprinted in Jellicoe, 1974: 541-71.
1972    "The Phenomenon of the Septuagint," in *The Witness of Tradition (OTS* 12): 11-36. Leiden: Brill.
1973    , with FRITSCH, C. T. and JELLICOE, S., *A Classified Bibliography of the Septuagint*. Leiden: Brill. Literature to 1969.

BROCKINGTON, L. H.
1951    "The Greek Translator of Isaiah and his Interest in δόξα," *VT* 1: 23-32.

BROWN, J. P.
1971    "Peace Symbolism in Ancient Military Vocabulary," *VT* 21: 1-23.

BUCHSEL, F.
1938    "κρίνω," *TDNT* 3: 921-54.

BULTMANN, R.
1935    "ἔλεος," *TDNT* 2: 477-87.

CAIRD, G. B.
1968        "Towards a Lexicon of the Septuagint. I," *JTS*
            n. s. 19: 453-75.
1969        "Towards a Lexicon of the Septuagint. II," *JTS*
            n. s. 20: 21-40.

CARROLL, J. B.
1956        ed., *Language, Thought and Reality: Selected
            Writings of Benjamin Lee Whorf*. Cambridge:
            M.I.T.

CAZELLES, H.
1951        "A propos de quelques textes difficiles relatifs
            à la justice de Dieu dans l'Ancien Testament," *RB*
            58: 169-88.

COLWELL, E. C.
1962        "Greek Language," *IDB* 2: 479-87.

CRANFIELD, C. E. B.
1975        *A Critical and Exegetical Commentary on the
            Epistle to the Romans*. ICC. Edinburgh: Clark.

CRONBACH, A.
1962        "Righteousness in Jewish Literature, 200 BC -
            AD 100," *IDB* 4: 85-91.

DAHOOD, M.
1963        "Hebrew-Ugaritic Lexicography," *Bib* 44: 289-303.
1966, 1968, 1970  *Psalms I (1-50), II (51-100), III (101-
            150)*. Anchor Bible. Garden City: Doubleday.
1971        "Phoenician Elements in Isaiah 52:13 - 53:12," in
            GOEDICKE, H., ed., *Near Eastern Studies in Honour
            of William Foxwell Albright*: 63-73. Baltimore
            and London: John Hopkins.

DANIEL, S.
1966        *Recherches sur le vocabulaire du culte dans la
            Septante*. Paris: Klincksieck.

DE BOER, P. A. H.
1956        *Second Isaiah's Message (OTS* 11). Leiden: Brill.

DEISSMANN, A.
1927        *Light from the Ancient East*, rev. ed., ET of
            *Licht vom Osten*, 4th ed. London: Hodder &
            Stoughton.

DEIST, F.
1973        "Jes 11:3a: Eine Glosse?" *ZAW* 85: 351-55.

DEMOS, R.
1972        "A Fallacy in Plato's *Republic*?" in Vlastos:
            52-56.

DESCAMPS, A. and CERFAUX, L.
1949        "Justice et Justification," *DBSup* 4: 1417-60
            (OT), 1460-510 (NT).

DEUTSCH, R. R.
1969        *Die Hiskiaerzählungen*. Dissertation, Basel.
            Basel: Basileia.

DODD, C. H.
1935        *The Bible and the Greeks*. London: Hodder &
            Stoughton.

DODDS, E. R.
1959        *Plato: Gorgias - a revised text with introduction
            and commentary*. Oxford: Clarendon.

DRIVER, G. R.
1968        "Isaiah 52:13-53:12: the Servant of the Lord," in
            BLACK, M. and FOHRER, G. ed., *In Memoriam Paul
            Kahle* (BZAW 103): 90-105. Berlin: Töpelmann.

DUHM, B.
1968        *Das Buch Jesaia*. 5th ed., based on 4th ed.
            Göttingen: Vandenhoeck & Ruprecht.

DÜNNER, A.
1963        *Die Gerechtigkeit nach dem Alten Testament*.
            Bonn: Bouvier.

DUPONT, J.
1961        "τὰ ὅσια Δαυιδ τὰ πιστά (Ac 13:34 = Is 55:3)," *RB*
            68: 91-114; reprinted in Dupont, J., *Etudes sur
            les Actes des Apôtres*: 337-59. Paris: Cerf,
            1967.

EICHRODT, W.
1960        *Der Heilige in Israel: Jesaja 1-12*. BAT 17/1.
            Stuttgart: Calwer.
1961        *Theology of the OT*, Vol. I. London: S.C.M.
1967        *Der Herr der Geschichte: Jesaja 13-23, 28-39*.
            BAT 17/2. Stuttgart: Calwer.

EISSFELDT, O.
1965        *The Old Testament: An Introduction*. Oxford:
            Blackwell.

FAHLGREN, K. Hj.
1932        *$ṣ^e dākā$, nahestende und entgegengesetzte Begriffe
            im Alten Testament*. Uppsala: Almqvist &
            Wiksells.

FALK, Z. W.
1960        "Hebrew Legal Terms," *JSS* 5: 350-54.

FIELDER, M. J.
1970        "Δικαιοσύνη in der diaspora-jüdischen und
            intertestamentarischen Literatur," *JSJ* 1: 120-43.

FOERSTER, W.
1964        "σέβομαι," *TDNT* 7: 168-96.

FOHRER, G.
1960-64     *Das Buch Jesaja*, 3 vols. Zürcher Bibelkom-
            mentare. Zürich and Stuttgart: Zwingli.

FRAENKEL, E.
1950        *Aeschylus: Agamemnon, edited with commentary*, 3
            vols. Oxford: Clarendon.

FRISCH, H.
1949        *Might and Right in Antiquity*. Copenhagen:
            Gyldendalske.

FRITSCH, C. T.
1971        "A Theology of the Septuagint," *Proceedings of
            the 27th International Congress of Orientalists,
            1967*: 138-39. Wiesbaden: Harrassowitz.

1972a       "The International Organization for Septuagint
            and Cognate Studies," *JSJ* 3: 1-6.
1972b       "Studies in the Theology of the Greek Psalter,"
            *BIOSCS* 5: 7.
1973        See Brock, 1973.

GEHMAN, H. S.
1951        "The Hebraic Character of LXX Greek," *VT* 1:
            81-90.
1953        "Hebraisms of the Old Greek Version of Genesis,"
            *VT* 3: 141-48.
1954        "Ἅγιος in the Septuagint and its relation to the
            Hebrew Original," *VT* 4: 337-48.
1966        "Adventures in Septuagint Lexicography," *Textus*
            5: 125-32 (on 1 Samuel and Job).
1972        "Ἐπισκέπομαι, ἐπίσκεψις, ἐπίσκοπος and ἐπισκοπή
            in the Septuagint in relation to פקד and other
            Hebrew roots — a case of semantic development
            similar to that of Hebrew," *VT* 22: 197-207.

GELSTON, A.
1971        "Some Notes on Second Isaiah," *VT* 21: 517-27.

GLUECK, N.
1967        *Ḥesed in the Bible*, ET, with Introduction by G.
            A. Larue, of *Das Wort Ḥesed im alttestament-
            lichen Sprachgebrauche* (1927).  Cincinnati:
            Hebrew Union College.

GOODING, D. W.
1963        "Aristeas and Septuagint Origins: a review of
            recent studies," *VT* 13: 357-79.

GOMME, A. W., ANDREWES, A. and DOVER, K. J.
1970        *A Historical Commentary on Thucydides*.  Oxford:
            Clarendon.

GOSHEN-GOTTSTEIN, M. H.
1963        "Theory and Practice of Textual Criticism: the
            Text-Critical Use of the Septuagint," *Textus* 3:
            130-158.

GRAY, G. B.
1910        "The Greek Version of Isaiah: is it the work of a
            Single Translator?" *JTS* 12: 286-93.
1912        *A Critical and Exegetical Commentary on the Book
            of Isaiah, Vol. I, chap. I-XXVII*.  ICC.
            Edinburgh: Clark.

HANHART, R.
1962        "Fragen um die Entstehung der LXX," *VT* 12:
            139-62.
1970        Review of Hill, *Gnomon* 43: 764-68.

HARDIE, W. F. R.
1968        *Aristotle's Ethical Theory*.  Oxford: Clarendon.

HARVEY, J.
1962        "Le 'rîb-Pattern' réquisitoire prophetique sur la
            rupture de l'alliance," *Bib* 43: 172-96.

HAVELOCK, E. A.
1969        "DIKAIOSUNE. An Essay in Greek intellectual
            history," *Phoenix* 23: 49-70.

174

HENLE, R.
1965            ed., *Language, Thought and Culture*. Ann Arbor:
               University of Michigan.

HILL, D.
1967            *Greek Words and Hebrew Meanings: Studies in the
               Semantics of Soteriological Terms*. Society for
               NT Studies Monograph Series 5. Cambridge:
               Cambridge University.

HOMMEL, H.
1969            "Wahrheit und Gerechtigkeit. Zur Geschichte und
               Deutung eines Begriffspaares," *Antike und
               Abendland* 15: 159-86.

HORST, F.
1958            "Gerechtigkeit Gottes. II. Im AT und Judentum,"
               *RGG* 2: 1403-06.

HUFFMON, H. B.
1959            "The Covenant Lawsuit in the Prophets," *JBL* 78:
               285-95.

HUGHES, D.
1968            Review of Hill, *EvQ* 40: 118-20.

HURWITZ, M. S.
1957            "The Septuagint of Isaiah 36-39 in relation to
               that of 1-35, 40-66," *HUCA* 28: 75-83.

JACOB, E.
1958            *Theology of the OT*. London: Hodder & Stoughton.

JACQUES, X.
1967            "Le vocabulaire de la Septante. Vers une méthode
               de recherche et d'exposition," *Bib* 48: 296-301
               (review of Daniel).

JELLICOE, S.
1968            *The Septuagint and Modern Study*. Oxford:
               Clarendon.
1969            "Septuagint Studies in the Current Century," *JBL*
               88: 191-99.
1973            See Brock, 1973.
1974            *Studies in the Septuagint: Origins, Recensions,
               and Interpretations*, ed. with prolegomenon. New
               York: Ktav.

JEPSEN, A.
1965            "צדק und צדקה im Alten Testament," in Reventlow,
               1965: 78-99.

JEREMIAS, Joachim
1965            *The Central Message of the New Testament*.
               London: S.C.M.

JEREMIAS, Jörg
1972            "Mišpāṭ im ersten Gottesknechtslied," *VT* 22:
               31-42.

JOACHIM, H. H.
1955            *Aristotle: the Nicomachean Ethics - a Commentary*,
               ed. REES, D. A. Oxford: Clarendon.

JONES, D. R.
1964            *Isaiah 56-66 and Joel*. Torch Commentaries.

London: S.C.M.

JONES, Gw. H.
1972    "Abraham and Cyrus: Type and anti-type?" *VT* 22:
304-19.

JUSTESEN, J. P.
1964    "On the Meaning of ṢĀDĀQ," *Andrews University
Seminary Studies* 2: 53-61.

KAISER, O.
1963    *Der Prophet Jesaja: Kap 1-12.* ATD 17.
Göttingen: Vandenhoeck & Ruprecht, 2nd ed. ET,
*Isaiah 1-12: A Commentary.* London: S.C.M., 1972.
1973    *Der Prophet Jesaja: Kap. 13-39.* ATD 18.
Göttingen: Vandenhoeck & Ruprecht. ET, *Isaiah
13-39: A Commentary.* London: S.C.M., 1974.

KÄSEMANN, E.
1961    "Gottesgerechtigkeit bei Paulus," *Zeitschrift für
Theologie und Kirche* 58: 367-78; ET, "God's
Righteousness in Paul," *Journal for Theology and
Church* 1 (1965): 100-110.

KATZ, P.
1954    "Septuagintal Studies in the Mid-Century: their
links with the past and their present
tendencies," in DAVIES, W. D., and DAUBE, D.,
ed., *The Background of the NT and its
Eschatology: Studies in Honour of C. H. Dodd*:
176-208. Cambridge: Cambridge University.
Reprinted in Jellicoe, 1974: 21-53.
1961    "Septuaginta-Forschung," *RGG* 5: 1704-07.

KESSLER, W.
1960    *Gott geht es um das Ganze: Jesaja 56-66 und
24-27.* BAT 19. Stuttgart: Calwer.

KISSANE, E. J.
1943    *The Book of Isaiah*, Vol. II. Dublin: Brown and
Nolan.

KLEIN, G.
1976    "Righteousness in the NT," *IDBSup*: 750-752.

KNIGHT, G. A. F.
1959    *A Christian Theology of the OT.* London: S.C.M.

KRAFT, R. A.
1970    "Jewish Greek Scriptures and Related Topics," *NTS*
16: 384-96.
1971    "Jewish Greek Scriptures and Related Topics. II,"
*NTS* 17: 488-90.
1972    ed., *Septuagintal Lexicography.* Missoula:
Society of Biblical Literature.
1976    "Septuagint. B. Earliest Greek Versions," *IDBSup*:
811-815.

LARUE, G. A.
1967    "Recent Studies in Ḥesed," in Glueck: 1-32.

LEE, H. D. P.
1955    *Plato: Republic*, ET and Introduction. Harmondsworth: Penguin.

LEE, J. A. L.
1969            "A Note on Septuagintal Material in the Supple-
               ment to Liddell and Scott," *Glotta* 47: 234-42.

LLOYD-JONES, H.
1972            "Pindar *Fr.* 169," *Harvard Studies in Classical
               Philology* 76: 45-56.

LOFTHOUSE, W. F.
1938            "The Righteousness of Jahweh," *ExpT* 50: 341-45.

MAUCHLINE, J.
1962            *Isaiah 1-39.* Torch Commentaries. London: S.C.M.

McCARTHY, D. J.
1965            "Notes on the love of God in Deuteronomy and the
               father-son relationship between Yahweh and
               Israel," *CBQ* 27: 144-47.

McKAY, K. L.
1972            "Syntax in Exegesis," *Tyndale Bulletin* 23: 39-57.

McKENZIE, J. L.
1968            *Second Isaiah.* Anchor Bible. Garden City:
               Doubleday.

METZGER, B. M.
1963            *Chapters in the History of NT Textual Criticism.*
               Leiden: Brill.

MORAN, W. J.
1963            "The Ancient Near Eastern Background of the Love
               of God in Deuteronomy," *CBQ* 25: 77-87.

MORRIS, L.
1955            *The Apostolic Preaching of the Cross.* London:
               Tyndale.

MOWINCKEL, S.
1956            *He that Cometh.* Oxford: Blackwell.

MUILENBURG, J.
1956            "The Book of Isaiah, chap. 40-66," *IB* 5: 381-773.

NIDA, E.
1964            *Toward a Science of Translating.* Leiden: Brill.

NORTH, C. R.
1952            *Isaiah 40-55.* Torch Commentary. London: S.C.M.
1956            *The Suffering Servant in Deutero-Isaiah.* London:
               Oxford University.
1964            *The Second Isaiah.* Oxford: Clarendon.

OLLEY, J. W.
1975            "Biblical Exegesis in a Cross-cultural Context:
               the Study of the Septuagint," *South East Asia
               Journal of Theology* 16/1: 1-11; 16/2: 30
               (errata).
1976            "A Forensic Connotation of *bōš*," *VT* 26: 230-34.

ORLINSKY, H. M.
1939            "The Kings-Isaiah Recensions," *Jewish Quarterly
               Review* 30: 33-49.
1941            "On the Present State of Proto-Septuagint
               Studies," *Journal of the American Oriental
               Society* 61; reprinted in Jellicoe, 1974: 78-109.

1947  "Current Progress and Problems in Septuagint Research," in WILLOUGHBY, H. R., ed., *The Study of the Bible Today and Tomorrow*: 144-61. Chicago: Chicago University. Reprinted in Jellicoe, 1974: 3-20.

1956  "The Treatment of Anthropomorhisms and Anthropopathisms in the Septuagint of Isaiah," *HUCA* 27: 193-200.

1959  "Qumran and the present state of OT text studies: the Septuagint text," *JBL* 78: 26-33.

1961  "The Textual Criticism of the OT," in WRIGHT, G. E., ed., *The Bible and the Ancient Near East*: 113-132. London: Routledge & Kegan Paul. Reprinted in Jellicoe, 1974: 239-258.

1967  "The so-called 'Servant of the Lord' and 'Suffering Servant' in Second Isaiah," *VTSup* 14: 1-133.

1970  "Nationalism - Universalism and Internationalism in Ancient Israel," in FRANK, H. T., and REED, W. L., ed., *Translating and Understanding the Old Testament: Essays in Honor of Herbert Gordon May*: 206-36. Nashville and New York: Abingdon.

1974  "The Septuagint: the Oldest Translation of the Bible," in *Essays in Biblical Culture and Bible Translation*: 363-382. New York: Ktav.

1975  "The Septuagint as Holy Writ and the Philosophy of the Translators," *HUCA* 46: 89-114.

OTTLEY, R. R.
1904-06 *The Book of Isaiah according to the Septuagint, Vol. 1: Introduction and Translation; Vol. 2: Text and Notes*. Cambridge: Cambridge University.

PAVESE, C.
1968  "The new Heracles poem of Pindar," *Harvard Studies in Classical Philology* 72: 47-88.

PAYNE, D. F.
1967  "Characteristic Word-Play in 'Second Isaiah': A Reappraisal," *JSS* 12: 207-229.

1971  "The Servant of the Lord: Language and Interpretation," *EvQ* 43: 131-43.

PEDERSEN, J.
1959  *Israel: its Life and Culture, I-II*, 2nd ed. London: Oxford University.

POWELL, J. E.
1949  *Herodotus*. Oxford: Clarendon.

QUELL, G.
1935  "The Concept of Law in the OT," *TDNT* 2: 174-78.

RABIN, C.
1968  "The Translation Process and the Character of the Septuagint," *Textus* 6: 1-26.

REICKE, Bo
1968  "Paul's Understanding of Righteousness," in RICHARDS, J. M., ed., *Soli Deo Gratia: NT Studies in Honour of W. C. Robinson*: 37-49. Richmond: Knox.

178

REUMANN, J.
1966        "The Gospel of the Righteousness of God," *Int* 20:
            432-52.

REVENTLOW, H. Graf
1965        ed., *Gottes Wort und Gottee Land*. Göttingen:
            Vandenhoeck & Ruprecht.
1971        *Rechtfertigung im Horizont des Alten Testaments*.
            Munich: Kaiser.

RODGERS, V. A.
1971        "Some thoughts on δίκη," *Classical Quarterly* 21:
            289-301.

ROSE, H. J.
1958        *A Commentary on the Surviving Plays of Aeschylus*,
            2 vols. Amsterdam: Noord-Hollandsche Uitgevers.

ROSENBERG, R. A.
1965        "The God Ṣedeq," *HUCA* 36: 161-77.

SACHS, D.
1971        "A Fallacy in Plato's *Republic*," in Vlastos:
            35-51.

SANDAY, W. and HEADLAM, A. C.
1902        *A Critical and Exegetical Commentary on the
            Epistle to the Romans*. ICC. 5th ed. Edinburgh:
            Clark.

SAWYER, J. F. A.
1972        *Semantics in Biblical Research*. SBT 2/24.
            London: S.C.M.

SCHMID, H. H.
1968        *Gerechtigkeit als Weltordnung: Hintergrund und
            Geschichte des alttestamentlichen
            Gerechtigkeitsbegriffes*. Beitrage zur
            historischen Theologie 40. Tübingen: Mohr.

SCHOORS, A.
1973        *I am God Your Saviour: a form-critical study of
            the main genres in Is. xl-lv. VTSup* 24. Leiden:
            Brill.

SCHRENK, G.
1933        "ἄδικος," *TDNT* 1: 149-63.
1935        "δίκη," *TDNT* 2: 178-225.

SCHWARZCHILD, S. S.
1972        "Justice," *EncJud* 10: 476-77.

SCHWER, W.
1950        "Barmherzigkeit," *Reallexikon für Antike und
            Christentum* 1: 1200-07. Stuttgart: Hiersemann.

SCOTT, R. B. Y.
1956        "The Book of Isaiah, chap. 1-39," *IB* 5: 151-381.

SCULLION, J. J.
1971        "ṢEDEQ-ṢEDAQAH in Isaiah cc. 40-66," *UF* 3:
            335-48.
1972        "Some difficult texts in Isaiah cc. 56-66 in the
            light of modern scholarship," *UF* 4: 105-28.

SEELIGMANN, I. L.
1948        *The Septuagint Version of Isaiah: a discussion of its problems.* Leiden: Brill.

SEVENSTER, J. N.
1968        *Do You Know Greek? How Much Greek Could the First Jewish Christians Have Known?.* *Novum Testamentum Sup* 19. Leiden: Brill.

SHOREY, P.
1918        "Righteousness (Greek and Roman)," *Encyclopaedia of Religion and Ethics* 10: 800-04. Edinburgh: Clark.
1971        "Plato's Ethics," in Vlastos: 7-34.

SKINNER, J.
1902        "Righteousness in OT," Hasting's *A Dictionary of the Bible* 4: 272-81. Edinburgh: Clark.

SMITH, S.
1944        *Isaiah Chapters XL-LV: Literary Criticism and History.* Schweich Lectures 1940. London: Oxford University.

SNAITH, N.
1944        *The Distinctive Ideas of the Old Testament.* London: Epworth.
1967        "Isaiah 40-66: A Study of the Teaching of the Second Isaiah and Its Consequences," *VTSup* 14: 135-264.

STUHLMACHER, P.
1966        *Gerechtigkeit Gottes bei Paulus.* 2nd ed. Göttingen: Vandenhoeck & Ruprecht.

SWETE, H. B.
1914        *An Introduction to the Old Testament in Greek,* revised by OTTLEY, R. R., 2nd ed. Cambridge: Cambridge University. Reprinted New York: Ktav, 1968.

SZUBIN, Z. H. and JACOBS L.
1972        "Righteousness," *EncJud* 14: 180-84.

TANGBERG, K. A.
1973        "Linguistics and Theology," *Bible Translator* 24: 301-10.

THACKERAY, H. St.J.
1902a,b,c   "The Greek Translators of the Prophetical Books," *JTS* 4: 245-66, 398-411, 578-85.
1906        "The Greek Translators of the Four Books of Kings," *JTS* 8: 262-78.
1909        *Grammar of the OT in Greek,* Vol. I. Cambridge: Cambridge University.
1921        *The Septuagint and Jewish Worship.* Schweich Lectures 1920. London: Oxford University.
1929        "Septuagint," *International Standard Bible Encyclopaedia*: 4: 2722-31. Reprinted Grand Rapids: Eerdmans, 1946.

THOMAS, D. W.
1968b       "A consideration of Isaiah LIII in the light of recent textual and philological study,"

*Ephemerides Theologicae Lovanienses* 44: 79-86.

TORREY, C. C.
1951      "Isaiah 41," *Harvard Theological Review* 44: 121-36.

TOV, E.
1976a     "Septuagint. A. Contribution to OT Scholarship," *IDBSup*: 807-811.
1976b     "Some Thoughts on a Lexicon of the LXX," *BIOSCS* 9: 14-46.

TREDENNICK, H.
1959     *Plato: The Last Days of Socrates*, ET and Introduction. Harmondsworth: Penguin.

TURNER, N.
1955     "The Unique Character of Biblical Greek," *VT* 5: 208-13.
1963     *Syntax*, Vol. III of MOULTON, J. H., *A Grammar of New Testament Greek*. Edinburgh: Clark.
1964     "Second Thoughts: VII, Papyrus Finds," *ExpT* 76: 44-48.

TUR-SINAI, N. H.
1961     "A Contribution to the Understanding of Isaiah i-xii," *Scripta Hierosolymitana* 8: 145-88.

VERGOTE, J.
1938     "Grec biblique," *DBSup* 3: 1320-69.

VLASTOS, G.
1971     ed., *Plato: A Collection of Critical Essays. II: Ethics, Politics, and Philosophy of Art and Religion* (Modern Studies in Philosophy; Garden City: Doubleday); including his own article, "Justice and Happiness in the *Republic*": 66-95.

VON RAD, G.
1962     *OT Theology*, Vol. I. Edinburgh & London: Oliver & Boyd.
1966     *The Problem of the Hexateuch and Other Essays*. Edinburgh & London: Oliver & Boyd.

WATSON, N. M.
1960     "Some observations on the use of δικαιόω in the Septuagint," *JBL* 79: 255-66.

WERNBERG-MØLLER, P.
1973     Review of Sawyer, *JTS* n. s. 24: 215-17.

WESTERMANN, C.
1966     *Das Buch Jesaia, Kap. 40-66*. ATD 19. Göttingen: Vandenhoeck & Ruprecht. ET, *Isaiah 40-66: A Commentary*. London: S.C.M., 1969.

WEVERS, J. W.
1954a,b   "Septuaginta-Forschungen," *TR* nF 22: 85-138, 171-90.
1968     "Septuaginta-Forschungen seit 1954," *TR* nF 33: 18-76.

WHITLEY, C. F.
1972     "Deutero-Isaiah's Interpretation of ṣedeq," *VT* 22: 469-75.

181

WOLFF, H. W.
1974        *Anthropology of the Old Testament*.  London:
            S.C.M.

ZIEGLER, J.
1934        *Untersuchungen zur Septuaginta des Buches Isaias*.
            Alttestamentliche Abhandlungen XII/3.  Münster:
            Aschendorffschen.
1959        "Die Vorlage der Isaias-Septuaginta (LXX) und die
            erste Isaias-Rolle von Qumran (1QIs$^a$)," *JBL* 78:
            34-59.

ZIESLER, J. A.
1972        *The Meaning of Righteousness in Paul: A
            Linguistic and Theological Enquiry*.  Society for
            NT Studies Monograph Series 20.  Cambridge:
            Cambridge University.

ZIMMERLI, W. and JEREMIAS, J.
1954        "παῖς θεοῦ," *TDNT* 5: 654-717.

# INDEX OF BIBLICAL REFERENCES

(MT verse numbers are given.  Pages in
italics signify major discussion.)

*Genesis*
47:29   142

*Exodus*
2:25   74
23:7f   45-46, 127
33:21f   100

*Leviticus*
19:15   73
20:18   158

*Deuteronomy*
6:25   127, 160
16:18   110
24:13   127, 160
28:12   79
29:18   144
32:18   100
32:34   79

*Judges*
5:11   55

*1 Samuel*
12:7   55

*2 Kings*
chaps. 18-20   92
20:19   159

*Isaiah*
chaps. 1-39   16, 18, 111,
   112, 133
chaps. 1-35   92, 129-31
1:2-4   88
1:11-17   90

1:17   *59-60*, 61, 73, 96, 114,
   122
1:18-20   67, 75
1:19f   111
1:21-28   *66-68*, 75, 111, 112
1:21   112, 133
1:23   59, 73
1:24f   111
1:26   112, 133
1:27   65, 74, 85, 103, 112,
   113, 115
2:1-4   147
2:3f   100
2:4   111, 113
2:5   50
2:10   120
2:19   120
2:21   120
2:22   100
3:10   119
3:11   158
3:12   59
3:15   122
4:2   156
4:5   50
5:7   103, 112, 113, 133
5:16   103, 112, 133
5:23   *45-46*, 61, 62, 73, 91,
   102, 112, 113, 119, 133, 138
7:20   157
8:14   100
8:20   80
9:2   50

*Isaiah (cont.)*

9:5    94, 95
9:6    95, 104, 113
9:7    66, 112
9:16    59
10:1f    73
10:2    96
10:17    50
10:18    159
10:20    92, 122
10:21f    66
10:22    133
11:1-9    104
11:1-7    112
11:1-5    66, *95-96*
11:2f    120
11:3f    112
11:4f    105, 133
11:4    *95-96*, 103, 114, 133, 159
11:5    113
11:6-9    95
13:10    50
13:11    122
13:19    156
14:1f    111, 147, 148, 149
16:3-5    94
16:5    92, 95, 112, 113, 133, 143
16:10    159
17:12f    100
chap. 19    147
20:2    86
21:3    122
23:7    102
23:9    156
23:12    122
24:1-5    150
24:5    119

24:15    149, 150
24:16    119, 138, 149, 156
24:20    122
25:3f    122
25:5    102
25:9    85
26:1    156
26:4    100
26:7    119
26:8    150, 158
26:9f    133
26:9    50, 147, 150, 158
26:15    159
26:16    46
26:18    120
chap. 28    *68-71*, 75, 111
28:1    156
28:11    1
28:16f    107
28:17    65, *68-71*, 112, 116
28:26    103
29:13    120
29:17    159
29:21    119
30:1    88
30:3    157
30:9    88
30:18    116
30:26    50
30:29    100
chap. 32    *103-05*
32:1-4    70
32:1f    69, 79, 95
32:1    *103-05*, 112, 113, 119
32:7    87
32:8    119
32:15-20    79
32:16f    *104-05*, 111, 112, 113
32:17f    94

*Isaiah (cont.)*

32:17   133

33:1-8   75, 111

33:1   79, 80, 102

33:5-15   *79-80*

33:5f   104, 113

33:5   158

33:6   65, *79-80*, 102, 120

33:14   122

33:15   76, 112, 113, 122, 133

33:19   79

33:20-22   79

chap. 34   86

34:1   100

34:5   103

34:8   86, 87

34:11   157

34:14   69

35:2   159

35:4   158

chaps. 36-39   8, *91-95*, 129-31

37:24   159

38:3   92, 93

38:10-20   92, 93

38:18f   91, *92-93*, 116

38:18   142

38:19   65, 91

39:8   65, 91, *94*, 114

chaps. 40-55   16, 18, 71, 72, 78, 92, 111, 112, 129-31, 134-35, 138

40:5   71

40:6   143

40:10   158

40:15   150

40:27   74

41:1-13   *105-07*, 115

41:1-5   51, 106, 111

41:1   51, 56, 100, 103, 107, 149, 150

41:2   134

41:5   150

41:10   103, *105-06*, 119, 134, 156

41:11   56

41:21-29   51

41:25   148

41:26   52

41:27   148

42:1-9   111, 151

42:1-6   99

42:1-4   95, 98, 113

42:1   111

42:3   92

42:4   60, 100, 115, 147, 150

42:6   73, 87, 100, 103, 134, 147

42:9   158

42:10, 12 ,  149

42:16   50

42:17-20   61

42:17   149

42:21   59, *60-61*, 62, 134

42:22   83

42:24   60

43:4   100

43:8-15   51, *52*, 55

43:9   *51-52*, 53, 62, 92, 100, 138

43:19   158

43:24-26   *53-54*, 122

43:26   51, *53-54*, 57, 62, 63, 73, 138

43:28   53

44:1, 2   53

44:4   158

44:6-8   51

44:8   100, 134

44:21f   51

*Isaiah (cont.)*

45:6   56-57
45:8   85, 99, 158, 160
45:9-13   55
45:13   87, 103, 134
45:14f   149
45:15-25   111, 148
45:15   56
45:16f   55, 58, 149
45:16   56, 111, 149, 150
45:18-25   *54-58*, 85
45:19   86, 134
45:20-25   51
45:21   119, 138
45:22f   115
45:23   115, 134
45:24   115, 134, 158
45:25   51, *54-58*, 62, 63, 138
46:12f   71, 99, 115, 134
46:13   84, 158
47:3f   *102*, 114
48:1   92, 103, 134
48:2   156
48:13   105
48:16   86
48:18   99, 134
49:1   98, 100, 149, 150
49:4   158
49:6   147
49:13   156
49:25f   86
50:4-11   46
50:4-9   155
50:7   100
50:8   45, *46-48*, 61, 62, 138
50:9-11   101, 111, 148
50:10f   150
50:10   50

chap. 51   47, 113
51:1-8   68, *96-101*, 111, 113
51:1   91, *100*, 102, 113, 134, 157
51:4-7   111
51:4-6   148
51:4f   60, *100*, 115, 147, 150
51:4   113
51:5-8   84, 158
51:5   134, 149, 150
51:6   134
51:7   96, *99*, *101*, 113, 134, 151
51:8   134
51:11   85
51:14   101
51:22f   86
51:22   101
51:23   101, 122
52:1   156, 159
52:13-53:12   48
52:13   49
53:4   49
53:5   46
53:6   90
53:8f   50-51
53:9   49
53:11   45, *48-51*, 61, 62, 119, 138
53:12   49
54:7f   143
54:10   143
54:11-17   *107-09*, 112
54:13f   94, 111, 113
54:14   103, 113, 134
54:15f   111, 115
54:15   148, 149
54:17   47, 103, *107-09*, 113, 119, 134
55:3   111, 144-45
55:4   100

*Isaiah (cont.)*

55:6f   72

55:7   72, 115

55:10f   158

chaps. 56-66   16, 18, 71,
    81, 83, 92, 111, 112,
    129-31, 136-37, 138

56:1-8   147

56:1-2   *71-72*

56:1   65, 68, 99, 112,
    113, 115, 136, 142,
    158, 160

56:6f   149

56:8   111, 149

57:1   114, 119, 122, 144,
    156

57:11   120

57:12   136

57:16   156

57:18   74

58:2f   90

58:2   103, *109-110*, 113,
    119, 136, 156, 158

58:6   122

58:8   136

58:11   158

chap. 59   *72-78*, 111, 112

59:3   122

59:4   91, 102, 103, 112,
    114, 122, 136

59:6   122

59:8f   94

59:9-20   68

59:9   112, 136

59:11   103

59:13   122

59:14f   92

59:14   112, 113, 136

59:16   65, *72*, 84, 116,
    136

59:17   84, 115, 116, 136

59:18   150, 158

59:19   120

chap. 60   147

60:1-14   99

60:1   159

60:3   100, 147, 150

60:5   100

60:7   81

60:9   100, 149, 150

60:10-12   100, 101

60:14   101

60:15-21   82

60:17   94, 99, 113, 136

60:18   122

60:19   57

60:21   81, 82, 85, 119, 138,
    158

chap. 61   *80-85*

61:2   86, 87

61:3   *81-82*, 112, 114, 136

61:4   156

61:8   65, 68, *80-85*, 92, 94,
    111, 114, 122

61:10f   81, *83-85*

61:10   68, 99, 112, 114, 136

61:11   112, 113, 114, 115, 136

62:1   50, 84, 86, 99, 136

62:2   57, 136

62:6   86

62:8   86, 105

62:11   86, 158

62:12   86

chaps. 63-64   *86-91*, 116

63:1   84, *86-87*, 103, 115, 130,
    136

63:4-6   *87-88*

63:5   73

63:7f   115

63:7   65, *86-89*, 115, 130, 143,
    158, 160

63:14   81

63:15   74, 158

*Isaiah (cont.)*
63:16    88
63:17    91, 120
64:3f    *89*
64:4    136
64:5f    *89-91*, 102, 113
64:5    136, 158
64:6    102, 113
64:10    156
65:7    158
65:22    82
65:25    122
66:5    148
66:14    120
66:16    73
66:19    150

*Jeremiah*    142
2:2    145
2:30    47
5:3    47
22:3, 15    110
31:29    49
31:31-34    99
33:6    94

*Ezekiel*
5:13    86
chap. 18    110
18:2    49
18:19f    142
18:24    90
36:5f    86
38:19    86

*Hosea*
6:4    144, 145
10:12    50, 103

*Joel*
2:23    103

*Amos*
5:7-15    73
5:7, 24    110
7:7-9    68

*Psalms*    119, 142
4:6    157
10:18    59
11:3, 5, 7    48
17:1    157
17:7    160
24:5    160
30:10    93
31:1, 5    94
31:19    48
33:18    93
36:10    150
40:11    94
45:5    94
60:8    86
71:22    94
72    15, 66, 95
72:3    94, 156
72:7    94
75:11    48
85:11f    94
86:17    157
89:2    160
89:15    94
89:39f    144
89:50    144
99:7    86
103:6    55
106:7    160
106:31    103
107:43    160
108:8    86
111:3, 8    94
112:4    48
119: 7, 62, 106, 164    110

*Psalms (cont.)*
141:5    48
147:11    93

*Job*
9:16    73
13:22    73
33:28    68

*Proverbs*    119, 142
3:11    47
17:15    *46*

*Lamentations*
3:23    160
4:20    144
5:7    49

*Daniel*    142

*2 Chronicles*
6:42    144, 160

*Matthew*
12:21    159

*Acts*
13:34    144

*Romans*
11:26    157

*1 Peter*
2:6    157

# INDEX OF NON-BIBLICAL GREEK SOURCES

Aeschylus   *33-34*, 42

Aristophanes   *37*

Aristotle   21, *27-32*, 33,
    36, 41, 42-43, 83, 141,
    155
    *Rhetorica ad Alexandrum*
    27, *31-32*

Callimachus   160

Demosthenes   141

Dio Cassius   33

Dionysius Halicarnassensis
    *38*

Herodotus   *34-36*, 42

Homer   141

Inscriptions   *39*, 41,
    145, 155, 160

Baruch   63

4 Ezra   156

Prayer of Azariah   63

Isocrates   *32-33*, 41

Josephus   19

Philo   19

Pindar   *26*

Plato   21, *22-27*, 28, 29, 30,
    32, 33, 41, 42, 43, 117, 141,
    154, 159, 160

Plutarch   *39*, 43

Polybius   *38*, 42, 43, 157

Sophocles   *34*

Thucydides   *36-37*, 40, 41, 42

Xenophon   *37-38*, 41, 154, 160

Papyri   *39-40*, 155, 160

Prayer of Manasseh   63

Wisdom of Solomon chap. 5   77